The
Atheist
Muslim

The
Atheist
Muslim

A JOURNEY
FROM RELIGION
TO REASON

ALI A. RIZVI

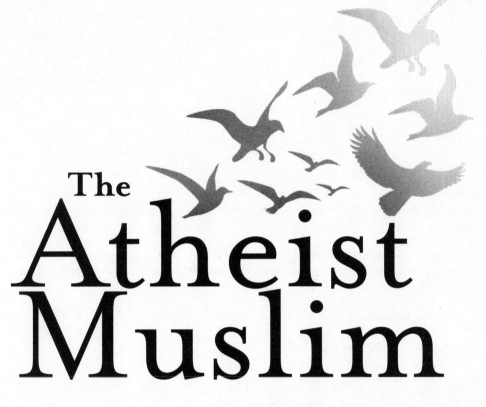

ST. MARTIN'S PRESS ◆ NEW YORK

www.stmartins.com

Text design: Meryl Sussman Levavi

Certain names have been changed.

Library of Congress Cataloging-in-Publication Data

Names: Rizvi, Ali A., author.
Title: The atheist Muslim : a journey from religion to reason / Ali A. Rizvi.
Description: New York, NY : St. Martin's Press, 2016.
Identifiers: LCCN 2016024634 | ISBN 9781250094445 (hardback) |
    ISBN 9781250094452 (e-book)
Subjects: LCSH: Rizvi, Ali A., | Atheists—Middle East—Biography. | Physicians—
    United States—Biography. | BISAC: RELIGION / Atheism. | POLITICAL SCIENCE /
    Political Ideologies / General.
Classification: LCC BL2765.M628 R59 2016 | DDC 211/.8092 [B]—dc23
LC record available at https://lccn.loc.gov/2016024634

Our books may be purchased in bulk for promotional, educational, or business use. Please contact your local bookseller or the Macmillan Corporate and Premium Sales Department at 1-800-221-7945, extension 5442, or by e-mail at MacmillanSpecialMarkets@macmillan.com.

First Edition: November 2016

10 9 8 7 6 5 4 3 2 1

For Zoë

Contents

ONE

Smoke Break

I'm in the fifth grade at the American International School in Riyadh, Saudi Arabia, and our teacher wants us to make paper snowflakes. Brimming with excitement, we all fold up our pieces of paper, cut into them, open them up, decorate them using glue and glitter, and label them with our names. They will be displayed on the bulletin board in the hall, after which we get to take them home to show our parents.

Thing is, it doesn't snow in Riyadh. I've never even *seen* snow—and I won't until I move to Canada, well into my twenties. But this is an American school, and it's two weeks to Christmas break. Trees with hand-made ornaments are up everywhere. Music teachers are busy preparing students for the winter recital. And classroom walls are adorned with cutouts of elves, snowmen, and reindeer.

My school has over two thousand students of about eighty nationalities, all from expatriate families, mostly American and Canadian. The Saudis aren't allowed by law to attend it. This is more or less consistent with the generally minimal interaction foreigners have with the locals anyway—and the government seems to like it that way. Consequently, our exposure to the Saudis' culture and customs is limited, as is theirs to ours. So it makes sense that Westerners who find themselves isolated in this cultural desert halfway across the world would want something to keep their kids connected to the way things are back home.

Well, almost.

You have to say "winter" or "holiday" instead of "Christmas"—winter break, winter recital, holiday party, and so on—and you can't display anything religious like crosses or images of Jesus. But the rest of it's pretty legit.

From time to time, government officials drop by to see if our school is in compliance with their rules. And today—on snowflake day—an officer from the ministry just happens to be dropping in for an inspection.

He approaches our snowflakes on the bulletin board, and he doesn't look happy. Scowling, he turns around to say something to our teacher. She hands him a pair of scissors, at his request. Then, he proceeds to snip one of the points off each of the paper snowflakes, leaving the disfigured, asymmetrical five-pointed figures on the board, not even bothering to pick up the amputated scraps of paper that have fallen to the floor.

As you'd expect, it isn't long before my teacher finds herself staring into the faces of twenty confused kids trying to make sense of what they've just witnessed. What could possibly be so threatening about *snowflakes*? Why are five points okay but not six?

"What is the Star of David?" we ask her, after she has finally—and hesitantly—given us the real answer to a long string of persistent "whys" characteristic of children our age. And what's so repugnant about it that a grown, literate man, presumably of sound intellectual faculty (he's from the Ministry of Education, after all), can't even stand the sight of paper snowflakes made by a bunch of eleven-year-olds just because both structures happen to have the same number of points?

"It's *their* symbol," the kid sitting next to me tells us, practically whispering.

I'm puzzled, disoriented, and slightly traumatized about having my creativity mauled. But most of all, I've just been given my first ever introduction to the Jews—and I am *terrified*.

I get home, itching to ask my father, a geography and history whiz, about the Jews. He asks me to get my illuminated plastic globe of the world that we bought earlier this year from both his and my favorite place in the city—the Jarir Bookstore in Riyadh's Al Akariyah Mall. He tells me a little bit about the history of the Israeli-Palestinian conflict, and guides me to find Israel on the globe. I look, and it isn't there. He then brings down a world atlas, also from the same store. Again, no Israel. It isn't on either map. Strangely, the maps haven't just ignored its existence and called all of it Palestine like they do on TV; instead, it appears as a blue, nameless notch in the Middle East, blending into the Mediterranean—literally wiped off the map.

I'm not telling you this to assert one position or another on the Middle East. Of course, I know today that Israel isn't synonymous with "all Jews" and vice versa. But I want you to understand how people often grow to believe things the way that they do, and how fear can entrench those beliefs so deeply in one's mind—especially a child's mind—that they become all but intractable.

What happened with me was actually the best-case scenario, considering the circumstances. I was a Pakistani child going to an international school. Both of my parents were highly educated university professors. My father had earned his doctorate in Canada, and my mother earned hers in the United States. They were progressive, rational, and well traveled. Both had lived and taught in several countries before they got married and had me. Like the other expatriates in Saudi, they had very little interaction with the locals outside of their places of work. They were liberal Muslims who valued pluralism and quality education that went beyond the textbook—and they wanted to instill that in us, their four children. This was a key reason they sent us to this expensive, private school.

Now, imagine the experience of an average Saudi child who will live in Saudi Arabia most or all of his life, like his parents did. He attends public Saudi schools—which the children of expatriates are not allowed to attend. Officials from the Ministry of Education—like the one who visited my classroom that day—don't just do spot-checks in his school to see if everything's running as it should. They actually *write* his school's curriculum, and significantly influence what goes in his textbooks.

We got a peek into the content of these textbooks shortly after the 9/11 attacks, after an investigation into the factors that may have led the hijackers—fifteen of whom were Saudi out of a total of nineteen—to do what they did. For example, a textbook for tenth-graders entitled *Monotheism*, published in 2000, featured passages like, "The Hour will not come until Muslims will fight the Jews, and Muslims will kill all the Jews." Students weren't just asked to learn these ideas—they were required to memorize the passages verbatim.[1]

Concerned, the United States put pressure on the Saudis to reform their education system. The author of several of these books, a deeply revered religious scholar named Saleh Al-Fawzan, was furious. In an interview with Saudi newspaper *Al Jazirah*, he said,

> The Jews and Christians and the polytheists have shown their heartfelt hatred and try to prevent us from the true path of God. They want to change our religion and our teaching to disconnect us from Islam so they can come and occupy us with their armies. It is bad enough when it comes from the infidels, but worse when they are of our skin. They say we create parrots, but they are the real parrots repeating what our enemies say of Islam.

Other Saudi officials, however, were more conciliatory. Over the next four years, they kept insisting repeatedly that the system had been reformed and the textbooks changed. And then Freedom House, a human rights think tank, got hold of some of these "reformed" books published in 2005 and 2006 and put out a report. Its findings were astonishing.[2]

A fill-in-the-blank question in a first-grade textbook read, "Every religion other than Islam is _____. Whoever dies outside of Islam enters _____."

The correct answers: "false" and "hellfire," respectively.

A fifth-grade textbook taught lessons on friendship and loyalty: "It is forbidden for a Muslim to be a loyal friend to someone who does not believe in God and His Prophet, or someone who fights the religion of Islam," and, "A Muslim, even if he lives far away, is your brother in religion.

Someone who opposes God, even if he is your brother by family tie, is your enemy in religion."

In the eighth grade, students learned about dealings with Jews and Christians. "The apes are Jews, the people of the Sabbath; while the swine are the Christians, the infidels of the communion of Jesus."

By the twelfth grade, the students were ready to graduate and go out to face the world. "Jihad in the path of God—which consists of battling against unbelief, oppression, injustice, and those who perpetrate it—is the summit of Islam. This religion arose through jihad and through jihad was its banner raised high. It is one of the noblest acts, which brings one closer to God, and one of the most magnificent acts of obedience to God."

Let me reiterate here—these were the *reformed* textbooks, printed several years after 9/11.

My experience on snowflake day really shook me up at the time. My memory of it is crystal clear to this day. Eventually, though, I was convinced that I'd moved on from all that backward silliness and prejudice. I was educated. Enlightened. I'd grown up with friends from all over the world. My parents had raised me right. I was smart enough to realize, if I'd been born in a Jewish or Christian or Hindu family, I would be raised in *those* religions. Being Muslim was just an accident of birth. Being good or bad is about your actions and deeds—not where you're from or what your parents happen to believe. That's just common sense.

Right?

Ten years later, I'm sitting in a convenience store in Mississauga, Ontario—a city just west of Toronto that first started up as one of its suburbs. My parents have now moved permanently to Canada. I'm still attending medical school in Karachi, Pakistan, but I've got the summer off and I've come here to spend it with them.

I'm working at the store to make a bit of cash, completely oblivious to the South-Asian-working-at-a-convenience-store stereotype here in the West, despite being a fan of Apu's character in *The Simpsons*. Either way, I wouldn't really care. It's 1996, and one Canadian dollar equals almost thirty rupees, which goes a long way back in Karachi. It's not too busy, the weather is amazing, and I've got a lot of time to study. (In medical school, you're always studying.)

It's after lunch, and I'm walking back from the record store two shops away, where I've just picked up the new Metallica tape, *Load*. Their last album, eponymously named *Metallica*, had all of my high school anthems on it. This is their first album after that. It's been five years.

I've always loved metal. It's aggressive, rebellious, smart, and it pisses off all the right people—teachers, preachers, and the *mutawwahs*, the religious policemen who used to go around the malls back in Saudi and hit your mom on the head with a stick if her headscarf slipped too far off her forehead. They hated the music. They said it was the *Shaitaan*, the devil, putting his word into our ears. But all the kids were listening to it. Riyadh had lots of tape and CD stores, and the *mutawwahs* didn't like it one bit. My favorite was a place called 747, right at the corner of the Olaya and Talateen streets, located at the base of the Green Towers apartment buildings that some of my friends lived in. The store was huge, had virtually everything, and was cheap because all the tapes were pirated. It was also a favorite of the *mutawwahs*, but for completely different reasons. They targeted it frequently because it had become a popular secret meeting spot for young boys and girls. Ultimately, it became men-only.

I had a dual-tape Sanyo system that I'd brought along to my university hostel room in Karachi. It was almost always at full volume, blasting out angry voices drenched in a massive wall of rich, distorted guitars, screaming hope and possibility.

"Don't damn me when I speak a piece of mind."

An irrepressible, growling Axl Rose from Guns N' Roses, speaking truth to power.

"'Cause silence isn't golden when I'm holding it inside."

Fuck yeah.

But back here in Canada, it all feels different. It's comfortable, it's open, everything seems to work, and you can say whatever you want without someone whisking you off to the *mutawwah* station or following you to your house. I pop in the new Metallica tape, and it seems they just don't have it anymore. There's no tension, no hunger, no urgency. There's an impalpable but tangible feel of complacency in the air. It's almost . . . boring.

It's fantastic.

A Middle Eastern–looking man walks in. I know he's been here before, but I've never spoken with him. He wants a pack of cigarettes, a lottery ticket, and a soda (they call it "pop" here, but at this point in my life, I've spent more years at an American school than in any Canadian city).

"What is that you're reading?"

I'm pretty sure that's an Arabic accent.

"Oh, this?" I smile. "Medical Microbiology, by Jawetz." I show him the cover. "I didn't do too well on my micro finals this year, so I have to redo the exam before starting the next year."

"So you're a doctor?"

"Ha, no, not yet. Hopefully in two more years, if I don't screw up any more of my exams."

He laughs, warmly. "Oh, I'm sure you'll do fine."

Then, the question that almost every medical student has been asked by almost every parent with a child in high school or college.

"My son is studying science in university. He's very smart, and also wants to go into medicine. What can he do to increase his chances of getting in?"

I rattle off my usual answer—that there's no real shortcut, you have to study hard, get good grades, research experience, and so on.

"Where is he thinking of applying?" I ask.

"It is still early," he replies. "I would like him to come to Canada for medical school."

"And where is he now?"

"Back home, in Israel."

And, suddenly, he looks different.

I start to feel a little cold. I feel my heartbeat, racing, in my throat. My palms are clammy and my muscles tense up. I'm sitting on a stool in a narrow space behind the cash register. My ambulatory ability is restricted, and I feel vulnerable. I'm in full fight-or-flight mode, and it shows on my face—I'm sure of it. I'm surprised at my reaction, and puzzled by my inability to control it. I am embarrassed—and a little angry.

This isn't me.

I'm a reasonable person. I'm not even religious at this point. Bizarre thoughts are darting through my mind. Hey, Seinfeld is Jewish, and I love Seinfeld! And Einstein, Woody Allen—they're my heroes. Wait, one in five people in Israel are Arabs. Maybe this guy's not Jewish at all—maybe he's an Arab. But no, why should that matter? What if he *isn't* an Arab? What if he *is* a Jew? Why should that even make a difference? I wonder if he supports the settlements. Has his son served with the Israel Defense Forces? Or maybe he's like Chomsky or Tony Judt—one of us. Huh? What does that even *mean*? "One of us?" Are you serious?

"Oh, yes, for sure. He should definitely try here," I tell him, awkwardly.

"And where are you studying?"

"In Karachi, Pakistan. Before that, I lived in Riyadh—also the Middle East." I offer a forced smile. It doesn't help. In this particular context, highlighting our prior geographical proximity doesn't exactly evoke warm, fuzzy feelings of neighborliness. He's not quite as convivial as he was before my twenty-second mental meltdown. But despite having read my reaction perfectly, he remains polite—a quality that briefly makes me think he's more Canadian than Jewish—until I promptly tell my brain to shut up.

"Well, good luck, and thank you." He takes the cigarettes out of the bag and starts walking away, rapping them firmly on his palm twice before starting to open the pack. I call out as he pushes open the door.

"Hey, mind if I join you? I have my own."

"Sure," he says. "Come on out."

After a few short, quintessentially Canadian exchanges about the weather, I come clean.

"You're the first person from Israel I've ever met."

I tell him what they think about people like him in Saudi Arabia. He knows, but he hasn't heard the stories. He's laughing and shaking his head, more entertained than outraged. And when it comes to religious beliefs, it turns out we're not so different after all.

We're both atheists.

It's 2001, a little over two years since I graduated from medical school and moved permanently to Canada. I've done my U.S. licensing exams (transferring your qualifications to Canada as a foreign medical graduate isn't a simple process, unfortunately), and I have just enrolled in graduate school.

I think clinical medicine is an incredibly noble profession, but I've always had an avid interest in—and a knack for—science. Whenever science students ask me about going into medicine, I advise them to first understand what it really entails. For the most part, medicine is more public service than science. In medicine, you have to follow protocols. In science, you help create them. In science, trying out new things and being creative is encouraged. In medicine, getting too creative could get you sued, or worse.

I'm in the biochemistry program because of my fascination with molecular genetics, and will go on to earn my Master of Science degree from McMaster University in Hamilton, Ontario, before returning to medicine and specializing in pathology. But at this point, I don't know that. Starting off, my goal was to do a Ph.D., but the harsh realities of living on a paltry stipend for five or more years of my adult life have caught up to me—an important point I now hasten to add to my science-versus-medicine advice speech to balance out the idealism. For now, I'm happy.

My daily commute is about forty-five minutes to the lab and forty-five minutes back. I've just gotten into the car on a bright Tuesday morning. It's September 11.

By the time I turn on the radio, the first plane has already hit. It is being treated like an accident, but I instantly know it isn't. As I'm merging onto the highway, the second plane hits the South Tower. Now everyone knows what's going on, but the lady on the radio is being very careful. It's the usual, obligatory list of disclaimers: remember, the Oklahoma City bomber was a white man, and so was the Unabomber. And what about those guys who blow up abortion clinics? You never know, right?

All they know, they say, is that two large passenger planes have flown straight into the World Trade Center buildings, one in each tower, within less than twenty minutes of each other. One reporter says it could be a terrorist attack, but it's also possible that "the air traffic control system completely crashed."[3]

I switch stations.

Nearly all of the music stations are running a live CNN or CBC feed. Everyone's trying to be responsible in their reporting, and they're doing a remarkably great job at it. But these aren't the people I'm going to run into on the street, or be interviewed by at the border the next time I drive down to the States. So I switch over to Howard Stern, my usual morning commute go-to, who is broadcasting live from Manhattan.

Howard still hasn't figured out exactly what's going on. One of his staffers says it looks like there's smoke coming out of the second building too.

"No, no, no, no," counters cohost Robin Quivers. "It's a reflection. It's a reflection."

Soon, they receive confirmation that there was indeed a second plane.

"We're totally too lax in this country," Howard says. "We gotta bomb the hell out of them. You know who it is. I can't say, but I know who it is."

A caller dials in. "This is them towelhead *bastards*! You can't say that, but I can say that. It's time we take these towelhead bastards and throw 'em outta the damn country!"

Then, one after the other, the towers collapse.

"Atom bombs! *Atom bombs!*"

"Nuclear strikes all over those countries . . ."

"The first second I hear it was one of these towelhead or dothead bastards, I'm going to go out there and start goin' to those A-rab stores and I'm gonna start kickin' ass and get those assholes out of the whole frickin' neighborhood . . ."

"I call all Americans to get your arms together, baby, get out on the streets and go to your local frickin' deli . . ."

"You see how they wiped out the twin towers? Wipe out their country! Don't worry about the kids or the old people. Babies? Who cares about their babies?"

Because I fall broadly into the towelhead/dothead category, this is disturbing. But at least it's real. It's raw, without pretense. Now I actually feel like I'm getting the news in real time. Regular New Yorkers are calling in. A cab driver. Someone who lives two buildings away from the towers. Someone with friends who worked there. Someone who's concerned about pandemonium breaking out on the streets—looting, rioting, violence.

I arrive at the lab. Everyone is speculating, wondering how much worse it could get. "They're saying fifty thousand people work in both of those buildings," someone says. "And now they've hit the Pentagon." I walk over to my bench and start setting up for the day. The Internet is still a relatively recent phenomenon at this point, and we have a total of two desktop computers in the lab connected to it by way of a jumble of wires. No one has even heard of Wi-Fi. Some people have cell phones, but at this point, they're just, well, phones. So far, I've only heard about what's happening. I haven't seen the images.

I load up the CNN home page, and there it is. Stills of fire and thick black smoke billowing out of the towers, moments before they collapsed to the ground. A picture of people running down the street, noses and mouths covered, smothered under a dark cloud of gray dust. Pieces of paper flying around, completely intact. I wonder why they didn't burn.

Back in the summer of 1988, I was in Pakistan with my family when the president, Zia Ul-Haq, was killed in a plane crash. One of the more popular stories that got out was about his personal Quran, which survived the crash with minimal charring, apparently just enough for it to qualify as a miracle. The way people ranted about it was bizarre to my eighth-grade mind. "Did you see? Not a *word* damaged in his Quran! *Masha'allah!* Praise God!" *What's so impressive about a god that allows thirty-two people to perish in the sky, instead choosing to protect a book?* I thought. And a book with billions of other copies in print around the world, at that. But there were grown, educated adults around me going on and on about it. There was probably something I was missing. Maybe I'd understand it when I got older.

Well, now I'm older, and this was no miracle. There is plenty of undamaged, nonsacred paper floating purposelessly through the dust clouds this morning—really mundane, nonrevelatory stuff like stationery, office memos, and financial statements. I refresh the page. And I see the one picture I will never forget.

There's a close-up of the burning part of the building, and there are people hanging out of the windows, clinging to the outside. It's zoomed in so close that their faces are blurry, but you can tell some of them are about to jump. People who came to work just two hours ago, like any other morning, now have to decide whether they want to be burned to death, or simply fall to it a thousand feet below. It will be some time before I see the actual video footage of people jumping. For now, I'm staring at the still photo, my eyes frozen in place.

Our lab tech walks over to me, a middle-aged man from Beijing, China, with a heavy accent. He is also a physician who trained in his own country, but isn't able to pursue medicine here, I assume owing to language difficulty. He sits next to me and leans in close.

"What are they saying in Pakistan?" he whispers, half smiling.

"Well, I'm sure some people there are happy," I reply, keeping my voice down as well. I'm being honest. I'd been in Lahore just two years before, and Osama bin Laden was already a hero there after the 1998 U.S. embassy bombings by Al Qaeda in Kenya and Tanzania. President Clinton had sent out two cruise missiles to kill Bin Laden—but missed. The fact that America was unsuccessful in hitting him back was a huge morale booster for many Pakistanis, only amplifying the already frenzied state of collective ecstasy the population was feeling after becoming the first ever Muslim-majority country to go nuclear just three months before the embassies were hit. We'd just gotten the "Islamic bomb"—and from where we were standing, things were looking pretty good.

No one in Pakistan liked America back then. The country was still reeling from having to take in over three million refugees during the U.S.-supported Afghan war against the Soviet Union. With the war came large amounts of weapons—weapons that were supposed to be channeled to Afghanistan, but often found their way to Pakistani locals, both during and after the war. The country was awash in Kalashnikovs (AK-47s), handguns, rocket launchers, land mines—you name it. Weapons were in ample supply, at giveaway prices, and, of course, all in the wrong hands.

The resulting "Kalashnikov culture" continues to destabilize Pakistan to this day, and many blame the United States for it. First, the United States propped up Zia Ul-Haq—the military dictator who ousted and executed the democratically elected prime minister, Zulfikar Ali Bhutto (father of Benazir). Then, after the war, it cut and ran without helping to clean up the mess. Pakistanis still blame America for the violence within their borders, harboring a deep distrust of the superpower (even if almost all of them would jump at the chance of getting a green card). They wanted someone to strike back at all those complacent people in America, protected on either side by Earth's largest oceans, comfortably ignorant of the terrible things their elected government was doing to others around the world. But now they had the Islamic bomb, and a hero in Bin Laden, himself U.S.-trained, who could stand up to America's cruise missiles. Even those who didn't like him didn't really *mind* him.

"Well, he is just a bearded mullah like the others," a friend's U.S.-educated father once told me, swirling his scotch. "But he's the only one with the balls to stand up to the *goras*, the white people." He took a swig. "*Beta*, son, they got the Soviet Union, they got Iraq, Afghanistan—you know what that means, right?" He shrugged his shoulders like it was obvious. "Pakistan is next. They want to destroy Islam. Now that Muslims have an atom bomb, they will double down, you just watch. Don't fall for all this propaganda."

My colleague is smiling, and comes even closer. Pointing to my computer screen, he whispers, "In China they say this is good." He's referring to the Hainan incident in April that year, where a U.S. surveillance plane collided midair with a Chinese fighter jet a few miles off China's southeastern coast, killing its pilot. China detained the American flight crew, angering the United States. The United States, on the other hand, expressed regret, but specifically stated that it was not an apology, which is what the Chinese wanted. And although U.S.-Chinese relations are particularly strained in 2001, this is far from the only issue the Chinese have with the United States.

You might wonder if the tech and I have talked about this before. After all, why else would he approach me and calmly express his approval of this terrible event mere hours after it occurred? We haven't talked about this—or much else—before. He has assumed, though, without knowing any of my political views, that I—the brown, foreign grad student—would get it. He has come close to me and kept his voice down so the *goras* don't hear, precisely because "they" wouldn't understand—not the way that "we" do.

He isn't the first to approach me this way. Over the coming weeks, several more foreigners and immigrants will come up to me and start talking about how America finally got a taste of her own medicine, assuming I think the same. They would never say it elsewhere, but talking to me is a safe bet—I'm one of them, so I "know." It turns out that a lot of people have a lot of issues with the United States, and not all are unfounded.

Talking to one of my friends from medical school in Karachi that weekend is even more confusing. He is still back in Pakistan. He was three years junior to me, and is about to graduate this year. He is an American-born Pakistani who will interview for medical residency spots in the United States over the winter and start his first year in internal medicine next summer. He, like many others back home, thinks this was, as they say, the chickens coming home to roost. But that's not all.

"Look, everyone knows it wasn't Al Qaeda. Let's just get that out of the way," he types into the chat window. He has the same contradictory stance that many other Pakistanis—including Western-educated professionals—have about the attacks: that they are a justifiable retaliation to America's anti-Muslim foreign policy, but it also isn't Muslims who did it. It's either the Jews or the U.S. government. Right.

But this picture, of people hanging off the outside of the towers—I can't figure out how this could bring a sense of resolution for people like my lab colleague. How do you look at these images, of people consciously and deliberately deciding to jump to their deaths, and think, "Okay, this is good, now we're even, I feel better"? I'm reminded of all those great Scorsese movies from the '90s like *Goodfellas* and *Casino*. Every character in those movies is scum, and there are no good guys anywhere for miles. But you just find yourself rooting for the one whose story you know best. It's simply a matter of what's presented to you. Loyalty, it seems, is a function of proximity. And when you've grown up living among Saudis, in a Pakistani family, going to an American school, you aren't just proximate to one side. You realize how primitive and tribal the idea of loyalty really is, whether it's coming from a colleague happy to see innocent

Americans incinerated alive, or callers to the Howard Stern show, itching to kick out all the towelheads and nuke their babies.

With time, the diagnosticians diverge, as they always do with any issue in America, into the right and the left. The right is clear: this was a naked act of aggression—a declaration of war by terrorists. They started it, and we must respond.

But no, the left says. We need to be more nuanced. These people are simply responding to America's atrocities around the world. We're the imperialists here—we colonized them, we've built ourselves up at their expense, we've left them powerless under the boot of the military-industrial complex. We must look at the underlying grievances driving this. What are the "root causes" at play here?

This is the crux of the debate here in the West. I wish it were as simple as trying to make sense of things, looking for rational explanations, or speculating about the geopolitical or economic benefits these actors are in pursuit of.

But a few weeks later—when it's confirmed that fifteen of the nineteen hijackers were from Saudi Arabia, not to mention Bin Laden himself—it all starts coming together. I try to figure out what grievances the Saudis might have against the Americans, who have given them near-unconditional support, turned a blind eye to their subjugation of women and non-Muslims, protected them in the First Gulf War of 1991, and helped place them, gallon by gallon, among the twenty countries in the world with the highest per capita GDP. I know if I dig deep enough, I'll find something to explain this.

But I don't need to.

Despite being kept segregated from Saudi culture as a foreigner during the decade I spent there; despite my interaction with the locals being sporadic at best; despite having reasonable, educated parents to talk sense into me on the odd occasion that I crossed paths with the *mutawwahs* or that Ministry of Education monitor; despite attending school with kids from many countries around the world and being exposed to a variety of cultures and ideas; and despite being a religious skeptic—I had a visceral, near-hostile, completely *irrational* reaction to the Israeli man at the store the moment I knew where he was from.

But those hijackers—they grew up right in the middle of what I had just gotten a mere taste of. It was *focused* on them, like rays from a hot desert sun converging through a magnifying glass and burning into their skin, from the day of their birth, through each advancing grade in school, with each advancing textbook from the first to the twelfth grade, beckoning them every day to fight the infidels and wage jihad against enemies of Allah—all within a quarantined world where even a snowflake was a threat to their faith, their heritage, and their identity.

Shocking? This wasn't shocking. It was inevitable.

TWO

Root Causes

If you had to guess, where would you say this quote is from?

> The Ambassador answered us that it was founded on the Laws of the Prophet; that it was written in their Koran; that all nations who should not have acknowledged their authority were sinners; that it was their right and duty to make war upon them wherever they could be found; and to make slaves of all they could take as prisoners; and that every Mussulman [Muslim] who should be slain in battle was sure to go to Paradise.

These words might read like they're referring to a declaration from the Islamic State (ISIS) or an excerpt from a recent Al Qaeda manifesto. They may even sound like part of a *fatwa* from an Iranian cleric.

But they are neither.

They're actually the words of Thomas Jefferson, back when he was the United States' ambassador to France. The passage is from his report to then Secretary of Foreign Affairs John Jay, about a meeting he and John Adams had with Tripoli's envoy to London, Sidi Haji Abdul Rahman Adja, in 1786—more than two and a quarter centuries ago.[1]

Obviously, this is before the Islamic State or Al Qaeda. It's before the creation of Israel or the Arab-Israeli conflict. It's before Ayatollah Khomeini and the Iranian revolution; before Saudi Arabia; before the Taliban; before drone strikes; before the Cold War or the World Wars; before Herzl founded the Zionist movement; before Americans knew what jihad or even Islam was; before the United States had ever engaged in any military operation overseas; and—importantly—well before the existence of any established U.S. foreign policy.

Yet these words—about the laws of the Quran, taking slaves, waging holy war, and martyrdom—read as if they could just as well have been plucked from any international newspaper in the last week. How is it that this passage, over two hundred years old, still rings with such relevance today?

A good place to start would be 1784, about two years prior to Jefferson's letter. The Revolutionary War had just ended, and Great Britain had just signed the Treaty of Paris with a newly founded United States, recognizing the new nation's independence and borders. This, of course, came with a cost. American trade ships venturing into the Mediterranean had thus far enjoyed the protection of the British navy, but this was to be no more. They needed protection from state-supported pirates (corsairs) from the North African Barbary States of the Ottoman Empire (corresponding to Morocco, Algeria, Tunisia, and Libya today), who routinely raided trade ships entering the Strait of Gibraltar and sold their crew members into slavery or held them for ransom. By some estimates, as many as 1.2 million[2] people from Europe and America had been enslaved in North Africa between 1530 and 1780. (This is about a tenth of the number of slaves taken *from* Africa in roughly the same time period, but pretty stunning nonetheless.)

Britain and France, the biggest powers in Europe, were able to protect their ships by essentially bribing the Barbary States with tribute payments, or annuities—an arrangement that worked very well in keeping both parties happy. The Barbary States got lots of money each year, and the capacity of the French and British to easily make these payments awarded them an increased share of Mediterranean trade relative to those who couldn't afford them.[3]

Once the United States declared independence, the British were only too happy to inform the Barbary powers that American ships were now fair game. And it wasn't long before Algiers' ruler, Dey Muhammad, captured several American ships in 1785, leaving the United States—navy-less and in its infancy—unable to pay the required tribute.

Already, America was suffering losses it could not afford. This is the importunate situation that ultimately landed Jefferson and Adams in a room with Sidi Haji Abdul Rahman Adja. They wanted to know why Tripoli was doing this. "We took the liberty to make some enquiries concerning the ground of their pretensions to make war upon nations who had done them no injury," they reported. And Adja's answer illustrated, with stark clarity, precisely what this ground was.[4]

It would be inaccurate to say, though, as it's often said in some conservative circles, that the ensuing conflict was some kind of holy war. This isn't the kind of thing the Founding Fathers seemed interested in. Jefferson, influenced by the Enlightenment and English deists like Henry St. John Bolingbroke, is known for taking a razor blade to the Bible. That's not just figurative. He got an actual razor blade and physically sliced out all references to the supernatural and miraculous, such as to the Virgin Birth and the resurrection of Christ, leaving only its moral lessons. He told his nephew Peter Carr in 1787, "Question with boldness even the existence of a god; because, if there be one, he must more approve the homage of reason, than that of blindfolded fear."[5] And in his 1785 book *Notes on the State of Virginia*, he wrote, "It does me no injury for my neighbor to say there are twenty gods, or no god. It neither picks my pocket nor breaks my leg."[6] Those two lines were seized upon by the Federalist Party, which attacked him viciously during a particularly bitter presidential campaign in 1800, maligning him as a "howling atheist" and an "infidel."[7] He still won.

It isn't inconceivable to think that the encounter with Adja might have made Jefferson think back to the Quran he had purchased twenty years prior as a law student, in 1765. Jefferson's Quran, as it's now known, is one of the earliest translations of the holy book into English, by George Sale. It is the book upon which Keith Ellison, America's first Muslim congressman, was controversially sworn in, in 2007. Jefferson's interest in the Quran didn't go unnoticed by his opponents either.

I remember being amused when Newt Gingrich expressed worry in 2011 that his grandchildren would grow up to see a "secular atheist" America dominated by "radical Islamists."[8] His comical, contradictory concern about the United States' supposedly eroding Christian roots actually has precedent with Jefferson, who, like Barack Obama, was accused of being both an atheist *and* a Muslim by his opponents. And Jefferson's rejection of traditional Christianity in favor of Unitarianism, his interest in the Quran as a legal document, and his advocacy of religious tolerance and civil rights for Muslims gave them additional ammunition against him in the 1800 election.[9]

Now, it would also be inaccurate, as it's often done in some liberal circles, to romanticize Jefferson's relationship with Islam. It is admittedly speculative to say that Jefferson's report to John Jay quoting Adja's vile description of Islamic theology—without any comment or reservation—connotes a sense of recognition and familiarity with the tenets of jihad that Jefferson might have had. But it is plausible when you take other factors into account. Even as Denise Spellberg, author of *Thomas Jefferson's Qur'an: Islam and the Founders*, makes the case that Jefferson fought to make the United States more inclusive of Muslims, she acknowledges that his views of Islam were "mostly negative."[10] The introductory notes in Sale's translation of the Quran framed it primarily as a book of law—presenting Muhammad not only as an impostor and infidel, but also the "legislator of the Arabs."[11] As an ardent advocate of the separation of state and religion, Jefferson's introduction to Islam as a law student was through Sale's translation of the Quran, in which state and religion are intimately interlinked. And then, twenty years later with the Barbary conflict, he witnessed this mixing of the two in action. How could this have sat with him? The reader who still thinks Jefferson was partial to the Quran merely by virtue of owning one should also consider this: the Quran contains many of the same supernatural and miraculous elements as the Bible—virgins giving birth, staffs turning to snakes, angels, the devil, and more. If Jefferson abhorred them to the extent of literally using a razor to excise them from the Bible, why would the exact same stories survive his disdain in the Quran?

Although we can speculate, there is a good reason we don't know the definitive answers to these questions: Jefferson never directly expressed his religious beliefs in public. In the years following the London meeting, the United States secured peace treaties with the Barbary States, starting with Morocco, then Algiers, and finally Tunis and Tripoli. At no time did Jefferson ever frame America's conflict with them as a religious one. His primary interest was in working out a system allowing the United States to trade freely in the Mediterranean. That's it. "Jefferson did not demand regime change of the Barbary states, only policy change," wrote Christopher Hitchens. "And as far as I can find, he avoided any comment on the religious dimension of the war. But then, he avoided public comment on faith whenever possible. It was not until long after his death that we became able to read most of his scornful writings on revelation and redemption . . . And it was not until long after his death that *The Life and Morals of Jesus of Nazareth* [the Jefferson Bible] was publishable."[12]

One of Thomas Jefferson's proudest achievements was the Virginia Statute of Religious Freedom, proposed in 1779 and enacted into law in 1786. So proud was he of the statute—which stripped the Church of England of its status as Virginia's official state church and went on to become a key precursor to the First Amendment of the U.S. Constitution—that he had it listed in his epitaph, second only to "Author of the Declaration of American Independence." His commitment to religious freedom is sometimes interpreted as an appreciation for religion, which it really wasn't; it was more a function of his wish to keep church and state separate, and prevent the establishment of a state religion, as was ultimately achieved with the First Amendment. Indeed, Jefferson was a key proponent not just of freedom of religion, but freedom *from* religion. Commenting on the statute in his autobiography, he wrote:

> Where the preamble declares that coercion is a departure from
> the plan of the holy author of our religion, an amendment was
> proposed, by inserting the word "Jesus Christ," so that it should
> read "a departure from the plan of Jesus Christ, the holy author
> of our religion;" the insertion was rejected by a great majority,
> in proof that they meant to comprehend, within the mantle of
> its protection, the Jew and the Gentile, the Christian and

Mahometan [Mohammedan], the Hindoo, and Infidel of every denomination.[13]

Throughout the Barbary conflict, the Founding Fathers focused squarely on pursuing the United States' national interests with regard to free trade. It wasn't about values or ideological differences. It was simply about getting the job done. These battles weren't "holy wars," according to historian Frank Lambert; they were "an extension of America's War of Independence."[14] But the Founding Fathers were also under no illusions about how the Muslim pirates saw the conflict. This is why the Treaty of Tripoli, signed into law by President John Adams in 1797, contains these now-famous words in Article 11:

> As the Government of the United States of America is not, in any sense, founded on the Christian religion; as it has in itself no character of enmity against the laws, religion, or tranquility, of Mussulmen; and, as the said States never entered into any war, or act of hostility against any Mahometan nation, it is declared by the parties, that no pretext, arising from religious opinions, shall ever produce an interruption of the harmony existing between the two countries.[15]

And there you have it. Widely cited as a foundational element of secularism in America, Article 11 of the Treaty of Tripoli was a direct result of the United States' first-ever brush with self-proclaimed Islamic jihadists. And when a newly inaugurated President Thomas Jefferson refused to pay additional tribute money to Tripoli's *Pasha*[16] in 1801, it became the independent United States' first-ever international war.

It would be somewhat fair to dismiss Adja's words to Adams and Jefferson on the premise that ultimately the Barbary Wars were economic at their roots, not religious. However, it would be less fair to infer, as Frank Lambert does, that "neither the pirates nor the Americans considered religion central to their conflict"[17]: Jefferson's report clearly reflected the envoy's overt religious motivation, and the Treaty of Tripoli prominently acknowledged and addressed it.

No one can say for sure whether the Tripolitans were genuinely driven by their religious beliefs or were just using religion to justify their actions—but this doesn't really matter. I've always been interested in another question: where did Adja's ISIS-esque words come from? They certainly weren't a response to U.S. foreign policy or globalization. And they quite obviously could not have been a reaction to AIPAC (American Israel Public Affairs Committee), the Iraq War, or post-9/11 "Islamophobia." Clearly, the Barbary Wars predate many of the political grievances widely claimed to be the "root causes" of jihadist outrage. Yet the battle cry today remains the same as it was then. These words are virtually identical to those spouted ad nauseam by jihadists today who rationalize their bellicosity against infidels as a reaction to these U.S.-centric factors, utterly nonexistent at the time. How to make sense of this?

Well, the common denominator here also just happens to be the elephant in the room.

Allahu Akbar.

What do these words mean to you? These days, they may very well bring up a feeling of dread, of fearful anticipation at what's to come. A brutal beheading, maybe. A suicide bomber's final call before he detonates his dynamite-laden vest on a crowded train. The last sound heard by a blindfolded gay teenager in Iraq—both from his captors and the cheering crowd below—as he is thrown off the top of a tall building. Or, perhaps, the last words of a man who flies an airplane full of innocent people into a skyscraper. "Shout, *Allahu Akbar*," read part of a four-page document found in the baggage of 9/11 hijacker Mohamed Atta. "Because this strikes fear in the hearts of the non-believers."[18]

Now let me tell you what these words once meant to me.

My life began with them. I was born in Lahore, Pakistan, to Shia Muslim parents in the 1970s. Mere seconds after I took my first breath, these words—*Allahu Akbar*, or "God is great"—became the first ever to be whispered into my ears. I am one of millions around the world who began life with this ritual. Growing up, I associated these words with good things. Five times a day, for decades, I heard them ring out from the minarets of mosques, echoing through the cities I grew up in—Lahore, Tripoli, Riyadh, and more—as part of the *adhaan*, the alluringly melodic public call to Muslim prayer. At least in the immediate world around me—the world my parents, friends, and community had created for my siblings and I to grow up in—these words represented gratitude and appreciation to the Almighty for all he had given us. They were recited at celebrations and milestones, at births of children, at weddings, birthdays, and college graduations. We would say them in times of hope, of strength, and of weakness.

But when I hear these words today, they sound ominous. They forebode something dark, tragic. And they don't just strike fear into the hearts of nonbelievers. By far, most of the victims of Islamist violence are Muslims themselves. How did things get this bad?

Well, it depends who you ask. Some will tell you it's because there was a resurgence of Islamic fundamentalism in the late 1970s and early 1980s. And to be sure, this period did see significant change in the Middle East and the larger Muslim world. This was when Saudi Arabia—the historical birthplace of Islam and its Prophet Muhammad—achieved its status as the biggest oil-exporting country in the world. The tremendous amount of wealth it gained was also spent very generously on exporting *Salafi* Islam, the ultraconservative strain of Sunni Islam that drives militant Islamic groups like Al Qaeda and the Islamic State to this day. The late 1970s also marked the start of the Soviet war in Afghanistan, in which the United States supported the Afghan *Mujahedin* (which literally means "practitioners of jihad") and glamorized and exploited the fighters' religious and nationalistic sentiments to gain ground in the Cold War, well into the 1980s. And, of course, 1979 was the year of the Iranian Revolution, which ushered in the theocratic fundamentalist Shia Islamic rule of Ayatollah Khomeini, enthroning him as a key player in the region. It put both the sectarian rivalry between Sunni and Shia, and the ethnic rivalry between Persian and Arab, into overdrive. It was no wonder that we were suddenly hearing *Allahu Akbar* ring out from so much of the Muslim world as a battle cry.

And all of this had billions of dollars behind it. In 1977, Zia Ul-Haq, Pakistan's ruling military dictator, usurped power from (and later executed) the democratically elected prime minister, Zulfikar Ali Bhutto. Looking for allies who would help him quash dissent and help cement his position, Zia turned to the Islamists. With the help of Saudi funding, he opened up *madrassahs* (religious schools) across the country to indoctrinate and train thousands of children. Saudi Arabia, lush with oil riches and eager to promote its fundamentalist Salafi Sunni Islam, financed the *madrassahs* handsomely, jumping on this timely opportunity to push back not only against the Iranian Shia ayatollahs but also against the godless, atheist Soviets, in one go—all the while reasserting its position as the foundational nexus of "true" Islam. The word *Salafi* comes from *salaf*, meaning "ancestor"—and refers specifically to the earliest generations of Muslims, from the time of Muhammad himself. Salafism is a rigid doctrine prescribing the revival of this early Islam, believed by its adherents to be the religion's purest form.

The Mujahedin's faith-fueled jihad proved to be quite a weapon. And the United States, seeing its own two-for-one opportunity to hit both the Soviets and the Iranians with it, happily went along. With the United States and Saudi Arabia now perfectly aligned in purpose (although for different reasons), Zia suddenly found himself at the helm of one of the most strategically important countries in the world. The dollars poured in, the jihadists became freedom-fighting heroes—and the United States rarely missed an opportunity to play up the holy-war angle.

"We know of their deep belief in God, that they're confident that their struggle will succeed," U.S. national security adviser Zbigniew Brzezinski declared during a visit to Pakistan in 1979. Addressing the Afghan Mujahedin, he said, "That land over there is yours. And you'll go back to it someday, because your fight will prevail. And you'll have your homes, your mosques, back again, because your cause is right, and God is on your side."[19]

It sounds completely crazy when you think about it now: an oil-rich Saudi Arabia, aligned with an Islamist military dictator in Pakistan, unabashedly mobilizing Islam and creating thousands of jihadists—with enthusiastic support and funding from a United States that considers propping up jihad to actually be *in its national interest*. But it's also easy to see why it made sense at the time. It was the Cold War, and this was the best weapon the United States had. Who knew back then what the young students from those *madrassahs* had in store for the future? Indeed, the word for "students" in Pashto—the native language in the area—is *taliban*.

Others, however, will tell you that much of this is an illusion. Apart from these sporadic pockets of fanaticism, this alleged resurgence is all about regional politics, and never really represented the Muslim world at large. They will point out that some of the world's largest Muslim populations— in Indonesia, India, Bangladesh, Turkey—remained relatively insulated from this fundamentalist madness, at least at the time. Even in Pakistan, a majority of the population is fairly moderate. Fundamentalist religious parties, despite being loud and somewhat influential, rarely ever get more than a small fraction of the vote in the national elections. They will re- mind you that women have been elected heads of state in Pakistan and Bangladesh several times. Can the United States make the same claim?

In his seminal 2001 essay "The Politics of Rage: Why Do They Hate Us?" published just over a month after 9/11, Fareed Zakaria noted that these "moderate" Muslim countries seemed to have less anti-American sentiment than those in the Middle East. "Only when you get to the Middle East do you see in lurid colors all the dysfunctions that people conjure up when they think of Islam today," he wrote. "In Iran, Egypt, Syria, Iraq, Jordan, the occupied territories, and the Persian Gulf, the resur- gence of Islamic fundamentalism is virulent, and a raw anti-Americanism seems to be everywhere. This is the land of suicide bombers, flag-burners, and fiery mullahs."[20]

This makes sense. I spent most of my youth in Saudi Arabia, which is run somewhat like a hotel by the House of Saud, the obscenely rich royal family. This is a place where women aren't allowed to drive, any criticism of the government can land you in jail or worse, and no one is allowed to practice any religion except conservative Sunni Islam. Public beheadings, floggings, and even crucifixions are carried out for crimes like sorcery, blogging, or staging nonviolent protests.[21] As in any other society, the population has its problems and its complaints, but there is no open channel to voice them. Any opposition to the government, or even criticism of it, can be deadly. There is no real political party to join, no freedom of the press, no platform for dialogue. Elections are exceedingly rare, virtually meaningless, and do nothing to bring about any significant change.

But there is one place where people can express themselves more openly: the mosque. Throughout the region's history, Arab dictators have cautiously used religion to their advantage, encouraging it just enough to be able to control the masses, but stopping just short of letting it become a threat to their rule. In Saudi Arabia, it is at the *khutbah* (religious sermon) after Friday prayers, and the conversations following it, that the average Saudi really gets to participate. The consequence of having just this singular channel for any kind of open expression is predictable. All of the frustrations, grievances, and problems of the people—political, economic, and social—get packaged up and channeled through a single medium, neatly wrapped up in *Allahu Akbar*.

This is quite true for much of the Arab world. It is at least partly why the only real political opposition to many of these governments comes in the form of devoutly religious groups. It is also why Islamist groups are often at the front of the line to fill the vacuum when a dictator is displaced or weakened—as happened in Iraq, Egypt, Libya, and, most recently, Syria. Religious speech isn't clamped down on as much as other forms of political speech; this is why religious groups were the only ones able to organize an opposition during dictatorial rule in these countries. They provided the only prominent platform for dissent.

And when religious expression is your only path for dissent, *everything* becomes a jihad.

So, did this era truly represent a widespread resurgence of fundamentalism, or is it just that a small but really loud fringe of people was finally given wealth, power, and a voice? Talk to young Muslims raised in North America, and many will tell you the latter. "Those fanatic blowhards are a miniscule minority," they'll say. "They aren't representative of the vast majority of Muslims."

If you take the words "miniscule" and "vast" out of those statements, I might actually agree with them. Growing up in a fairly moderate,

progressive Muslim family, I was told myriad political reasons for this supposedly recent rise of militant Islamic fervor in the world. My parents and
their friends would discuss it at length during parties and get-togethers.
Every root cause under the sun was blamed for the growing fanaticism we
saw around us—politics, culture, power, greed, U.S. foreign policy, British
colonialism, Arab nationalism, Israel, the media—you name it. But no
one seemed to want to connect it to the religion. It was anything, and
everything, but the religion itself. Despite being the only common denominator, Islam had nothing to do with it at all, they'd say.

I didn't find this hard to believe. My family and friends were good
people. They worked hard and made an honest living. They had made
great sacrifices to get where they were, and they were dedicated to giving
their children the best lives possible. Their religious faith had guided
them. God wanted them to be good people and do good things. And they
did. Their lives had started the same way mine did—with the words *Allahu Akbar* recited into their ears at birth. They truly believed God had
answered their prayers. They had good health, successful careers, financial security, and the ability to provide for their loved ones. They were
grateful to God for all of this. How, then, could it be possible that the same
Allah they worshiped, the same Quran they recited, could drive other
people to hate, destroy, kill? It *had* to be something else. It was obviously
not the faith. It couldn't be. The fanatics had hijacked and distorted
the faith of their parents, grandparents, and ancestors, making it—and
them—look bad to the rest of the world. No *true* Muslim would ever do
that. It had to be an outside force, a foreign hand, an enemy of Islam that
was trying to destroy it; these jihadist fanatics weren't *real* Muslims.
This was a political thing, a cultural thing. It had nothing to do with
Islam. And I believed them. I *lived* there, for God's sake. I was surrounded
by Muslims. If they were so bad, I wouldn't have a hope in hell. But
things just weren't that bad. I used to go to school, play with my friends,
and ride my bike like any other kid anywhere in the world.

And it seemed as if that culture thing had something to it. I had already lived in Libya, Saudi Arabia, and Pakistan by the time I hit my
teens. I had also visited Tunisia, Syria, Turkey, and Bahrain. They were
all countries with Muslim-majority populations, yet vastly different. They

pronounced Arabic words differently, despite three of them being Arabic-speaking. Women were allowed to drive everywhere except Saudi Arabia, and dressed more liberally in Turkey and Tunisia. You could get thrown in jail and beaten if you were caught with alcohol in the Saudi city of Al Khobar—but if you drove just forty minutes east to Bahrain, you could easily drink, and no one cared.

Some things, however, didn't change. The *adhaan* was the same everywhere. The Quran and the Prophet Muhammad were passionately revered everywhere. By middle school, my siblings and I had learned to read and even write Arabic fluently. But I could barely speak or understand it. That may sound bizarre, but it is the story of millions of Muslims around the world.

All in all, I spent over a decade in Saudi Arabia. Again, this land is the historical birthplace of Islam, its Prophet Muhammad, and its holy book, the Quran—foundational elements of the religion that are revered universally by over a billion and a half Muslims in the world, regardless of sect or denomination. The Saudi monarch isn't just called the king, but also holds the title "Custodian of the Two Holy Mosques," referring to the two holiest sites in Islam, in Mecca and Medina. This is the land that Muslims all around the world face when praying five times a day.

Growing up in Riyadh, I started feeling early on that something wasn't right. We all knew about the public beheadings, but never dared to watch them. In Riyadh, these are still carried out at a public square that expatriates lightheartedly refer to as "Chop Chop Square." In her book *Green Sands: My Five Years in the Saudi Desert*, Martha Kirk provides a fairly accurate account of how it all goes down. "The crowds tend to be emotional, almost to the point of hysteria, and at times, in irrational frenzies, they push the foreigners (or non-Moslems) in their midst to the front of the crowd," she writes. We knew about this, but as Kirk notes further, we also had other reasons not to go: "One story circulated that if the prisoner who is to be decapitated is a non-Moslem and of some other nationality, the crowd may attack anyone of that nationality who happens to be in their midst."[22]

Here's some perspective: In August 2014, the same month that the world was reeling with shock at the beheading of James Foley at the hands of the Islamic State, Saudi Arabia beheaded nineteen people, including some for the crimes of sorcery and smuggling cannabis.[23] The Saudi government, claiming the Quran and *Sunnah* (traditions of the Prophet Muhammad) as its constitution, also amputates the limbs of those charged with theft. Religious minorities are not allowed to practice their religions. The women in the country suffer some of the most egregious human rights abuses of any in the world. In addition to being banned from driving, they require the permission of a male guardian simply to work or travel. Victims of rape are often charged with fornication or adultery and sentenced to flogging if unable to produce four male witnesses to "prove" the "crime."

As I grew older and gradually became more aware of the environment outside the shelter of my immediate family and school, I started to note the discrepancies. I tried adamantly to reconcile this society around me with the religion I was being raised in. Over and over again, I was told by my relatively progressive family and friends that the culture around me had "nothing to do with true Islam." This land—the land that had first brought Islam into the world, they would tell me—had Islam all wrong.

In most Muslim households, the Quran sits at the highest place possible. In our house, it rested on top of the tallest bookshelf in the house, in the living room. It cannot be recited or physically touched unless an act of ablution and purification called *wudhu* is first performed. It cannot be recited or touched by menstruating women. It is read in its entirety during the Sunni *taraweeh* prayers in the holy month of Ramadan, and in many Muslim communities, it is held over the heads of grooms and brides as a blessing when they get married. A child completing her first reading of the Quran is a momentous occasion—parties are thrown, gifts are given. Second only to the Bible, the Quran is one of the world's most widely revered books.

But the majority of Muslims in the world cannot understand any of it.

Most of the world's Muslims do not understand Arabic. Before the Internet, I rarely met anyone—including the devoutly religious—who had really read the Quran in his or her own language. Like my parents, they simply went by what they had heard from their elders. We couldn't Google or verify translations instantaneously like we do now. In some conservative Muslim circles, it was even considered sacrilegious to translate the book into any other language—it was as good as altering the word of God.

With the Internet, however, came exposure. Suddenly, every twelve-year-old child could search multiple translations of the Quran online by topic or keyword, in dozens of languages. Nothing was hidden; it was all right there to see.

Understandably, this is how we make sense of most things today. When British soldier Lee Rigby was stabbed and hacked to death in broad daylight on a street in southeast London in 2013, one of his murderers, Michael Adebolajo, referenced the holy book to justify his actions. "We are forced by the Qur'an in . . . *Surah Al-Tawbah* and many, many other *ayahs* [verses], which state we must fight them as they fight us," he said in a video made by a witness.[24] All we had to do was a simple online search, and we would know exactly what Adebolajo was talking about. The Quran is a single book, consisting of 114 chapters, called *surahs*. Each *surah* is composed of *ayahs*, or verses. Reading *Surah Al-Tawbah*, the ninth *surah* in the Quran, you would find in verses 29 and 30 (written 9:29 and 9:30, or 9:29–30) the command to fight Christians and Jews until they either convert or pay the *jizyah* tax—as the Islamic State later did in cities like Mosul, Iraq. Similarly, when the Islamic State claims divine sanction for crucifying dissidents by citing verse 5:33 from *Surah Al-Maaidah*, or beheading its enemies by citing 47:4 from *Surah Muhammad*, we can look them up for ourselves in seconds, and instantly connect the dots.

Needless to say, this wasn't something I could do as a kid in the late 1980s, prior to the Internet. My siblings and I had an after-school tutor who taught us the Quran in the classical Arabic in which it's written. Again, like many non-Arabic-speaking Muslim children, I had learned how to read and recite Quranic Arabic without knowing its meaning. In order to change that, I asked my parents to buy me two well-regarded English translations—one by Muhammad Marmaduke Pickthall, an English convert to Islam whose translation was published in 1930; and the other by N. J. Dawood, an Arabic-speaking Iraqi Jew whose translation was popular for its easy readability.

At the time, there was a small Shia community in Riyadh, primarily made up of South Asian expatriates like us. The Shia sect of Islam follows the tradition of Muhammad's cousin and son-in-law, Ali ibn Abi Talib, the man I am named after (as are countless other Shia men—"Ali" is the "Joe" of the Shia world). Almost immediately after Muhammad's death in 632 CE, a conflict arose over who his successor would be. Some of his companions nominated Abu Bakr, Muhammad's close friend and father-in-law, who went on to become the first of four caliphs recognized and revered to this day by Sunni Muslims worldwide. Others, however, wanted Ali ibn Abi Talib to succeed the Prophet. This sect ultimately became known as *Shia-tul-Ali*, or "followers of Ali," shortened to *Shia*. Today, Ali is recognized by Shia Muslims to be the first of their twelve Imams (or six, for the Shia subsect, the *Ismailis*); and Sunnis also recognize Ali as their fourth caliph. As of 2009, Sunnis compose about 87 to 90 percent of the world's 1.57 billion Muslims, and Shias compose about 10 to 13 percent. A majority of the world's Shias—between 68 and 80 percent of them—live in just four countries: Iran, Iraq, India, and Pakistan.[25]

Every year during *Muharram*, the first month of the Islamic calendar, Shias commemorate the killing of Muhammad's grandson, Husayn, and his family, in 680 CE at Karbala, Iraq. Husayn, the third Imam of the Shias, was the son of Ali and Fatima, Muhammad's daughter. The family of Fatima, believed by Shias to be the only biological progeny of Muhammad to survive to adulthood, is called the *Ahl Al-Bayt*, a phrase literally translating to "people of the house." To Shias, these biological descendants of Muhammad are infallible, and free from sin. The Shias often use verse 33:33 in the Quran to partly back up their claim. The verse references the Ahl Al-Bayt by name and says God himself wants to remove *ar-rijs* (sin) from them. To the Sunnis, however, Ahl Al-Bayt in the context of this verse actually refers to Muhammad's wives—and this admittedly makes more sense if you read the verses before and after it, which clearly reference the *nisaa an-nabi*, the "wives of the Prophet."

Although Ali had worked cooperatively for the most part with the three caliphs before him and was a caliph himself, his son Husayn found himself in direct conflict with the *Umayyad* caliphs who gained power after his father's death. When Husayn refused to swear allegiance to Yazid, the caliph at the time, Yazid proceeded to behead him and kill most of his family and companions on the tenth of Muharram, a date known as *Ashura*. Even today, over 1300 years later, this incident is mourned quite ostentatiously by Shia Muslims worldwide.

During the ten days leading up to Ashura, Shias dress in black and attend *majalis*, or nightly gatherings where a religious scholar delivers a lecture about some aspect of Islamic history or philosophy, followed by a recollection of the events of Ashura, focusing on a different member of Husayn's family each night. On hearing this, the audience openly weeps, and then engages in a ritual of self-flagellation, that is, beating themselves in mourning. In most cases, this self-flagellation, called *maatam*, is a light to firm hitting of the chest to a rhythm accompanying the recitation and singing of *nawha*—melodic chants of tragic poetry and prose emotion- ally describing the killing of the Imam Husayn and other members of Muhammad's family by Yazid's army. As Ashura nears, however, many Shias dial up the intensity, using razors and knives to cut their skin and literally bleed for the Imam. Commonly, children partake in this ritual, encouraged by their parents.

In Riyadh, however, our Muharram rituals were dramatically atten- uated. Saudi Arabia doesn't allow the practice of any other religion ex- cept Sunni Islam. There are no churches, no Hindu temples, and certainly no synagogues—but the practice of Shia Islam or the presence of Shia mosques is especially odious to the Saudis. Many Saudis consider Shias to be heretics or apostates; the Shias are the people who, after all, devi- ated from Islam when they rejected the successorship of the first caliph. For Saudi Salafists, this isn't just a *difference* from Islam, like Hinduism or Christianity. It's a *blasphemy* of it.

The Saudis knew that many of us were Shia. They were okay with that, as long as they didn't catch us practicing it. Still, to avoid any undue dis- crimination, my father changed the Arabic spelling and phonology of our family name, a well-recognized Shia name, just in case. My last name, pronounced *Riz-vee* in Urdu and Persian, or *Ra-da-wi* in Arabic (written رضوى), became *Riz-fee* (written رزفى). We conducted our *majalis* in hiding, usually in someone's house or apartment, and disguised it as a dinner party. A large room would be cleared of furniture, and rugs and sheets spread out for people to sit on the floor. Videotapes of the sermons would be played on the TV, and someone always had the remote control ready to change the channel in case there was a raid. We had to keep our voices down while reciting or singing *nawhas*, and keep our chest-beating very light, so it sounded like soft, rhythmic clapping. The *majalis* were held in a different residence every night. All of us contributed.

The good news was that all my friends would be there. Like going to church, or other forms of religious congregation, these were communal, social events that I have fond memories of. I come from a musical family. Today, my brother and my cousins are professional musicians, and I sing and play in a band myself. This is no coincidence. My siblings and I were known in the community for our musical abilities, and we would excitedly wait for Muharram every year and prepare our *nawhas* for each of the ten days, working out the vocal arrangements and chest-beating *maatam* tempos for our performance (apart from the chest beating, any other musical accompaniment was considered inappropriate, or even sinful). My proud parents would serve as the audience for our rehearsals.

The religious mourning took a backseat to the social celebration, which isn't exactly unprecedented. To what extent, for example, can the somberness of Christ's crucifixion really compete with the excitement at the start of the Good Friday long weekend? It was a similar concept at play here. Just like children growing up singing in church choirs, we learned how to sing at these *majalis*. Oh, and there was also great food, and my favorite tea—steaming hot, pink, Kashmiri-style chai. To this day, some of my happiest memories come from the Shia mourning season.

The bad news, however, was that I wasn't very adept at Urdu, the Pakistani/Indian language that the scholar on TV delivered his lectures in. Everyone in my school spoke English, and my Urdu was limited to the frustrating confines of a very elementary, strictly conversational vocabulary. Sitting there for forty-five minutes and hearing an old bearded man speak incomprehensibly through a tinny JVC television speaker for ten nights in a row could get really grating.

So I started to bring in my Quran. The *majalis* were lectures in religion, and I could never properly understand them. Instead of wasting that time, I figured, I would just bring in my English Quran and read while everyone listened to the speaker.

"That could come across as rude, Ali," my dad told me. "Like you're not paying attention."

"Well, the guy's on a TV screen. And I'm not exactly reading a Bertrand Russell book in there. I'm reading the Quran. Who's going to stop me from reading the Quran?"

He seemed convinced. From then on, I would read the Quran, the book I'd been raised to believe was the perfect word of God, in a language I could understand, at the *majalis* for the next few Muharrams. And that's when things really started to change.

I found endorsement for almost all of the Saudis' actions in the Quran. The beheading of disbelievers (used interchangeably with "nonbelievers") was right there in verses 8:12–13; the amputation of hands for theft in verse 5:38; domestic violence in 4:34; the killing of polytheists in 9:5; and so on. I was dismayed. I began to ask more questions of my elders. Is this something they had been keeping from me? To be sure, there are things you don't tell children until they have reached a certain age. Was this one of them? I wanted them to explain all of this. But when I would present these verses to them, they seemed just as taken aback as I was. They would seem surprised, and more often than not, would allege that I was mistaken. They would insist that I show them exactly where I read the verse I was quoting. When I would show them both of my heavily bookmarked Qurans, they seemed even more shocked. This is when I realized that they didn't know the verses themselves. As it turns out, very few in the moderate and liberal Muslim community we used to keep company with had even *read* the Quran. And they were suspicious of the translations.

"This Pickthall, he was an English man. Why should we trust his translation? How do we know he had the right intention?"

The other translator, Dawood, fared worse. "He's a Jew! Come on, don't be so gullible. How could you possibly think an Iraqi *yahoodi* would have our best interest at heart?"

I must admit, these tactics worked. When someone tells you you're stupid for believing a certain narrative, your first instinct is to do anything *not* to appear stupid. And it seemed futile to put up a fight, because the conversation would never end:

- If the translation was correct, it was being "misinterpreted"—but there was no explanation as to what the correct interpretation was.
- If the interpretation was plausible, it was "specific to that time" or simply "out of context"—again, with no explanation as to the correct context.
- If it was all-out false or wrong, it was because it was "metaphor," and I was "taking it too literally"; indeed, it seemed as if the more questions I asked, the more "metaphorical" the Quran got—anything in the text that had been proven false over the centuries was deemed a "metaphor."
- If I pointed out that many of the Saudis, Egyptians, and other Arabic-speaking nations also interpreted the book in the way I was describing, I was promptly reminded that the Saudis had been bought by America and Israel a long time ago, and remember, those Egyptians even had a *treaty* with the Jews.

And if all else failed, they'd say these were "just words" unless "interpreted correctly," something along the lines of what we hear from apologists like Reza Aslan today.[26]

Needless to say, rendering the Quran's words meaningless and giving no objective parameters for what a truly correct interpretation would look like effectively made the book immune from any possible criticism.

It was a neat little trick, but I was happy to be challenged. It made me dig deeper into how the scripture could be interpreted, how the problematic passages could be rationalized, and what the historical context for some of these verses really was (see chapter 7).

A second upside to this was the realization that my family and friends were truly decent human beings. As much as their denialism could be frustrating in an argument, their flat-out refusal to accept that their religion prescribed bad things meant, to me anyway, that they were good people. And they weren't good people *because* of their holy book; they were good people *in spite* of it. They were also unwilling to accept at face value any verse or passage that didn't align with their personal ethics and morality. This was also telling: they didn't *get* their morality from the Quran; they used their *already-present* morality to *interpret* it—or at least to interpret what they thought was in it. *Why not cut out the middleman? I thought. You already have what you're hoping to get from a book that tells you that you need the book in order to get what you already have without the book in the first place, right?*

And I did seriously consider these convoluted rationalizations for some time. The reason was simple. Letting go isn't easy. I had been raised in Islam. Islam—or at least my parents' interpretation of it—directed the moral order of my family, my culture, and the society that surrounded me. I was well aware of the dire consequences of questioning it, especially in a country like Saudi Arabia. In a society where changing your mind can literally mean losing your head, even one's subconscious would make meticulous cost-benefit calculations before allowing one to make the leap.

In time, however, I became convinced that what I had been told was wrong. My elders would tell me, "Ali, it's not just religion that causes trouble in the world. What about greed? Power? Hate? What about racism and xenophobia? What about nationalism?"

I would find it amusing that in order to defend religion as a *good* thing, they would lump it into the same category as these *terrible* things. This was quite telling. So I would agree with them. I would say, "Oh, yes, I completely agree with you that religion is right up there on that list with greed, hate, and xenophobia." And they would shake their heads as if I'd misunderstood them, yet be unable to articulate how. They knew I hadn't. If anything, I feel religion is so divisive precisely because it encompasses elements of *all* of these things. My well-intentioned elders didn't know it, but they were conceding the point. They knew the reality of it—but they didn't *know* they knew. And that—that is the very definition of denial.

Now, it's one thing to say religion is the cause of every ill. Of course it isn't, and no reasonable person could claim that. But it's another to *never* hold religion accountable for *any* ill, effectively according it a status of honor and immunity that these very same apologists would never give to any of the other terrible things on that list that they themselves put religion on.

And all of this would make me wonder: Was this really about extremists corrupting the religion? Or was it about moderates sanitizing it? I was seeking explanations, but got excuses. Between then and now, they've only become more pronounced. Here are some of the more common ones.

"Islam is a religion of peace."

This is by far the most recognizable refrain, drummed into me over and over since I was a child. I was even told that the word *Islam* means "peace," which isn't really true. Although it sounds similar to *salam*, which does mean "peace," *Islam* actually means "submission" or "total surrender," derived from the verb *aslama*, which means "to surrender."[27]

To me, the question was, how would one define Islam, the *religion*? Defining Islam—or any religion, for that matter—by the actions of its adherents is problematic. Saying most Muslims are peaceful so Islam must be peaceful doesn't cut it. The immense diversity of the Muslim world includes believers ranging from the unflinchingly pacifistic to the murderously violent, both crediting their religion for their behavior. Moreover, just as it would be inaccurate to say that bacon-eating Jews are evidence that Judaism allows the eating of pork (it doesn't), it is inaccurate to say that certain behaviors indulged in by large numbers of Muslims—like adultery or drinking alcohol—are endorsed by Islam (they aren't). The actions of the religious are not the definition of their religion.

However, if you define Islam by the contents of the Quran—a universally recognized canonical document of the religion that is foundational to every sect and faction across the Muslim world—a credible conversation is certainly possible. The Quran, as discussed earlier, contains numerous verses of prescribed violence—amputation of hands for theft, the slaying of polytheists, eternal torture and hellfire for vocal disbelievers, and so on. But it also contains peaceful verses urging believers to care for orphans, provide for the poor, and treat others well.

My friend Maajid Nawaz, a reformed former member of the Islamist group *Hizb-ut-Tahrir*, often points out that Islam is neither a religion of war nor a religion of peace; it is simply a religion, like any other, that has been interpreted in a variety of ways over the years by a variety of different people.[28] This makes sense. Like the Bible and other holy texts, the Quran is full of contradictions. In some places, the book is vague enough to lend itself to a generous range of interpretive approaches; but in others, its words are clear as day. The verse prescribing hand amputation for theft, for example, couldn't be more unambiguous.

Where it really breaks down is how you approach the contradictions. Those who approach the Quran like any other book, with no partiality to faith or divinity, find it easy to appreciate the good, criticize the bad, and move on. But what about those who believe this is the perfect, infallible word of God? How would they deal with the contradictions?

This is where it gets interesting. A natural consequence of combining an unwavering belief in divine infallibility with discrepant, mixed messages is the emergence of powerful defense mechanisms. Some simply deny the presence of any contradictions outright; it is God's word after all, and it has to be perfect. Others compartmentalize the conflicting messages, picking and choosing what they want to follow, acknowledging that the rest is beyond their comprehension. God works in mysterious ways, they say. And some go to great lengths to interpret contradictory verses in a way that makes the violent verses seem peaceful, bringing what they see as some consistency. More often than not, these are distortions, not interpretations (see chapter 7). Finally, there are those who read the violent verses much more literally. They may employ traditional, recognized techniques of Quranic exegesis such as *naskh*, or abrogation, using the more violent verses from Muhammad's later life in Medina to nullify the more peaceable earlier verses from Mecca.

Like many others, I quickly realized that this last group was the most dangerous—but it wasn't because they chose a more violent interpretation of the religion. It was because their approach was much more *plausible*. Why?

Well, if you approach the Quran as an infallible, flaw-free book of peace, you have to work much harder to "interpret away" the obviously violent passages and make them seem benign. It takes an incredible amount of intellectual acrobatics, as many of us know from seeing that requisite Islamic scholar come out after every jihadist attack, going to great lengths to tell us why a phrase like "strike the necks of the disbelievers" is completely consistent with Islam being a religion of peace if only placed in its correct "context." This context is usually claimed to be self-defense in war, which, again, isn't strictly true (more also on this in chapter 7).

But if you focus on the more violent verses, the contradictions are much easier to reconcile. Here's why: The good things in the Quran are not unique to Islam. Giving charity, being kind to others, and not stealing, for example, are values that predate the Quran by centuries. Everyone from Confucius to the Greeks wrote about them, and human beings had been working together collaboratively and treating each other well for thousands of years before Muhammad was even born.

The violence in the Quran, however, is relatively unique to Islam—or to the Abrahamic religions in general. Muslims who revere concepts like jihad and martyrdom don't have to jump through hoops to reconcile the peaceful stuff with the violence the way apologists do. This is for two reasons.

First, they see everything they're doing as good. To them, feeding a hungry orphan is at par with eliminating the blasphemer from their ranks. Both actions, to them, serve to make their society more righteous, and are pleasing to Allah.

Second, they simply believe that the prescription to do good only applies to like-minded Muslims and their allies. Yes, they are to execute apostates and adulterers in their midst for their sins, to enslave Yazidi women, and to slay the polytheists. But they are also to ensure that their own orphans are fed, the believing women protected, and the poor given their due of *zakah*, the obligatory Islamic charity tax. It's actually quite simple. The fighting verses are about how to deal with the outsiders and the sinners; and the benevolent verses about how to deal with their own. No contradiction.

This is one of the only ways that a Quran seemingly full of contradictions can be deemed both infallible *and* consistent, making it both plausible and compelling. And that's why it's dangerous.

At this point, the "religion of peace" crowd can't compete with this kind of straightforward simplicity in its explanations—and until they do, they will never be able to make a convincing argument for their case. Kunwar Khuldune Shahid, a courageous Pakistani writer who publishes regularly in papers within and outside Pakistan, says that liberal Muslims who maintain that the scripture can be interpreted in many ways must acknowledge that literalism is one of them. "How exactly does one decide whose comprehension is accurate, when it's a direct case of 'my interpretation versus yours'?" he asks. "This is precisely why countering religious fundamentalism through a twisted and self-convenient brand of the same religion can never work, for it would always allow the radical brand to exist."[29]

The inconvenient truth here is, those that claim that Islam has been "hijacked" or is being "exploited" by violent militants bring up more questions than they answer. The most obvious one is this: If Islam is so peaceful, what is it about it that attracts such unsavory, violent characters to co-opt it? What else is there to the story?

"It's politics, not religion."

On his CNBC show in 2004, Tim Russert asked Christopher Hitchens and Andrew Sullivan to talk about the role of religion in the international conflicts the United States was involved in.[30] Hitchens spoke first, bringing up the Israel-Palestine issue. "American support has, up to now, gone to the Wahhabi [Saudi] royal family that pumps out anti-Semitic [and anti-American] propaganda but is considered our ally in the Middle East; to Israeli settlements run by Messianic fanatics who wouldn't be able to do this if it weren't for American aid; and to extreme Christians, mainly in the United States, who hope that out of this conflict they can bring on Armageddon and the Apocalypse." Hitchens believed that the relatively straightforward solution to this problem—division of the land between the Jews and Arabs living in it—was "made impossible" because of monotheism. "It's poisoned by it."

"No," said Sullivan, a believing Catholic, insisting it wasn't monotheism, but the fusion of monotheism with politics that was the poison. "The issue is not the relevance of faith," he said. "The issue is the fusion of faith with *political power.*"

Sullivan's argument is one I've heard endlessly, and still do in the case of Islam. It isn't an altogether bad one. There's almost always a political element—usually a desire for political influence, power, or dominance—driving these conflicts between religious groups. Most of us have likely heard liberal Muslims, particularly North American Muslims, claim that their religion has been hijacked, that terrible acts are being carried out "in the name" of their religion, or that all these miscreants are using their religion "as an excuse" to advance what really happens to be their politically driven agendas.

But what's missed in these discussions is the take-home point that Hitchens articulated perfectly in response to Sullivan's protest: "But if your belief is that Jesus [is going to come] back very soon [and] is going to kill everyone who doesn't agree with him—how do you keep that out of politics? *The belief is political.*"

He was spot on. The Abrahamic religions are *inherently* political.

The Israel-Palestine conflict is probably the best model to demonstrate this, so let's stay on it for a bit. What we're talking about here are ideological belief systems that use reward and punishment, on Earth and beyond, to affect people's individual and collective behavior. We're talking about authoritarian dictates prescribing how to live, eat, deal with authority, form a government, have sex, raise children, and punish those who don't comply. We're talking about legal codes, both personal (the Ten Commandments) and societal (*halakha*, *Shariah*). We're talking about economics, trade, and more.

Nationalism, terms of law and order, and territorial claims are at the very root of what makes something political. Islamic jihadism, a doctrine of holy war, is centrally driven by a nationalism that is fiercely and violently protective of the religion against attacks (including from cartoonists and novelists), or of encroachment on Muslim lands. Zionism, also a nationalist movement, has a territorial claim at its very heart—one also supported by many evangelical Christians who believe the Jews must first return to Israel in order for Christ to return. Of course, the Jews are mere pawns in this eagerly anticipated end-times scenario, making this belief simultaneously anti-Semitic *and* pro-Israel. Add to this the unfortunate fact that "pro-Israel" automatically means "anti-Muslim" to millions of

Arabs and Muslims across the world, and it becomes all but impossible to see where religion ends and politics begins.

To think that the religious can be separated from the political in conflicts like this is naïve. If we roll the snowball back up the hill a few centuries, we see that much of what we consider to be the *causes* of this conflict today are actually the *effects* of previous hostilities. This continues, on repeat, until you trace it back to the books. Says Exodus 23:31–32 in the Old Testament:

> I will establish your borders from the Red Sea to the Sea of the Philistines, and from the desert to the River. I will hand over to you the people who live in the land and you will drive them out before you. Do not make a covenant with them or with their gods.

Sound familiar? And Deuteronomy 1:8:

> See, I have given you this land. Go in and take possession of the land the Lord swore he would give to your fathers—to Abraham, Isaac and Jacob—and to their descendants after them.

Of course, there's more. Genesis 15:18–21 promises the land of Israel to Abraham and the Chosen People. Numbers 34:1–12 describes the borders of the Promised Land in great detail, and it's no surprise that they are quite similar to the borders of Israel today.

Simply citing these passages will often get you a firestorm of backlash and accusations of being reductive, simplistic, or not examining the full historical context of these documents. If only I were to dive in a little deeper, they tell me, I would see that the current situation in Israel and Palestine—which looks and feels identical to the descriptions in these passages—is utterly and completely unconnected to the passages. This, of course, is obvious nonsense.

It's also almost exactly what I've been hearing from my fellow moderate and liberal Muslims since I was a child—that despite the complete and obvious corroboration of my observations by what I've read in the scripture, I am still somehow mistaken.

Verse 5:51 of the Quran says:

> O you who have believed, do not take the Jews and the Christians as allies. They are [in fact] allies of one another. And whoever is an ally to them among you—then indeed, he is [one] of them. Indeed, Allah guides not the wrongdoing people.

Am I to believe that this verse, or verses 9:29–30 directing Muslims to fight Jews and Christians, or the famous *hadith* (an account of Muhammad's words or actions, as recorded by his companions, separate from the Quran) of the Gharkad tree saying the "last hour" will not come until the Muslims "kill [the Jews],"[31] have no effect *whatsoever* on the thinking of people who genuinely believe the Quran to be the perfect, infallible word of God?

To me, denying religion's role seems to be a way to criticize the politics of these situations while remaining apologetically "respectful" of people's religious beliefs for fear of offending them. You may have heard it said more than once: "I am against radical jihadism, not Islam, for Islam is a religion of peace." Or, "We oppose the Zionists, not the Jews, for they are the people of the book." But Zionism and jihadism aren't just political movements separate from Judaism and Islam. They are central to and *driven* by these religions. There is no good secular argument for Israeli settlements in the West Bank, yet settlement construction continues despite explicit bipartisan opposition to it by every U.S. administration since Lyndon B. Johnson.[32] The liberation of Palestine is claimed to be a solely nationalistic goal, but finding a pro-Palestinian rally without someone shouting *Allahu Akbar* is about as rare as finding a Palestinian Christian suicide bomber. And even if you look at other conflicts, sure, maybe the Islamic State is reacting to U.S. foreign policy or British imperialism (they certainly aren't known to be fond of the Sykes-Picot Agreement), but one wonders, what can this possibly have to do with enslaving underage Yazidi girls, killing Turkmen Shias, throwing gays off rooftops, or executing apostates? My argument isn't that religion is the *only* factor driving these atrocities, but rather that of several factors involved, religion is one—and a key driver.

Religious beliefs can also have a significant impact on secular politics. In a 2013 Pew research poll of the American general public, 44 percent answered "yes" when asked if they believed God gave Israel to the Jews. This included 55 percent of all American Christians and 40 percent of all American Jews. And among white evangelical Christians, a whopping 82 percent said they believed God gave the land of Israel to the Jewish people.[33] In a separate Pew poll, over a third said they believed the return of Jews to Israel was essential to facilitate the return of Christ.[34] As you may imagine, these beliefs do influence how people vote. And 44 percent is a sizeable voting bloc, whether you're running as a Democrat or a Republican. Not only are these religions political by their very nature, but their practitioners also dramatically influence both domestic and foreign policy in the United States.

Interestingly, the explanation the pollsters gave for why so many more Christians than Jews supported the proposition was as follows: "Some of the discrepancy is attributable to Jews' lower levels of belief in God overall."[35] This is not surprising. As religious belief wanes, so do the rigid positions that make solutions impossible.

Hitchens was right on this. The religion/politics dichotomy is a false one. It isn't that politics has no role; it's that politics is simply inseparable from the Abrahamic religions. Religion *is* politics. That was the case during the Barbary confrontation in 1786, and it's the case with the Israel-Palestine conflict now. Throughout history, religion has simply been an excuse looking for a conflict.

"It's culture, not religion."

This is another false dichotomy that almost all Muslims have heard at some point, whatever their degree of religiosity. For the most part, it's simply a matter of perspective.

As an example, consider women who wear the *burka* (full body cloak) and/or *niqab* (face veil). They are almost exclusively Muslim women who do it for religious reasons. But women who wear only the *hijab* (headscarf) will often claim that the niqab is not required and is altogether un-Islamic—a "cultural" practice. Other Muslim women who don't cover their hair at all will tell you the hijab itself isn't required for Muslim women, but women should still not mix with men, date, or attend coeducational schooling. And then you would have all-out feminist Muslim women, some of whom don't just demand full equality with men, but insist that Islam gave women full equal rights 1,300 years before the feminist revolution. They'll tell you that socially conservative Muslim women are just part of a patriarchal "culture" that really has nothing to do with *true* Islam, which, to them, is all about gender equality.

Growing up in Riyadh, my siblings and I learned early on what was religion and what was culture. My parents had a ready reference point in the Saudis. Anything that both the Saudis and we practiced was real religion. This included praying, fasting during Ramadan, and visiting Mecca for *Hajj* (the yearly Muslim pilgrimage) or *Umrah* (similar to Hajj, but smaller scale with fewer rituals and no time specification). Some of it was sectarian, such as our *majalis* and their *taraweeh*, an extended form of Ramadan prayer exclusively practiced by Sunnis. But other things, they told us, were just Saudi or Arab culture, like the burka, niqab, and the violent corporal punishments. These practices had nothing to do with us, and were un-Islamic, they'd say. This, I later found, was not true.

Those who make the "it's culture, not religion" argument are essentially doing what the "it's politics, not religion" crowd does: trying to find a way to criticize acts they find deplorable without being seen as disrespectful of religion, or worse, blasphemous to it.

Take child marriage, for instance. In 2008, a Saudi court in the conservative Qasim province of the country refused to grant an eight-year-old girl the divorce she sought from her fifty-eight-year-old husband.[36] As expected, there was near-universal outrage in response, not least among Muslims themselves. The husband was called sick, perverted, and disgusting, with several creative yet unprintable interventions proposed as to what should be done with him and certain elements of his anatomy. "This is a horrific cultural practice," people would say. "It has nothing to do with Islam."

Except that it does. "The Prophet married Aisha when she was six years old and consummated his marriage with her when she was nine years old," states a *hadith* recorded in the *Sahih Bukhari* collection, volume 7, book 62, number 88 (written 7:62:88). "And she remained with him for nine years (until his death)."

This is not a one-off *hadith*. There are at least twenty more that reference Aisha's young age at the time of her marriage to Muhammad. Verse 65:4 of the Quran gives instructions on how to divorce certain women, including "those who have not yet menstruated," a verse interpreted widely by many influential scholars in both the Sunni and Shia sects to mean that marrying young children is permissible. This is why Saudi Arabia has no formal age limit on marriages. It is also why Iran's Ayatollah Khomeini, still widely respected by Shias worldwide, lowered the age of marriage for girls from eighteen to nine, specifically allowed intercourse with girls as young as nine, and actually endorsed "touching with lust" and other forms of nonpenetrative sex play with even younger girls—in his words, "even if she is a nursing baby."[37]

On several occasions, I brought up the topic of Muhammad's marriage to Aisha in front of Muslim friends who were lambasting the old Saudi husband. Their reaction to the Prophet's marriage was notably different. It ranged from complete distrust and rejection of my sources to excuses like, "It was different back then," or "Girls at that time matured faster." The Prophet's marriage to Aisha simply wasn't seen in relation to Saudi laws allowing child marriage. The latter was deemed a sick cultural perversion—but the former, an identical act, was considered either untrue or acceptable when seen from some kind of "contextual" perspective. The oft-quoted description of the Prophet as the perfect human being to emulate for all time wouldn't apply to this particular topic. In this particular case, it was the "it was different at that time" excuse.

Another example illustrating the false religion/culture dichotomy is that of female genital mutilation (FGM). The prevalence of this practice in several Muslim-majority countries, particularly those in Africa, is astonishingly high. In Egypt, the largest Arab country in the world, over 80 percent of women have undergone the procedure. In countries like Somalia and Djibouti, the prevalence is above 95 percent.[38]

In 2014, the American scholar of religions Reza Aslan declared on CNN that FGM is "not an Islamic problem. It's an African problem." Two other points he made turned out to be unintentionally related. First, he said, "Nowhere else in the . . . Muslim-majority states is female genital mutilation an issue." And then, "[in] Indonesia, women are absolutely 100 percent equal to men."[39]

Why is this interesting? Well, Indonesia is the largest Muslim-majority country in the world, with a population of about 250 million, close to 90 percent of who are Muslim. And when it comes to this one particular practice, Aslan isn't far off: women and men in Indonesia *do* happen to have roughly equal rates of childhood genital cutting. At least 86 percent of Indonesian girls have undergone FGM, and 90 percent of households think the practice should continue.[40]

Even though we've seen that the world's largest Muslim country and the world's largest Arab country both have FGM rates higher than 80 percent, does this really mean it's related to Islam? Or is it merely a "cultural" practice as Aslan claims? Well, here's the thing: there are four *madhab*, or schools of jurisprudence, in Sunni Islam: *Hanafi, Shafi'i, Maliki,* and *Hanbali.* In the Shafi'i school, FGM is mandatory, or *wajib.* In the other three, it is optional, but preferred.[41] Nowhere is it denounced or condemned. There are also several *ahadith* (plural of *hadith*)[42] promoting the procedure, and as expected, those who practice it consider them very authentic, and those who don't, don't. Along with countries like Indonesia where the Shafi'i school is heavily subscribed to, FGM is also practiced among the *Bohra Ismaili* Shias in South Asia and the Kurds in Iraq.[43]

The next argument is usually that FGM predates Islam, which is true; and that FGM is mentioned nowhere in the actual Quran, also true. Now, this is also true of male circumcision (more aptly, male genital mutilation or MGM), practiced across all sects and factions on baby boys born to Muslim families. MGM also predates Islam by several millennia, and is also mentioned nowhere in the Quran. Like female cutting, it is mentioned only in the *hadith.* But would anyone argue that MGM has "nothing to do with Islam" on the same basis?

To the rationalist who knows religion is man-made, the separation between religion and culture is even more spurious than that between religion and politics. Cultures give rise to religions, and religions shape cultures. Even genuine cultural innovations within a religious group like the driving ban on Saudi women aren't completely unrelated to the theology; they fit comfortably into the larger picture of prescribed patriarchal control, completely in sync with the mind-set behind the Quranic command that men have authority over women, in verse 4:34.

If I had to articulate the distinction between religion and culture, I wouldn't say they are separate entities. I would say they symbiotically enable each other. Cultures are dynamic by nature, continuously evolving. Religion dogmatizes them. It cements them in their place, freezes them in time, and prevents them from moving forward. By locking culture up into a time warp, religion makes it look like the bad guy, absolving itself of blame. Cultures carry potential for change. Religionizing them effectively kills off that potential.

To paraphrase an eloquent but anonymous Reddit user: saying that culture is the problem and not religion is like saying, "It's not falling out of the airplane that kills you. It's the ground."[44]

"These people are not true Muslims."

The aftermath of the 2011 killing of Osama bin Laden by U.S. Navy SEALs was a confusing time for some Muslims, particularly those in the West. Many of those I knew had spent years dismissing Bin Laden as a terrorist who was "not a true Muslim." Yet, after his body had been dropped into the sea from the side of an aircraft carrier, there was concern about whether he had been given a proper Islamic burial.[45] The Obama administration insisted that the sea burial had been conducted according to Islamic requirements—the body had been washed and wrapped in a plain white *kafan* (shroud), religious remarks had been read, and the remains dropped into the water within twenty-four hours of the man's death. But despite all indications that this was a dignified burial for a Muslim, some still didn't seem to think it was dignified *enough*—even though they didn't really consider him a "true" Muslim until his killing.

I've encountered the "not a true Muslim" retort countless times. The arguer first makes a general statement about all Muslims, and then reframes it in order to somehow render it immune from any refutation. This is an informal fallacy known as the *No True Scotsman* fallacy, first described by the philosopher Antony Flew, who asked us to imagine a Scotsman shocked after reading a story in his morning paper about the actions of an English sexual predator on the loose. "No Scotsman would do such a thing," he tells himself. The next morning, he sees another story about an even more heinous sex crime, this time committed by a Scotsman. Not ready to admit he was wrong, he says, this time, "No *true* Scotsman would do such a thing."[46]

This is a common problem when it comes to discussions about Islam, especially because different kinds of Muslims often have vastly different ideas about what it means to be a Muslim. A common conversation with Muslims in the West may proceed like this:

> *Person A: Islam means peace and Muslims do not kill innocent people.*
> *Person B: But the Islamic State kills innocent people, and they even say "Allahu Akbar" as they do it.*
> *Person A: Well, then they're not* true *Muslims.*

The obvious issue here is, there is never any consensus on who the "real" Muslims are. To a moderate Muslim in the West, the Islamic State aren't true Muslims. To the Islamic State, Shias aren't true Muslims. To both the Shias and the Sunnis, *Ahmadis*—a sect that believes a prophet or messiah actually came after Muhammad—aren't true Muslims. And to the Ahmadis, the Islamic State aren't true Muslims.

This is another reason why, as mentioned earlier, it is problematic to define Islam by the actions of its adherents, and better to define it by the contents of the Quran, which each of these sects holds as foundational to their faith. Other elements like the *hadith* or documented biographies of Muhammad vary widely from sect to sect. Once the Quran becomes the central reference point, a substantive conversation can take place. Yes, it's true that there are numerous interpretations of the book across all sects, but these can be debated more effectively when there is consensus on the source. The status of the Quran is the only thing that all believing Muslims agree on.

"Most Muslims are peaceful, so Islam is peaceful."

This defense frequently accompanies the "Islam is a religion of peace" position discussed earlier, and makes the mistake of conflating the actions of Muslims, which are exceedingly diverse, with the tenets of Islam, which are codified in immutable scripture. Many Muslims drink alcohol and have premarital sex too—this doesn't mean Islam endorses those actions. Conversely, only 42 percent of Muslims in my home country of Pakistan—which has the second-largest Muslim population in the world—pray the five daily prayers actually mandated for most Muslims by the Quran and the *hadith*.[47] What's Islamic and what Muslims do are often two different things.

Since childhood, I have heard examples of the great scientific and mathematical discoveries of Muslim scientists, like the great ninth-century astronomer Ibn Ishaq al-Kindi and Ibn al-Haytham (Alhazen), the father of optics, during Islam's "golden age." The achievements of these men were truly revolutionary, but had as much to do with Islam as Christianity had to do with the achievements of Newton, or Judaism with the achievements of Einstein. In fact, just as Galileo and Darwin got themselves into trouble with the Church, some of the early Muslim scientists and philosophers often found themselves in conflict with Islamic theologians for their leanings toward rationality over revelation.

I figured out early on that this position—of giving Islam credit for the achievements of Muslims—didn't work. Could anyone seriously allege that the hundreds of Nobel Prizes won by Christians and Jews could be credited to their beliefs in Christianity or Judaism? Of course not. Most of these scientists were secular in their beliefs, and achieved what they did in spite of religion, not because of it.

But when it comes to religious violence, there *is* a direct line that can be drawn from a verse that says "beat your wife if you fear disobedience" (verse 4:34) to the actual action of hitting one's wife. Similarly, a verse that directs you to fight the Jews and Christians until they convert or pay a heavy tax (9:29–30) can directly be connected to the actual action of fighting Jews and Christians until they convert or pay a heavy tax. No one is saying that those who don't hit their wives aren't faithful

Muslims. But those who do it aren't being un-Islamic in any sense. They are acting in accordance with the verse that allows it. (The various interpretations of this verse are discussed further in chapter 7.) In the same way, while it is clear and obvious that all Muslims are not violent jihadists, it is also true that all violent jihadists are Muslims, and, as discussed earlier, use plausible interpretations of scripture to justify their actions.

With this, one can see what I've always thought of as an obvious defense mechanism on the part of many Muslims, to say nothing of religious people in general. Where there is no direct link, as with Islam and scientific achievement, every attempt is made to try and establish one. But when there *is* a direct link between scripture and action—as in the case of jihadist violence or hitting one's wife—it is not only denied, but those who do point it out are labeled ignorant, or even bigoted. That, of course, isn't a counterargument; it's evidence of a lack of one.

"This has nothing to do with Islam."

In February 2015, Craig Stephen Hicks was arrested for murdering his three young Muslim neighbors over what a police investigation determined was a parking dispute. However, speculation continued as to his "real" motivation to commit the crime. The problem was that Hicks was a vocal atheist who posted frequently about his disdain for irrational beliefs on social media networks. Interestingly, he seemed to be an equal opportunity offender who actually seemed to think at times that Muslims were unfairly singled out. In one instance, he supported the controversial 2010 Park 51 project of building an Islamic community center close to Ground Zero in Manhattan, writing on his Facebook page that U.S. Christians who thought Muslims were using this mosque to "mark their conquest" were being hypocritical. "Everywhere I've been in this country there are churches marking the Christian conquest of this country from the Native Americans," he wrote.[48]

His seemingly impartial opposition to all religions was also noted by CNN religion editor Daniel Burke, who pointed out that Hicks actually seemed to *defend* Islam in certain instances, like in his criticism of conservatives concerned that Obama is a Muslim, which he didn't see as a big deal. "His views against religion are kind of—very anti-religious, but nothing specifically against Islam," said Burke.[49]

Of course, this wasn't going to be any consolation to the families of the three victims, Deah Shaddy Barakat, Yusor Mohammad Abu-Salha, and Razan Mohammad Abu-Salha. Hicks's crime was horrific, and despite the motive revealed by the police, there was no way to definitively say this wasn't a hate crime.

But then, something very telling happened. Several writers who typically bemoan the idea that Islam promotes violence came out to propose a link between the so-called "new atheism" and Hicks's crime. "THE CHAPEL HILL MURDERS SHOULD BE A WAKE-UP CALL FOR ATHEISTS," screamed a New Republic headline.[50] The author, Elizabeth Bruenig, pointed out Hicks's admiration for the writings of Richard Dawkins and Thomas Paine, alleging that there was some influence. And the aforementioned scholar of religions, Reza Aslan, sent out a bizarre tweet:

> Sorry @RichardDawkins no matter how many times you condemn #ChapelHillShooting we are just going to assume you haven't and don't.[51]

Journalist Glenn Greenwald also suggested a connection between the murders and atheism, tweeting:

> The Chapel Hill killer had "an obsessive interest in atheism," was a fan of Richard Dawkins (who condemned killing).[52]

This kind of response to these incidents isn't new. Of course, the writings of Richard Dawkins and Sam Harris are no more responsible for Hicks's actions than the writings of Noam Chomsky are for the actions of Osama bin Laden. The renowned terrorist not only praised and quoted Chomsky's views on U.S. foreign policy, but also owned some of Chomsky's books.[53] Does that in any way invalidate Chomsky's criticism of U.S. foreign policy? No. Does it place any responsibility on Chomsky for violence that may be perpetrated on American citizens by Al Qaeda–inspired Islamic jihadists? Not at all. And finally, does the fact that Bin

Laden's views on U.S. foreign policy were closely aligned with those of Chomsky imply any equivalence whatsoever of intention or purpose between the two men? Absolutely not. And the reason for this is clear: Not once has Noam Chomsky ever endorsed any kind of violence against anyone in his writings. If anything, he has always stood for the opposite.

Now, people like me—who grew up among moderate, peace-loving Muslims tired of repeatedly having to explain the violence committed in the name of their religion every day—are familiar with the opportunity that incidents like the Chapel Hill shooting present to some apologists. At some level, there is a strange sense of satisfaction from certain defensive Muslims and their allies—sometimes even all-out glee—when the usual patterns are reversed in this way. There's an understandable (if disturbing) feeling of vindication that apologists gain from these crimes that provide them with a rebuttal against the narrative that terrorism is an "Islam problem." Every time an event such as this happens, it's as if they get yet another item to add to an already not-very-long list of "What about . . ." debate points—like the violent Christianity of the twelfth century, abortion clinic bombers, and one-offs like Oklahoma City bomber Timothy McVeigh and Norwegian mass murderer Anders Breivik—to deflect attention from a strikingly clear pattern of hundreds of jihadist attacks happening on a daily basis, in multiple countries, in the name of Islam, with the killers citing supporting verses from the Quran and chanting *Allahu Akbar* at every instance. Instead, they get to say, "See? It's not *just* Islam." Obviously, this is misleading. It's almost an exploitation of anti-Muslim hate crime victims for the political purpose of curbing criticism of the religion.

It's plain to see that this equivalence is misplaced. Unlike the books of Dawkins or Chomsky, the literal words of the Quran, as we've seen, clearly encourage and endorse hate and violence against disbelievers, women, Jews and Christians, polytheists, and others (see chapter 7).

Here's what is so revealing about the Chapel Hill shooting aftermath: on the one hand, you have countless Islamic jihadists every day, plainly articulating the religious motivation behind their violent actions, quoting Quranic verses explicitly *endorsing* these actions, and yelling *Allahu*

Akbar before carrying them out. To the apologists, this has "nothing to do with Islam."

On the other, you have a one-off incident in which three Muslims are tragically murdered by an atheist who never declared his intentions, enjoyed books by Dawkins and Thomas Paine that don't even *remotely* prescribe violence, and whose motive was determined by investigators to be related to a parking dispute. To Greenwald and Aslan, this was somehow "linked to atheism."

And there you have it: the apologists outright deny any link when it's clearly there; yet vociferously claim the existence of a link where none exists.

Unlike religious scriptures, there is simply no atheist "doctrine" that prescribes or commands violence. We have yet to see a man quoting from *On the Origin of Species* and yelling, "Darwin is great!" before detonating himself on a crowded bus. Do atheists do bad things? Of course they do. But even Joseph Stalin, possibly the most evil atheist in history, didn't commit his crimes in the *name* of atheism. If anything, Stalin's murderous totalitarian ideology was manifestly closer to (one could say, even modeled on) the Abrahamic religions: accept me as your savior or face severe punishment; I'm watching your deeds, I'm monitoring your thoughts; doom awaits you if you do wrong, but do as I say and you'll be saved; and so on. It was utterly removed from, say, the free-thinking spirit of the philosophers of the Enlightenment, or the "new atheist" thinkers of today.

After the beheading of journalist James Foley by the Islamic State in August 2014, President Barack Obama stated in his remarks: "ISIL speaks for no religion . . . no faith teaches people to massacre innocents."[54] Unfortunately, this is only accurate if we share the same definition of "innocent" as the authors of the sacred texts of these religions, which we don't. In verses 9:1–6 of the Quran, for instance, one need only be a polytheist who won't capitulate to Islamic authority to be worthy of death. In the Old Testament, nonvirginal brides (Deuteronomy 22:21–22), sexually active gay men (Leviticus 20:13), and those who dare to work on the Sabbath (Exodus 35:2) are all to be killed by divine command. To the authors of these books, these are not innocent people. To us—needless to say—they are.

By the time Islamic State suicide bombers and gunmen took to the streets of Paris, killing and wounding hundreds a little over a year after Obama's statement, fewer people were buying the story. Once the statement of responsibility from the organization came forth, replete with direct quotes from the Quran, descriptions of non-Muslims as "pagans" and "crusaders," and characterization of Paris as a "capital of prostitution and vice,"[55] many non-Muslims were not only distrustful of the usual ensuing defenses of Islam by Muslims, but also frustrated. Whenever declared Islamic jihadists kill a large number of innocent non-Muslims, the first reaction from Western moderate Muslims often centers on trying not to make Islam look bad. One hears that the Quranic verses quoted are out of context, that members of the Islamic State aren't "true" Muslims, that Islam is a religion of peace, that most Muslims are peaceful, and of course, that the attacks have "nothing to do with Islam."

The fear of simply calling a spade a spade is seemingly ubiquitous, and almost exclusively happens with the case of religion. Consider for a moment how strange this is: a man yells *Allahu Akbar* and commits a terrible action, like a beheading. He claims his act was justified in the eyes of God. You go online and look up all of the passages he is quoting, as well as related ones. The words match his actions exactly. He has even articulated his intentions clearly and *told* everyone why he did it. But everywhere you turn, people are saying, no, it's got to be something else. Even if you show them the exact words the man quoted, they find a way to tell you it's unrelated. Some may even call you a racist or bigot simply for bringing the issue up.

Now, if he had said he was influenced by politics, nationalism, money, video games, gangster movies, or hip-hop, we would see the opposite. Everyone would easily take his claim at face value. We would have heated debates about guns, the regulation of video games, violent rap lyrics, and the dangers of American exceptionalism. Indeed, when any terrorist so much as mentions Iraq or Palestine in one of his speeches, the same nothing-to-do-with-Islam crowd immediately begins its anti-foreign-policy tirade. They don't wait to try and find "context" or "deeper meaning" behind the terrorist's stated motives. They simply take him at his word. However, if he is repeatedly and consistently citing his religious beliefs and devotion to Allah as his central motivation, they back off, stroke their chins, and suspect that there has to be something deeper at play: a "root cause."

The taboo against criticizing religion is still so astonishingly pervasive that centuries of hard lessons haven't yet opened our eyes to what has been apparent all along: it is often religion itself—not the distortion, hijacking, misrepresentation, or politicization of it—that is the root cause. Why all the defense mechanisms, then?

Because of fear.

There are 1.6 billion Muslims in the world. How do you say openly that their faith is driving these atrocities? If you criticize their beliefs or doctrine, will they take it as a personal attack on them? Will they accuse you of being a bigot? What if some far-right extremist gets angry and commits a hate crime against a Muslim neighbor? What if you get lumped in with his kind? And finally, what typically happens to critics of this particular religion? It's clear, from the Salman Rushdie affair to the Danish cartoonists to *Charlie Hebdo*, that the risks for them are quite high.[56] It is understandable why many Westerners—particularly liberals—would want to avoid saying anything.

Now, imagine the risks for those who want to take on the faith from within.

THREE

Letting Go (Part I):
The Born-Again Skeptic

I'm five years old, standing next to my dad in the large upstairs bedroom at my aunt's house in London, England. Everyone is gathered in the room—my parents, siblings, aunts, and uncles. My cousin and playmate, Sana, is lying on the bed. She has childhood leukemia, and her battle is coming to an end. We're all here to be with her in her last moments, to say good-bye. She is three years old.

Although this is not my first visit to England, it's the first I would remember, and with a great amount of clarity. It wouldn't be until years later, during my training as a medical student and subsequent cancer pathologist, that I would fully understand what I saw Sana go through the last few weeks—the terrifying bouts of pain, the heartbreaking way she cries for her mother when it hurts, the utter helplessness of feeling those horrible symptoms of cancer inside her tiny little body, symptoms that can reduce even grown men to tears. She is too young to understand why this is happening, and too innocent to comprehend, much less face, the inevitability of death.

And then, there are moments that would stay in my memory forever. One morning, all us kids are sitting at the breakfast table having Weetabix cereal and grape juice. Sana is sitting across from me. Her older brother says something funny, and everyone laughs. She adores her brother. She giggles, smiling wide, as a three-year-old does. But her gums are bright red. There's blood running across her teeth. She doesn't know she's bleeding. Our smiles fade, and she notices. The blood slowly trickles down the sides of her lips. She looks down and quietly starts crying. My aunt hurries over. Sana immediately turns to her, burying her face into her mother's shoulder, clinging to her sleeves as they walk away. Now sobbing, her face is wet with tears and blood. She is embarrassed by her cancer symptoms. Things were going well for her that morning. She was fitting in, enjoying breakfast with her cousins, being a normal kid. But something just had to go wrong again. No carefree moment can ever last, I learn that day, when you're a kid with cancer.

Holding on to my dad's forearm, I watch as my aunt and mother sit by Sana's bed, crying and praying desperately as she gasps for breath. She is pale and weak. She has likely been given large amounts of sedatives and painkillers to help ease her passing, but watching her now makes it clear that there's still some pain breaking through. Cancer doesn't discriminate. There's no reason she would have it any easier than anyone else. Cancer doesn't care if you're eighty, or three.

"*Baba*, what's happening to Sana?" I ask my dad. He looks down at me.

"She is returning to God," he says. "God is taking her back so she can be with him again, like she was before."

He makes it sound as if that's a good thing, but nothing that I'm seeing in this room feels like a good thing. My mother and my aunt are reading from the Quran, their faces drenched with tears.

"What are *Ammi* and *Khala* reading?" I ask my dad. "What are they praying so hard for?"

"They don't want Sana to go, Ali. They are praying to God, begging him to let her stay and to stop her pain."

God doesn't do either of those things that day. Her pain gets worse. She struggles harder and harder to breathe, her gasping becoming more and more pronounced. And then, finally, it stops. My three-year-old cousin, Sana, is dead. Everyone in the room is drained. Shaken. My aunt and uncle are inconsolable.

I'm angry. My five-year-old mind is seeing this as a gruesome game of tug-of-war between God and the rest of us. This unseen being who my parents have told me is all-powerful and can do anything he wants, is on one end of the rope, and barely even has to try. We are all on the other end, tugging with all our might. Obviously, it's hopeless. And he doesn't even pull the rope his way in one fell swoop to win. No. He lets us keep tugging for a while, stretching out the agony over time, gradually amping up our struggle like a trained torturer. We don't have even the remotest hope of winning. We never did. It's cruel, sadistic, and obscene. Yet they're praying to him, begging him to save Sana, but from whom? Himself? Surely they'll realize now how *rahmaan* (compassionate) and *raheem* (merciful) he really is.[1] If I, as a five-year-old, can see this is a scam, surely they will too, won't they?

But almost every ritual in the immediate days after Sana's death—from the funeral prayers to the burial ceremony—seems to involve God as a positive character, despite what he did to her. He is being prayed to. He is being asked to bless her and take care of her in heaven just hours after he painfully and callously took her away. I must be missing something. After all, I'm just a kid. They are grown-ups, with university degrees and well-paying jobs. Maybe there's something they're not telling me that would make sense of all of this. But I don't dare to ask the question. I know it's a really bad thing to doubt God. I've been told that I should fear God, but I've also been told to love God more than anything else. It's that fear-love combination, I would learn later, that is at the heart of what drives the battered woman syndrome, or the master-slave relationship.

"She's in heaven, Ali. It's the best place in the universe. God has called her back. Once you go there, you never die," they tell me. Why, then, don't we all go there right now? Why are we still here? Why are we so sad for her? Shouldn't we be happy? And how do you know in the first place? Have you *seen* heaven? Has anyone been there and come back to tell us about it? If God loves her so much, why did he make her suffer so horrifically before taking her? If we are taking so much comfort in God, why are we behaving as if he doesn't even exist at all? As if this is so *permanent*?

And right there—years before I would even know the meaning of the word skepticism—its seeds have been sown.

In 2013, a ferocious tornado ripped through Moore, Oklahoma, reducing much of the city to rubble. The storm killed twenty-four people, injured hundreds more, and caused about $2 billion in damages. Rebecca Vitsmun, a resident of the city, got out just in time. With her husband at work, she scooped up her toddler, Anders, and drove south until she was out of harm's way. When she returned, she saw that her house had been completely destroyed by the tornado. She took some pictures. Soon after she put them online along with her story, she was contacted by CNN for an interview. The clip of her interview with Wolf Blitzer went viral.[2]

"Well, you're blessed. Brian, your husband, is blessed. Anders is blessed," Wolf said to her on the air, with a number of decimated houses visible in the background. "We're happy you're here. You guys did a great job. I guess you've got to thank the Lord, right? Do you thank the Lord?"

Vitsmun was gracious in her response.

"I . . . I'm . . . I'm actually an atheist," she said, laughing, and prompting Blitzer to laugh awkwardly with her. "But we are here, and I don't blame anybody for thanking the Lord."

Once you've learned to be skeptical, it's almost impossible to unlearn it. Critical thinking fosters curiosity and widens the intellect. One finds value in truth and the process of seeking it. The skeptical bent I had acquired at the time of Sana's death would revisit me frequently over the following years, particularly when my family moved to Saudi Arabia. I would see tearful survivors of plane crashes on television, profusely grateful to God for saving them, and immediately wonder what the dozens of other passengers who had perished had done wrong to not deserve that honor. I would see post-soccer-game interviews with the winning team captain claiming God's blessing made them victorious, and wonder what the other teams could possibly have done to make themselves so unworthy of this divine endorsement. In simple, everyday rituals, like listening to my elders thanking God before dinner, I would wonder if a more honest prayer would be something like, "Thank you, Lord, for providing us with lots of extra, sure-to-be-wasted food tonight, instead of giving it to those kids in Ethiopia who are starving to death." Indeed, it was the early and mid-1980s, when Ethiopia was undergoing a deadly famine.

And then, there were the unburned books. Year after year, there would be a fire in a church or an explosion in a mosque that would kill people, but miraculously leave a Bible or Quran untouched. Smug, I-told-you-so faces on TV would quote Isaiah 40:8 from the Bible to explain the marvel: "The grass withers and the flowers fall, but the word of our God endures forever." And over in Riyadh, it was verse 9 of *Al-Hijr*, the fifteenth *surah* in the Quran: "Indeed, it is We who sent down the Quran and indeed, We will be its guardian." Thus worked the Almighty's miracle: let the people burn, but save those $6.99 paperbacks that can also be perused for free at nearly every mosque and in every hotel room.

I would feel strange asking God for things. I was part of a relatively well-off family, with well-educated parents sending me to a good school. It seemed my prayers usually came true whether I asked for something or not. Whenever I'd ask for my school exams to go well (it was almost exclusively during exams that I would be the most resolutely devout), I would secretly imagine God replying, "Yes, Ali, I will help you get an A on that chemistry test tomorrow as soon as I'm done setting off this Ebola epidemic in Africa. Then I'm all yours." I would chuckle to myself at the absurdity of it all. This happened almost on a daily basis. But none of the adults seemed to see it like I did. And I never dared bring it up with them.

Watching Rebecca Vitsmun speak to Wolf Blitzer after that tornado brought a lot of that back for me. This was a small Oklahoma town in which dozens of people, likely believing, Christian people, perished due to what is officially called an "act of God" by insurance companies. In a surprising U-turn from his usual antics, though, God chose to save an atheist from the bunch, who, upon being asked if she was grateful to him, said no, she wasn't, because he didn't exist.

Times are changing. Today, I know that acute lymphoblastic leukemia, the blood cancer that Sana had, is very treatable. There has been a tremendous amount of progress in the last several decades—in fact, survival rates are now up to 90 percent by some accounts.[3] Of course, the number of children who have benefited from these recent medical advancements is a tiny fraction of the countless children who died from it prior to, say, 1980. Think about that survival rate for a second: *90 percent*. This is what scientists and physicians have achieved in the last thirty-five years or so. Today, after informing parents that their toddler has blood cancer, they can then proceed to treat them successfully and allow them to live normal, fulfilling lives. It's no surprise that it's thought of as a miracle—one that many of these children's parents end up thanking God for.

But unlike today's pediatric oncologists, God was supposedly always there, for millennia upon millennia, before 1980. For children who had the disease before that, like Sana, these "miracles" were few and far between. They died like Sana did. The only thing that changed in the meantime was the breathtaking progress humanity has made in science and medicine. Unlike the tornado in Oklahoma, this progress wasn't an "act of God."

Even now, this obvious fact illustrates what made me appreciate science more than anything else: it's true, and it works whether you have faith in it or not.

Death is incredibly powerful. As a child, I would sometimes chase ants. The moment they sensed my feet on the ground, thumping toward them, they would run in different directions. They knew death was imminent, and they didn't want to be crushed. Clearly, ants do not possess any subjective awareness or consciousness; nor do they have nociceptors, the nerve endings that transmit pain. Yet they would know each time, definitively, that my shoes would kill them—and they didn't want to die.

This instinct of self-preservation is nearly universal among all living things. Even single-celled bacteria avoid damaging environments, and ultimately evolve to adapt to them when needed.

As human beings, we are one of the few rare species to possess not only this immensely powerful instinct to survive at any cost, but also the intellectual capacity to fully understand that one day—no matter what—we will die. This irresolvable conflict gives rise to adaptive defense mechanisms, which help us cope and maintain psychological homeostasis. Admittedly, it's a strange way to live, to simultaneously harbor both this potent survival instinct and the certainty of mortality. The idea of necessary, permanent death can make life seem somewhat pointless when you look at the big picture. We don't want that. We want our lives to have meaning.

And we want *justice*. Nature is cruel. Storms, hurricanes, and tsunamis kill millions. Famines and earthquakes often strike the most vulnerable and needy. Many living things must kill and eat other living things to survive. Competition for territory and resources can be downright deadly. Powerful, rich people can commit crime after crime without ever getting caught and die in peace, surrounded by family and friends. The poor and downtrodden are often abused, neglected, and die alone. And children get cancer.

Where to find justice in such a violent, unjust universe?

Late in 2015, one-year-old Gianna Masciantonio was taken by her parents Joe and Kristen to meet Pope Francis during his visit to Philadelphia, Pennsylvania. Gianna had a rare, inoperable tumor on her brainstem, called a juvenile xanthogranuloma. On meeting her, His Holiness kissed her on the head. Several weeks later, an MRI scan showed that the tumor had dramatically shrunk. The story made headlines across the world, and both Joe and Kristen Masciantonio, dedicated Catholics, attributed their daughter's progress to the Holy Father's kiss. Neighbors called it the "Miracle on Market Street."

Of course, this was patent nonsense. Few of the stories actually mentioned that Gianna was being treated aggressively at the Children's Hospital of Philadelphia for her tumor, and had received several courses of chemotherapy, the last ending immediately prior to her meeting with the Pope.[4] Yet it was the story of the divine papal kiss that made headlines, for understandable reasons.

In Yann Martel's classic novel *Life of Pi*, the lead character, Pi Patel, argues that a world with God is always a "better story" than a world without him. We like good stories, where good triumphs over evil; where our favorite characters overcome impossible obstacles to survive in the end; where we can stick around to see an ending that answers all our questions. We like stories where there is some sense of justice—where we know that the inevitable injustices we suffered in this cruel, stoic universe will not go unchecked. Where there will be accountability.

But this cannot happen if there is no hereafter. As the great Bertrand Russell wrote in his famous essay "Why I Am Not a Christian": "If you are going to have justice in the universe as a whole you have to suppose a future life to redress the balance of life here on Earth. So they say that there must be a God, and there must be Heaven and Hell in order that in the long run there may be justice." Russell illustrated this—what he termed a "curious argument"—using the example of opening a crate of oranges where the top layer was rotten. Would we assume that because the top layer was bad, the ones underneath were good to eat? Of course not. We would likely determine that the entire crate was a bad lot.[5]

Yet, strangely, we think differently when it comes to justice in the world. We think that because there is so much injustice in the world, the future world must be just, to balance it out. I learned early on that people like to go with the miraculous, otherworldly explanation, as the Masciantonios did. They want to know there is something bigger than them out there. As impressive as they might be, pediatric oncologists are still mere mortals, fellow human beings right here on Earth, destined to suffer the same fate as the rest of us. But with divine intervention, there is *hope*—I can take comfort in the idea that ultimately, everything will be fine. Life *will* be fair. Someone out there is taking care of us.

And when your daughter has been ripped out of your arms at age three, this could well be the only thing that keeps you going. In contrast to my response to it, Sana's death made her parents even stronger in their faith. After experiencing the death of my father years later, I understood this. When I was planning out this book, I sent my aunt the proposal to ensure that I was accurate in my memory of that event. She has long known I am an atheist, but we had never discussed the role Sana's death had played in my ultimately becoming one. "It's so interesting how the same event can set two people down such different paths," she told me. She understood where I was coming from.

I, too, understand where she's coming from. I haven't yet mentioned that a year after Sana's death, my aunt and uncle had another daughter who, like her late older sister, developed the same childhood leukemia, also at age three. She too did not survive. This, as you may imagine—or may be unable to—was devastating beyond anything these words can describe; yet it too did not shake their faith. Despite our disagreements, I developed an immense amount of respect for my aunt, uncle, and my cousin Emran, Sana's older brother, over the years. The way they stuck together and rebuilt their lives after losing two beautiful little girls to a merciless disease is nothing short of heroic.

Now, my rational side tells me that just because something gives us comfort doesn't necessarily make it true; that it is important to deal with the realities of the world and the universe as they are; and that rationality and reason are the only paths to discovering any kind of objective truth. All of that is correct. But if we expect people—especially those who have undergone these kinds of horrific, tragic experiences—to embrace these ideas purely on their merit, we're not just asking them to think differently. We're asking them to let go of their only hope of bringing some kind of justice and meaning to their lives after senseless tragedy. We're asking them to suck it up and accept the idea that yes, what happened to them was grossly unfair and unjust, but there's nothing that can be done about it.

The price of letting go can be immensely high. Giving up the security of faith and the idea of an ultimate justice is just one of many costs that an increasing number of Muslims around the world have to pay as they give up the religion of their parents. Recognizing this should help us better understand and empathize with those who are unwilling or unable to leave the comfort of their faith.

But it should also help us better appreciate the courage of those who have dared to give it up and construct a new compass for their lives.

In much of the Muslim world where I grew up, religion is more than just a belief system. It is inextricably embedded in every aspect of people's lives—it is the central foundation upon which family, community, and morality are built. And perhaps of most consequence, it is intractably intertwined with one's very sense of identity.

Today, as more and more young Muslims give up the religion of their parents, they find themselves facing life-shattering consequences. The simple act of exploring new ideas can leave them isolated from their very own lives. Many are disowned by their parents and lose their families. Their friends refuse to associate with them. Their communities ostracize them. Their societies exile them. Their governments often imprison them, where they may be persecuted, flogged, or tortured. Worst of all, there are thirteen countries in the world today—all Muslim-majority—that punish atheism by death,[6] and as of 2014, Saudi Arabia has declared all atheists to be terrorists.[7] But it isn't just the governments. Recent Pew research polls show that in countries like Pakistan, Egypt, and Malaysia, majorities of the population support the death penalty for apostates.[8] And in Bangladesh, an officially secular country, news stories about atheist bloggers being hacked to death have become disturbingly routine.[9]

But it's the personal toll that hits the hardest. Simply changing one's mind can mean leaving behind not only one's family and community, but also childhood memories, lifestyle, relationships, feelings of belonging, and, as discussed earlier, one's sense of security, safety, and comfort. When beliefs are so deeply ingrained in one's identity, a shattered faith almost inevitably results in a shattered identity—one that must be rebuilt fragment by fragment.

This is why they hold on to it so dearly. This is why any attack on the religion—which is not a person but simply a set of ideas like any other—comes across to them as a *personal* attack. When you put their beliefs under scrutiny, you're prodding at their entire sense of being. You're rocking the boat, criticizing and satirizing that one thing they need to cling to in order to keep their lives intact, their families together, and—in some cases—their heads attached to their bodies. Does this mean you should not criticize or satirize religious beliefs? No, quite the opposite—it's the only way to "break the spell," to borrow from Daniel Dennett.[10] But in order to do it effectively, it is important first to acknowledge what you're dealing with.

You can also see how strong this religion-identity amalgam is when you look at young ex-Muslims who have recently left the faith. An initial phase of disorientation, anxiety, and/or depression is exceedingly common. In his book *The Apostates*, Dr. Simon Cottee writes about Irtaza

Hussain, a young, twenty-two-year-old man who grew up in a Muslim family in the United Kingdom and ultimately left Islam.[11] His atheism led to a worsening of his already somewhat contentious relationship with his father, who first threatened to disown him, but later relented on the condition that the two would thenceforth avoid discussing faith. Despite this, Irtaza became more and more despondent, until one day his Facebook friends, myself included, saw a picture in our newsfeeds, of him sitting high up in a tree. He had taken the picture himself. Only his legs were visible, the camera was pointing down toward the ground, and a light blue rope fashioned into a noose was partially visible in the frame, hanging from his neck. The caption: "Just a jump away." Before emergency services could even get to him, he was dead.

Irtaza's story isn't unique. In his study of suicide, the French sociologist Émile Durkheim described the phenomenon of *anomie*, a kind of moral identity crisis characterized by instability and the breakdown of social connections between an individual and his/her community.[12] When young Muslims leaving the faith discard their previous moral compass based on Islam, it often leaves a vacuum, and it can take some time before they reformulate a renewed sense of identity and connection to their new milieu.

Those who find a community of like-minded peers seem to fare better. I once attended a party on Eid, a Muslim holiday, thrown by young ex-Muslims who were estranged from their families. None of them wanted to be alone on Eid, which made them acutely feel the absence of their loved ones. So they decided to spend it with one another. It was clear at the party that many of them were in transition and acting out. The strict religious rules dealing with diet and conduct that had bound them in their old lives were being flouted aggressively. There was bacon on virtually every dinner item. Large amounts of alcohol were being consumed without restraint. Two young women who had been wearing the hijab since childhood donned revealing clothing and heavy makeup as they flirted unabashedly with the men at the party—and with each other. The pendulum had swung the other way—and as pronounced as it was in some cases, I found it to be healthy. This group of young men and women had established a community for themselves that was like-minded and had similar experiences. They were battling their inhibitions and experimenting without fear of judgment or penalty. The men were making conscious, deliberate efforts to be tolerant of and appreciate what they'd always been taught to view with disdain. The women, who had been raised to erase any semblance of sexuality from their appearance, were now exploring it without reservation or reticence. Ultimately, many of them will find equilibrium and stability, and learn to define themselves in a new way. Others, like Irtaza, sadly, aren't as fortunate.

I would again remind the reader that these monumental upheavals in the lives of young, freethinking Muslims are solely the consequence of changing their minds about one thing—their religion. This is the price they have to pay—and we should always be mindful of this. One of the ugliest and most sinister aspects of any religion is this intricate entanglement of ideology with identity, and the often dire consequences for those who have the ability and the courage to successfully pry the two apart.

Imagine: If simply changing your mind came with that kind of cost, how open would *you* be to doing it?

What is it, then, that has empowered more ex-Muslims to start speaking out publicly in a way that they've otherwise never done in recent memory? What are some of the different factors that can help lower the cost of letting go?

Maryam Namazie is an Iranian-born feminist and human rights activist who started the Council of Ex-Muslims of Britain (CEMB) in 2007.[13] CEMB members have grown from a handful when it started to thousands today, not only in Britain, but also across the rest of the world. Similar organizations have also sprung up in other countries over the last decade, including two fast-growing ones in North America: Muslimish,[14] where liberal and questioning Muslims can interact with ex-Muslims securely; and Ex-Muslims of North America (EXMNA).[15] These organizations provide secure forums for ex-Muslims to connect, share their stories, and discuss ideas. They enable agnostics and atheists from Muslim backgrounds to find others like themselves in their own towns and cities, and speak face-to-face with one another, either in person during regular meet-ups or via online platforms like Google Hangouts. All of the groups are stringent about maintaining security for their members, being careful to vet their members when they join, and taking great care to prevent any circumstance that could result in their closeted members—particularly in Muslim-majority countries—from being "outed."

In preparation for International Human Rights Day in 2015, Namazie and CEMB began a campaign inviting ex-Muslims from around the world to use photographs, videos, and handwritten signs to explain why they left Islam. The movement was named *#ExMuslimBecause* and spearheaded by Rayhana Sultan, a CEMB member of Bangladeshi origin.

Although the campaign was announced several weeks before International Human Rights Day on December 10, the response was immediate and tremendous. Within twenty-four hours, #ExMuslimBecause became the number one trending hashtag on Twitter in the United Kingdom. Close to twenty thousand people participated in the first twenty-four hours, and six times as many in the first week. There were tweets from secret LGBT Saudis; women who had been forced into marriages; closeted atheists in Egypt and Pakistan tweeting under pseudonyms; young women disowned by their families in the United States; and more. I covered the campaign for the *Huffington Post* and compiled some of the most popular tweets as the hashtag went viral.[16] I wrote:

> What you'll see below is the often unheard, third side to the international conversation we have been witnessing since the Paris attacks—a conversation that represents an increasingly reverberating alternative narrative that is developing across the Muslim world, where atheism is on the rise . . . [These messages should] be read by everyone who wants to understand narratives from the Muslim world otherwise all too often silenced before reaching us.

I also included three important points to consider as readers read through the tweets. The first:

> Being part of Muslim families and communities, ex-Muslims not only receive the same bigoted treatment [sometimes

directed at] other Muslims, but are also persecuted (often severely) *by* Muslims who consider them heretics and apostates.

A significant factor that distinguishes ex-Muslim critics of Islam and far-right Western critics of Islam is the conflation of ideas and people. Most ex-Muslims have Muslim-sounding names and have lived in and come from the same places as their Muslim counterparts. Consequently, they are just as likely as other Muslims to be on the receiving end of anti-Muslim sentiment and/or harassment. But as discussed earlier, they are also frequently disowned by their Muslim families, marginalized by their Muslim communities, and imprisoned, tortured, or executed by their own Muslim governments. They are a minority within a minority.

The second:

> Ex-Muslims often find themselves caught between the anti-Muslim bigotry of the far right that demonizes all Muslims, and the apologism of the far left that conflates any legitimate criticism of Islam with "bigotry" or "Islamophobia" . . . Criticizing Islam . . . and demonizing Muslims . . . are very different things.

Many ex-Muslims do have lifelong Muslim friends and family who are supportive, moderate, or liberal, even if they disagree. This was a common theme in the #ExMuslimBecause tweets: most participants, while certainly unreserved in their criticism of the faith, made it a point to differentiate between criticizing Islam (an idea) and demonizing Muslims (a people). Human beings have rights and are entitled to respect. Ideas, books, and beliefs don't, and aren't.

The third:

> Many ex-Muslims feel betrayed by their liberal counterparts in the West. The fight against Islamic jihad should come from a position of moral strength, not xenophobic bigotry. This is a

fight that liberals should take on themselves before it's hijacked by the far right.

This is a crucial point that is discussed at length in chapter 6. Secularists in the Muslim world are often the liberals in their communities, but feel alienated by their Western liberal counterparts. In their well-intentioned attempts to try and protect Muslims in the West—whom they see as a persecuted and unfairly stereotyped community—many Western liberals inadvertently also end up empowering undemocratic Islamist governments in Muslim-majority countries who use this status of victimhood as a tool to oppress and persecute liberal dissidents within their own populations. Legitimately criticizing *illiberal* ideas and practices in the Quran—misogyny, homophobia, jihad, harsh corporal punishments like hand amputation, severe legal penalties for blasphemy and apostasy, and so on—gets one accused of being "bigoted" or "Islamophobic," even though the very same ideas would be resoundingly denounced by the very same individuals if found in, say, the Republican Tea Party manifesto or a neo-Nazi website. It's as if the same idea is bad if a KKK member says it, but perfectly fine when it appears in a certain holy book. When liberals equate criticizing Islamic doctrine with anti-Muslim bigotry, it leaves a vacuum that is too frequently filled by genuine right-wing anti-Muslim bigots who are even more disagreeable. Who gets stuck in the middle? Ex-Muslims.

Maryam Namazie herself stated during the campaign that she was not angry with Muslims. "My family are Muslims and very supportive of me," she tweeted. "Criticizing Islam/Islamism [is] not anti-Muslim."

Here are some of the most widely circulated tweets [abbreviated words expanded and punctuation/spelling corrected for clarity]:

> #ExMuslimBecause I was told I was a Muslim. But then I learned that religion is not a gene and being born to believers doesn't make you one.
> —@SamSedaei

> #ExMuslimBecause I know being a woman doesn't make me lesser. I shouldn't have to worship behind men, or be segregated from them.
> —@NiceMangos

#ExMuslimBecause No real God should need protection from bloggers and no real prophet should need protection from cartoons.

—@aliamjadrizvi [myself]

"#ExMuslimBecause I'd be sentenced to death if I was [outed] as an apostate in Saudi Arabia.

—@alina_mmz

#ExMuslimBecause I am not an abomination by virtue of being gay.

—@DudeInDistress

#ExMuslimBecause Atheist [bloggers] are being killed in my country #Bangladesh but my Muslim friends are directly or indirectly supporting it.

—@sh1shazal

#ExMuslimBecause I couldn't handle hearing my own family say that Shi'as, my neighbors and best friends, are kuffar [infidels].

—@riyamnm

#ExMuslimBecause My own mother told me I should be killed because I didn't believe the same things she did.

—@YasmienMills

#ExMuslimBecause The Quran, in my view, is literature that was written by men. We are yet to know who wrote it.

—@Ali_Jones89

#ExMuslimBecause I'm told Islam gives you freedom of thought and religion but at the same time punishes apostasy by death.

—@Zxop11

#ExMuslimBecause For some reason Islam bans alcohol and pre-marital sex but not slavery.

—@MalayBoy87

#ExMuslimBecause [I] was indoctrinated as a child and denounced my religion as soon as I was old enough to think for myself.

—@90degree_flow

#ExMuslimBecause I care about what is true.

—@FilthyApostate

#ExMuslimBecause I simply used my brain.

—@M37158

#ExMuslimBecause I was tired of trying to fit inside a box that was never made for me.

—@hossain_food

#ExMuslimBecause I prefer reality over myth and reason over igno-rance.

—*@musaaziz*

#ExMuslimBecause LGBT are humans and not my [enemies].

—*@AaalaKaatiba*

#ExMuslimBecause I have a deep yearning for knowledge about our world, nature, and the universe. Religion can't provide adequate answers.

—*@slumdoglove*

#ExMuslimBecause I couldn't debate or criticize Islam without my parents yelling or screaming at me, and threatening me.

—*@nukacola11*

#ExMuslimBecause People should have the right to leave whatever religion they want.

—*@Aren_Armenian*

#ExMuslimBecause I'd rather look through a telescope than read a book that says I came out of a man's rib to be lured by a talking snake.

—*@SecularlyYours*

#ExMuslimBecause I didn't want to live in guilt anymore.

—*@super_trampp*

#ExMuslimBecause Speaking my truth shouldn't be a death sentence.

—*@SuraiyaSimi*

#ExMuslimBecause . . . I am a #Saudi . . . enough said . . .

—*@AtheistHijazi*

#ExMuslimBecause I cannot fathom the idea that wretched morality of 7th century is unchangeable no matter how barbaric it is.

—*@DesiZeus*

#ExMuslimBecause Misogyny, homophobia, stoning people to death, and killing apostates don't suddenly become "respectable" when put in a holy book.

—*@LibMuslim*

This one had several iterations:

#ExMuslimBecause Bacon—what other reason could there possibly be?

—*@Wraithiest*

And one young woman sent a photograph to CEMB anonymously, holding in front of her face a spiral-bound notebook with the following words:

> Ex-Muslim because my dad, the sheikh, said, "There's no such thing as rape in marriage, in Islam, you're a liar," when I'd asked him to tell the man he'd married me off to at 17 to stop raping me. My own dad!

This powerful, revelatory campaign wasn't without its expected backlash, a lot of which, in my estimation, was due to genuine surprise. Most Muslims didn't seem to be aware that ex-Muslims were now significant enough in number to drive this hashtag to the top trending spot in Britain. Upon seeing this actually happen, some were angry, calling the campaign hateful and untimely, considering that it launched within a week of the November 2015 Paris attacks, when they said Muslims were at increased risk of harassment and even hate crimes.

I think these critics are misguided. Not to diminish the very real problem of anti-Muslim bigotry, but it only seems to be with Islam that whenever dozens of largely *non-Muslim* innocents are mercilessly murdered by Muslim men yelling "Allahu Akbar," the attention in the aftermath somehow immediately turns to the victimization of *Muslims*. I do understand why this is, but I would say one of the things that turned me off from Islam and religion in general is the trend that after almost every terrorist attack carried out in the name of Islam, the first reaction of some apologists is, "Oh no, I hope this doesn't make Islam look bad." And soon after that, we are treated to inevitable, increasingly clichéd, unconvincing statements like "Islam is a religion of peace," or "Terrorists have no religion," which now rarely resonate too far beyond the confines of a steadily shrinking echo chamber. I've always seen this as a seriously disordered sense of prioritization that—well intentioned or not—ends up valuing ideology over human beings.

The #ExMuslimBecause campaign was avidly backed by Richard Dawkins, the famed evolutionary biologist and atheist activist who is often accused of "racism" despite being an ardent supporter of thousands upon thousands of nonwhite ex-Muslims. The Richard Dawkins Foundation for Reason and Science was the first major secular group that took an initiative to reach out to ex-Muslims, fully funding and organizing a nationwide meeting with over 130 of them in Washington, D.C., in the fall of 2013. These young men and women, all atheists and agnostics from Muslim backgrounds—Arab, Persian, African, South Asian, Caucasian, and more—traveled from various cities across the United States and Canada to attend. The meeting, run and moderated by Alishba Zarmeen, a Pakistani feminist and secular activist (and, I should mention, my then-future wife), was also attended by the leaders of other national and international organizations like the Secular Coalition of America and the Center for Inquiry. For five hours, a jetlagged Dawkins took time out of his tightly scheduled U.S. book tour to listen to this community of young ex-Muslim outcasts, pledging his dedication and support. And two years later with the CEMB's campaign, he followed through.

Indeed, Dawkins frequently comes under fire for his seemingly strident approach to criticizing religion by many in the West, including some ex-Muslims. However, to thousands of closeted ex-Muslims actually living in the Muslim world that I have corresponded with over the last seven years, he is widely regarded as a hero. The aggressive, up-front approaches of people like Richard Dawkins and the late Christopher Hitchens seem somehow relatable and resonate with them. Remember—these are people who are unable to speak out openly about the abuse and oppression they have suffered at the hands of their governments, communities, and even families in the name of religion. So they are angry—and they often view conciliatory and "respectful" attitudes toward oppressive religious theology as a luxury affordable only to those privileged enough to live in open societies. They respect people like Richard Dawkins for breaking with many of his fellow Western liberals to take up the cause of real liberals around the world who are doing the heavy lifting where it really matters.

So, as expected, Dawkins was flabbergasted at the backlash to the CEMB's campaign. "People are saying #ExMuslimBecause is hateful," he wrote. "How can telling people why you left a religion be 'hate'? By what bizarrely twisted logic?"[17] He urged ex-Muslims around the world to continue to use the hashtag and share their stories.

There were also many Muslims who were very supportive of the campaign, like Sarah Ager, a British Muslim woman in Italy. "Ex-Muslims are also affected by anti-Muslim hate and bigotry," wrote Ager. "Islamophobia only increases if we hide the problems in our communities. Sadly, an awful lot of Islamophobia is fueled by the terrible treatment of ex-Muslims by Muslims themselves." Sarah, an interfaith outreach activist who converted to Islam from Christianity, said she related to ex-Muslims for a special reason. "People often ask why I support ex-Muslims. Well, I was able to leave my religion and choose another. Everyone should have that basic right and freedom."[18]

There are several factors that help lower the cost of letting go, from supportive parents to quality education. But being part of a robust, thriving community of like-minded peers, in my experience, is the single most important factor that helps young Muslims make that leap from religion to rationality; and giving that community a voice and a platform via the Internet and social media can empower them immeasurably.

Over two-thirds of the populations in countries like Saudi Arabia, Iran, and Egypt are under the age of thirty-five. To these young people, who have grown up under monarchs and dictators for decades, never having seen anything else, freedom of speech is often a completely alien concept. Just as people born and raised in the United States find it almost impossible to comprehend the idea of a government imprisoning and publicly flogging a man simply for expressing his ideas, it is unthinkable for many people in these countries to imagine living in a society where we can openly criticize our political leaders without any repercussions.

For them, social media platforms like Facebook, YouTube, and Twitter aren't just an entertaining extension of their real lives, as they are to us. They're a fantastical ingress into reality; virtual vessels into the real world, where you can say what you can't in real life and be exposed to the uncensored ideas of people around the world, where you can talk to them, even watch them. These forums represent an unprecedented portal into a world most of them never knew existed as little as ten years ago—one that allows them to live inside the outside world.

We hear every day about the steadily widening income inequality gap, by all means a serious issue that needs to be addressed. But when it comes to the more vaguely defined "opportunity gap," the story is significantly different. Of course, economics has a considerable influence on access to opportunity in the conventional sense. But the role technology plays in this cannot be understated.

As a recording musician, I remember what it took for my rock band in Pakistan to record and distribute a decent demo in the early to mid-1990s. We would cobble together whatever meager resources we had to be able to afford a shift or two in an average recording studio. Being billed at an hourly rate, our performances had to be thoroughly well rehearsed; time was short and pressure was high. Mastering usually cost extra, and the final recording quality was rarely good enough to compete with anything mainstream. Once we had our master tape, we would spend days making copies ourselves (cassette tapes took longer than CDs, but CD reproduction technology wasn't as accessible), or cough up more cash to have a duplication facility do it for us. Then we would physically have to go out and distribute these tapes and/or CDs at shows and elsewhere, and send them off by snail mail to local labels, hoping to get signed. And music videos? Out of the question. We were all relatively well off, higher-middle-class kids, but only the kids with the *really* rich parents could afford to make those. Note that this is in Pakistan, where everything was a lot cheaper and rock bands few and far between. For bands in the United States, this process was even more arduous and competitive.

Today, any talented teenager in Senegal can make a broadcast-quality recording on her smartphone and upload it as an MP3; shoot a high-definition music video (also on her smartphone) and upload it to You-Tube; distribute it worldwide for next to nothing; promote it using social media; and even make money from it. Of course there are still many obstacles in the way—but this is a tremendous opportunity that was available only to the privileged or lucky in the past. Now, this opportunity is available to almost anyone.

One of the most interesting aspects of Steve Jobs's biography relates to his pilgrimage to India in the 1970s. He intended it to be a spiritual exploration in accordance with the teachings of the world-famous guru,

Neem Karoli Baba. Unfortunately, the guru died shortly before Jobs could meet him. But Jobs stayed on, living on a potato farm and traveling around the country, deeply impacted by the immense poverty and suffering of its people. Apart from a little dollop of Buddhism, his love affair with India didn't last long. But the insight he gained from it was invaluable and unexpected. He told a biographer, "It was one of the first times I started thinking that maybe Thomas Edison did a lot more to improve the world than Karl Marx and Neem Karoli Baba put together."[19]

I sometimes feel as though we're living in an almost postimperial world. The far-left rhetoric against corporatocracy that I grew up with in the late twentieth century seems like a blur today. YouTube is full of videos uploaded by ordinary Gazan civilians—victims of both Hamas's jihadist agenda and the recklessness of the Israel Defense Forces—showing us a side of the Israeli-Palestinian war we never really saw before the advent of streaming video. The 2009 Green Revolution in Iran allowed us a rare glimpse into the country's hidden society postrevolution, courtesy of brave Iranian activists on Twitter. Wael Ghonim, the Egyptian activist who started the 2011 Tahrir Square protests in Cairo that ultimately took down Hosni Mubarak after thirty years of dictatorial rule, did so with the help of Facebook. Shortly after Mubarak stepped down, Ghonim told CNN that he wanted to meet Mark Zuckerberg in person to thank him. "This revolution started online," he said. "This revolution started on Facebook. This revolution started . . . when hundreds of thousands of Egyptians started collaborating content. We would post a video on Facebook that would be shared by 60,000 people on their walls within a few hours. I've always said that if you want to liberate a society, just give them the Internet."[20]

Think about that for a minute. Facebook is a U.S. corporation headed by a young Jewish atheist who started it in his Harvard dorm room. It has in its possession private information on over a billion people—not just their names, contact information, and geographic locations, but their personal preferences, likes, and dislikes—that it makes available to advertisers. To protesters in the 1980s, this would sound like an Orwellian nightmare. But to Egyptians in 2011, it was an instrument of revolutionary change. Google, Twitter, Apple, and other tech giants are part of the same dynamic. We are living in an age where open discourse, free exchange of ideas, and the empowerment of the individual have become aligned with corporate interests; where anticapitalist Occupy Wall Street activists used their iPhones to film their protests, fueled by morning caffeine rushes courtesy of Starbucks; where innovation is crowd-sourced with services like Kickstarter; and regular folk are empowered by Uber and Airbnb at the expense of long-established transportation and hotel industry giants.

This is a world where regular individuals with an Internet connection can change the course of history. The cables released by Julian Assange's WikiLeaks helped trigger the Tunisian Jasmine Revolution that led to the ouster of its dictator, President Ben Ali—the first domino to fall in the Arab Spring.[21] Libyan dictator Muammar Gaddafi angrily called out WikiLeaks by name soon after, and was right to be anxious.[22] A few months later, he saw his own forty-two-year rule come to a brutal end, along with his life.

Like anything revolutionary, though, the technology age is a double-edged sword. Today, our main enemies are stateless. The tech savvy of Al Qaeda and the Islamic State has transformed what was a regional war into a global one, a phenomenon even the world's most capable leaders are sometimes slow to catch on to. A day before the November 2015 Paris attacks, President Obama was feeling a little more hopeful about the war against the Islamic State. Noting that the caliphate hadn't made any significant territorial gains in some time, Obama said it had been "contained."[23] As we know now, this contention was obscenely countered the very next day.

Terrorism has also come of age with the millennial generation. The Islamic State of today is miles from the Al Qaeda it grew out of. Its supporters aren't coming from Afghanistan, Iraq, or Pakistan anymore. They're living in Belgium, France, Britain, and, as we saw with the attacks in San Benardino and Orlando, even the United States. They're not refugees or illegal immigrants. They're legal, passport-carrying, Western-born or naturalized citizens of our countries. So what does bombing them do now? The more you bomb over there, the more the appeal grows over here. And there's proof of that from the last three wars: the Islamic State itself is the visible result. ISIS isn't just a geographical entity. There are kids sitting across Western countries, right here in our cities and neighborhoods, being inspired and groomed by the group's wide-ranging social media expertise and slickly produced propaganda videos as we speak. These kids are not coming here from Syria. They've always been here.

But not everybody's joining up. The success of a campaign like #Ex-MuslimBecause; the burgeoning memberships of ex-Muslim groups like CEMB, Muslimish, and EXMNA; and the steadily growing audiences of pro-secular dissidents and reform activists from Muslim backgrounds show that there's something else brewing too—something you don't hear about as much because it has historically been suppressed by governments, moderates, and fundamentalists alike. As can be seen from their tweets and more, many young Muslims are reacting to this suppression, watching the Islamic State's antics around the world and how it's making them look, studying the scripture their parents taught them was infallible, and dealing with high levels of unemployment and economic difficulty due to their governments' corrupt, ineffectual policies. They are watching their leaders use religion and blasphemy laws to solidify their authority and restrict the freedoms of their people. This worked in the past, but not anymore. On websites like WikiLeaks, they learn things about their governments and the world that they have never seen in their newspapers. They discover the roles that their own leaders have played in bringing about the frustrations and difficult conditions they were told were the fault of the United States and Israel. They speak to their online friends living in open societies who tell them of free speech, gender equality, and LGBT rights. It's like someone who has been locked in a dark room since birth suddenly gaining access to a window and looking outside for the first time—only to see that she isn't the only one locked in.

Think about what they're struggling for: secularism, justice, equality, the right to elect their own leaders, the right to speak freely. And think about what they're willing to risk: isolation, imprisonment, torture, even death. All just to fight for the things that the rest of us take for granted every day.

In an article entitled "How ISIS Drives Muslims From Islam," *New York Times* columnist Thomas Friedman wrote about how he was seeing more and more Muslims letting go:

There is a significant group of Muslims who feel that their government-backed preachers and religious hierarchies have handed them a brand of Islam that does not speak to them. These same authorities have also denied them the critical thinking tools and religious space to imagine new interpretations . . . And some seem to be quietly detaching from religion entirely—fed up with being patronized by politically correct Westerners telling them what Islam is not and with being tyrannized by self-appointed Islamist authoritarians telling them what Islam is. Now that the Internet has created free, safe, alternative spaces and platforms to discuss these issues, outside the mosques and government-owned media, this war of ideas is on.[24]

Amen.

FOUR

A Tale of Two Identities

C onsider this passage:

> When you march up to attack a city, make its people an offer of
> peace. If they accept and open their gates, all the people in it
> shall be subject to forced labor and shall work for you. If they
> refuse to make peace and they engage you in battle, lay siege to
> that city. When the Lord your God delivers it into your hand,
> put to the sword all the men in it. As for the women, the
> children, the livestock and everything else in the city, you may
> take these as plunder for yourselves. And you may use the plun-
> der the Lord your God gives you from your enemies. This is
> how you are to treat all the cities that are at a distance from you
> and do not belong to the nations nearby. However, in the cities
> of the nations the Lord your God is giving you as an inheri-
> tance, do not leave alive anything that breathes.

In 2014, the world watched as a group of militant, fundamentalist
Muslims advanced dramatically through Syria and Iraq, seizing major
cities like Raqqa, Tikrit, and Mosul, and announcing the end of the

Sykes-Picot Agreement in a triumphant propaganda video.[1] Britain and France orchestrated this agreement secretly in 1916, dividing Arab lands as they saw fit to consolidate their influence over the region when the Ottoman Empire was in its final, crumbling throes.

Once the Islamic State declared the new caliphate, its members kept on doing more of what was working so well. They demanded allegiance from the residents of every city and town they took. Those who submitted—either by converting to their faith or paying the *jizyah*, a heavy tax imposed on some non-Muslims—were allowed to live peacefully. As for the rest, they put the sword to the men, took the women and children as plunder, and used them as they pleased—which included forcing Yazidi girls as young as nine into sex slavery.[2] Reading the passage, you would think it was excerpted from their rulebook.

However, as some readers may have recognized, that passage is not from the Quran. It is from the Old Testament/Torah, Deuteronomy 20:10–16. (The Torah comprises the first five books of the Old Testament: Genesis, Exodus, Numbers, Leviticus, and Deuteronomy.) It seems the Islamic State is making its territorial gains in much the same way as Moses and the Israelites made theirs back in the day.

This shouldn't be much of a surprise to those who have actually studied the holy texts of each of the three great monotheisms.

The first thing you notice is that God doesn't just speak Arabic, which is a relief. I was raised to think you could never truly understand the Quran without knowing the Arabic language inside out. This only applied, of course, if you didn't agree with all of it. The moment you did, your Arabic—no matter how rudimentary—was deemed fine.

Second, you notice the similarities, particularly between the Old Testament and the Quran. There is the almost identical creation story, the characteristically human violence, the stories of the prophets, the militarism and war, and a bizarrely harsh penal code—amputating hands, cutting off heads, and, in the case of the Old Testament, stoning people to death. (Interestingly enough, stoning to death is never mentioned in the Quran as it stands today—it's derived from the *hadith*. See chapter 7.) Even superficially, the parallels between Jewish and Islamic tradition stand out: *Salaam* and *Shalom* sound alike; pork is a no-no;

there's nary a foreskin for miles; and the prophets of both would today be nicknamed "Mo."

More significant, however, is the pattern of revelation. The Old Testament is said to have been revealed directly to Moses by God at Mount Sinai and the Tabernacle; some even believe it was a blueprint for creation, thus predating it. The Quran is said to have been revealed directly to Muhammad in much the same way, starting when he was forty years old, and continuing throughout his life.

The New Testament, on the other hand, is a different animal. Here, life on Earth seems much nicer than in its much more ruthless scriptural predecessor. It's all about loving your neighbors, forgiving your enemies, and turning the other cheek. There is considerably less violence, except after you die. Then, quite literally, all hell breaks loose, unless you let Jesus in. Why must you let Jesus in? Because he loves you, and wants to save you from the horror that he himself will inflict on you if you *didn't* let him in. Remember, this is religion, not rationality: if you stray from the Christian faith, you will still be loved on Earth; the brutal violence and torture will only begin *after* you die. And then, it will continue forever.

In his book *God Is Not Great*, Christopher Hitchens spends a chapter each on the scriptures of the monotheisms. After a chapter about the Old Testament being a "nightmare," and another on how the New Testament "exceeds the evil" of the Old, Hitchens lands on a relatively anticlimactic theme for his Quran chapter, describing the document as an "obvious and ill-arranged set of plagiarisms."[3]

What makes the Quran so boring to Hitchens is also precisely what makes it so dangerous. It combines the violence of the worldly life in the Old Testament with the violence of the afterlife in the New. It combines the militarism and warmongering in the Old Testament with New Testament ideas like submission ("Accept Jesus as your savior!") and martyrdom ("Jesus died for your sins!"), effectively birthing the concept of jihad. Finally, it is an expansionist religion: by taking the Christian command to proselytize (Matthew 28:19–20 and more), and combining it with the Old Testament's ISIS-like militarism, Islam has created an extremely effective, and frequently deadly, system of propagation. This is historically evidenced by its dramatic spread so quickly after being founded. The rapid expansion of Islam in a matter of decades—remember, this is a re-ligion commonly portrayed by its adherents to be a comprehensive sys-tem of living that takes years of careful study simply to understand—is very unlikely to have been achieved by friendly, smiling *sahabah* (compan-ions of Muhammad) distributing pamphlets to passersby in the desert.

Now, how many Jews today really see that Deuteronomy passage as anything but archaic, inane gibberish? In my experience, most aren't even aware such passages exist, and are frequently shocked upon hearing them for the first time. Ever since secularism and reform squeezed the Judaism out of "being Jewish," these texts, once thought to be the literal word of God by many, have largely been demoted to "divinely inspired" status. In practice, they simply collect dust on the bookshelf. This is not a bad thing, and also has sound basis. The advent of Abraham Geiger's Re-form Judaism movement in the nineteenth century provided a mechanism for innovation and evolution in the Jewish religion. For Reform Jews, the Torah was no longer the word of a god making appearances at Mount Si-nai, but the writing of human hands. Revelation was now a progressive and continuing process. Diversity and inclusion trumped tribalism and entitlement. Ethics took precedence over rituals. And today, on average, more Jews tend to be progressive and secular than Christians or Muslims.

In theory, this kind of thing isn't out of the question for Muslims. An in-creasing number of Muslims today—especially in the West—know very little about their scripture or religion as it is.

Do a Google Images search for "American Muslims." The overwhelm-ing majority of results show women in headscarves, men wearing Islamic skullcaps, and people dressed in loose clothing, praying or demonstrat-ing on the street. Unfortunately, the people seen to represent Muslims in the United States are often as misrepresentative of American Muslims as ISIS itself. How many American Muslims that you know are anything like the hijab-wearing, fully covered, or bearded members of Islamic organizations like ISNA (Islamic Society of North America) or CAIR (Council on American-Islamic Relations) typically seen on TV?

There are more American Muslims having beers at bars after work, dancing at clubs on a Saturday night, regularly spending the night at their girlfriend's or boyfriend's place, or having non-*halal* steaks and fast food than there are who actually pray five times a day. Most non-Muslims who have a Muslim friend or colleague at school or work know exactly what I'm talking about. Most American Muslims are as American as anyone else.

Rarely in this discourse do we hear about these American Muslims, who exist in plain sight. Dr. Mehmet Oz, for instance. Shaquille O'Neal. Comedian Dave Chappelle. Ahmet Ertegun, who founded Atlantic Records, established the Rock and Roll Hall of Fame, and introduced the world to iconic artists ranging from Ray Charles and Aretha Franklin to Led Zeppelin and Stone Temple Pilots. R&B star Akon. Jermaine Jackson, brother of Michael. Supermodel Iman, wife of David Bowie. Fazlur Khan, architect of the Willis (Sears) Tower and the John Hancock Center in Chicago. TV stars Aziz Ansari and Kumail Nanjiani, who are both atheists from Muslim backgrounds—Nanjiani having been raised Shia in Pakistan, like me. And journalist Fareed Zakaria, who embraces the Muslim identity despite describing himself as nonpracticing and "completely secular," with views falling "somewhere between deism and agnosticism."[4] These are not the people America thinks of when they hear "Muslim." Should they?

Well, it wouldn't make too much sense, would it? Whenever there is a news story that is Christianity- or Judaism-related, it is a pastor or rabbi called forth to comment, not a celebrity who simply *happens* to be Christian or Jewish. And what the prominent American Muslims on that list have done with their success is make their identities bigger than just "Muslim." You don't immediately think "Jew" when you hear the names of Jon Stewart or Jerry Seinfeld. Likewise, you don't immediately think "Muslim" when you hear of Dr. Oz or Shaq. These are not people who wear their religion on their sleeves.

For most Western Muslims, "Muslim" is just a birth identity, like "Arab," "Persian," or "South Asian." And any kind of rhetoric that reduces their identities to just "Muslim" doesn't help successful, hard-working Muslim-Americans rise *above* it. Instead, it throws them back, categorizing, ghettoizing, and tribalizing them.

When it comes to how we form our identities, birth gives us a head start. From the day we are born, we are assigned a racial or ethnic identity, a nationality, a biological sex, and often a familial religious affiliation that is obviously not belief-based just yet, but will unavoidably mark us (sometimes dramatically, as with rituals like genital circumcision). These "inborn" identifiers are *unearned* attributes that we did nothing to achieve, and that nobody can take away from us.

As we evolve and develop, we begin to add to this. Erik Erikson, the great German-American developmental psychologist, wrote of identity formation during adolescence, coining the term *identity crisis* to describe the state of turmoil and exploration we undergo at this stage. As adolescents, we deal with physical growth, sexual maturation, self-image issues, potential career choices, and explore an overwhelming number of options to decide how to shape ourselves into who we want to be. The central conflict of the adolescent, thought Erikson, was a contest between the formation of a strong identity and what he called *role confusion*, a state of not knowing who you are or what you believe. Canadian developmental psychologist James Marcia expanded on Erikson's work, describing four outcomes of the identity crisis in terms of level of exploration and level of commitment to a set of values.

According to Marcia, *identity achievement* is the successful confrontation, and subsequent resolution, of the identity crisis. The identity-achieved harbor a well-developed set of personal values resulting from high levels of both exploration and commitment; this is the group considered best equipped to take on the challenges of adulthood. *Identity foreclosure*, on the other hand, describes those who have passively adopted the beliefs and values of others, often their parents and families, without any active exploration of their own. These individuals are characterized by high commitment and low exploration. *Identity moratorium* is a state of continued unresolved crisis, where the exploration process is ongoing, but no resolution is achieved; these individuals know their options, but don't know what they want—high exploration, low commitment. Finally, *identity diffusion* is the low commitment, low exploration state in which individuals have neither attempted to explore who or what they'd like to be, nor committed to any definitive personal values or goals.

These states aren't fixed, and multiple states can occur at various points in a person's life. Some ex-Muslims, for example, may start with an identity-foreclosed state, accepting the religious beliefs and values of

their parents without question, only to be thrust into the identity moratorium state later in life, when exposed to the problematic parts of these
beliefs.

This can also go in a completely different direction. Psychologist
Cally O'Brien writes that the identity-foreclosed state is most susceptible
to a serious crisis in later life, having skipped crisis resolution early on.[5]
She gives the example of Sayyid Qutb, a key, influential leader in Egypt's
Muslim Brotherhood, who was convicted and executed for plotting the
assassination of Egypt's president, Gamal Abdel Nasser. Qutb was raised
in a very conservative, strictly observant Muslim family, and became radicalized after attending college in the United States, where he seemed
most disgusted at one aspect of American culture: female sexuality. In his
book *The America I Have Seen*, he wrote: "The American girl is well ac-
quainted with her body's seductive capacity. She knows it lies in the face,
and in expressive eyes, and thirsty lips. She knows seductiveness lies in
the round breasts, the full buttocks, and in the shapely thighs, sleek legs—
and she shows all this and does not hide it."[6] Qutb even saw this alleged
debauchery during a dance at a *church*: "They danced to the tunes of the
gramophone, and the dance floor was replete with tapping feet, enticing
legs, arms wrapped around waists, lips pressed to lips, and chests pressed
to chests. The atmosphere was full of desire."

On returning to an Egypt that was also becoming more Westernized
as it moved toward modernity, Qutb's radicalization increased and he
turned to violence. O'Brien suggests this may have been because he foreclosed too soon. "In theory, a person who has attained achievement
should not be threatened by the existence of others who deviate from his
or her views," she writes. "On the other hand, foreclosure is when a person settles on an outcome too early. Often, this is because they were not
exposed to alternatives, or were raised to think of possible alternatives as
evil from a young age."[7] (A brief digression before we continue: Note that
according to his book, Qutb's main gripes with the United States were not
its policies as much as the mixing of the sexes [even in churches!], mate-
rialism, secularism, and bare female skin. And he didn't just find this dis-
tasteful—he found it offensive enough to justify murderous violence
against the West and its supporters. The Muslim Brotherhood is widely

agreed to be the precursor to Islamic jihadist groups like Al Qaeda today. Hearing those who claim these groups wouldn't exist if we in the West hadn't aggrieved them in the first place, one wonders what this restraint on our part would look like. Less dancing in churches, perhaps? Is that what it would take?)

I think of identity foreclosure as an adherence to those "inborn" identifiers: sex, ethnicity, nationality, familial religious affiliation, and so on. They are there, they've always been there, and they'll always be there. There's no need to *work* for these labels as one would, say, for the label of doctor or accountant. All you need to do is be born. No need for exploration—just submission and commitment.

Then, there are "acquired" identifiers, those we actually *earn* by way of exploration, drive, deliberation, and effort—these are markers of Marcian identity achievement. As we evolve, we gain an education; form values and perspectives on our lives and the world based on what we learn from our experiences; earn a definitive social and/or financial status in our communities by working hard and making decisions; settle into our professions; and become parents, philanthropists, journalists, artists, engineers, businesspeople, physicians, and more. The more of this we do, the less likely we are to have foreclosed, and the less urgent our need to cling to our inborn identifiers.

Now, to some extent, we all take pride in our identities. This can be healthy if it's for the achievements we've worked to earn. But deriving pride from our inborn identifiers is precarious in a way best summed up by the brilliant, late comedian George Carlin, who said he could never understand ethnic or national pride. (Out of respect for his disdain for censorship, I will present his thoughts unaltered.) "Pride should be reserved for something you achieved or attained on your own, not something that happens by accident of birth," he said. "Being Irish isn't a skill. It's a fucking genetic accident . . . If you're happy with it, that's fine—do that, put that on your car: 'Happy to be an American.' Be happy. Don't be proud."[8]

The identity-achieved, having undergone a process of exploration, are not threatened by differing ideas or beliefs. Earning a sense of pride from one's hard-earned achievements can bring about progress, innovation, exchange of ideas, constructive dialogue, and healthy debate. But the identity-foreclosed have no choice but to fall back on their inborn identifiers for some sense of self-worth. Patriotism. Nationalism. Religious fundamentalism. Otherization. All of these notions are based on taking immense pride in what one has *not* worked to earn, with a dismissal of all other alternatives. Indeed, differences over inborn identifiers have been at the heart of many of the worst crimes, wars, and genocides in history.

When we look at the problem of "homegrown terrorism" in Western countries, we often reduce it to issues of economics and opportunity, speaking only of disenfranchised youth lashing out against a historically colonialist or imperialist power that continues to oppress and victimize its minorities. But time and time again, we're seeing that it doesn't play out that way. American Muslims tend to have higher education levels than almost all other religious groups, second only to Jews.[9] They are also more likely to have college degrees than the general American population.[10] On gender equality, Muslim women in the United States are more likely to have college or graduate degrees than American Muslim men, and a higher percentage of them have careers in professional fields compared to the general population.[11] In general, Muslims in America are doing really well. The most notorious U.S.-based terrorists—including the 9/11 hijackers, the Boston marathon bombers, the San Bernardino shooters, Fort Hood shooter Nidal Hasan, Orlando shooter Omar Mateen, American-born Al Qaeda mastermind Anwar Al-Awlaki, and others—were well off, with no discernible lack of opportunity. Some actually left extremely prestigious careers for the purpose of jihad. Hasan was a psychiatrist, and Al-Awlaki had a doctorate from the University of Nebraska. Even in Europe, many of the youths who carry out terrorist acts tend to be fairly comfortable, with decent jobs and middle-class incomes. The notorious ISIS executioner Mohammed Emwazi ("Jihadi John"), for example, had a graduate degree in computer science from the University of Westminster, and a successful career in information technology.[12]

Now, there is no doubt that high levels of unemployment in countries like France frustrate young Muslims, but this does not adequately explain what turns them into holy warriors ready to kill. So, instead of looking at the problem through a political or economic lens, it may be worthwhile to look at these young men's psychological development during adolescence. O'Brien thinks that the model proposed by Erikson and Marcia fits the profiles of many terrorists, who were "not exposed to the West in a positive context, whether by simple isolation or conservative family influence, until well after they had established a personal and social identity." Once exposed, they became radicalized, perceiving their identities and mental health—not to mention their vision of a "proper" and "morally correct order of society"—to be at risk.[13]

A 2008 paper by Seth Schwartz and his colleagues Curtis Dunkel and Alan Waterman finds that both identity foreclosure and identity diffusion are susceptible to radicalization.[14] The identity-foreclosed are often taught to hate (or deem inferior) outside groups from early childhood. Their families and communities encourage them to follow the "right path" without any deviation—which, by definition, means that identity exploration is strongly discouraged.

The second group the authors highlight as being particularly susceptible to being involved in terrorism is the identity diffusion group. The identity-diffused are individuals who score low on both exploration and commitment, and have not developed a personal identity. Their lives are riddled with aimlessness, uncertainty, and indecisiveness. Needless to say, groups that provide them with an identity, and give their lives purpose and certainty both on Earth and in the afterlife, can manipulate them fairly easily. They are "willing to go to their deaths for ideas that they have appropriated from others," write the authors, "rather than ideas that they have chosen through independent and thoughtful reflection."

Religious faith is so deeply ingrained into the cultural, social, and personal identities of people across the Muslim world, that any criticism of the religion or its fundamental elements—even from cartoonists like those at *Charlie Hebdo*—is immediately perceived as a personal attack, an attack on Muslims' collective or individual identity.

Even as far back as 1968, Erikson described this phenomenon in his book *Identity: Youth and Crisis*. "The fear of loss of identity," he wrote, ". . . contributes significantly to that mixture of righteousness and criminality which, under totalitarian conditions, becomes available for organized terror and for the establishment of major industries of extermination."[15]

Conventional explanations for Islamic terrorism—poverty, lack of education, lack of opportunity, and the grievance narrative, among others—don't seem to fit the story very well anymore. However, seen through the lens of identity formation or fear of identity loss, applying identity development theory appears to show a remarkable amount of consistency across the board.

People are much more than the ideas they believe in—or *think* they believe in. As Pakistani feminist Alishba Zarmeen points out, "Most humans are more moral than the scriptures they hold sacred."[16] Those who actually live their lives in accordance with the fundamentals of their holy books are a minority, even if sizeable, as in the case of Muslims. Sure, there is the question of the Quran being the infallible, direct word of God to be applicable for all time; but this was also once true of the Torah for many Jews. Moreover, there are already reform-minded groups and individuals who are beginning to challenge this assertion of divine authorship.

I once jokingly asked a writer friend how her identification as a "feminist Muslim" was any different from someone identifying as a black white supremacist or a meat-eating vegetarian. She replied that she didn't see this designation as inherently contradictory, because she identified with a range of feminist values as well as Islamic ones. I asked how she reconciles her feminism with some of the obviously misogynistic verses in the Quran, such as verse 4:34, which establishes male authority over women and advocates beating one's wife if one "fears disobedience"; or verse 2:282, which states that two women witnesses are equivalent to one man because "if one of the women errs, then the other can remind her." She openly admitted that she doesn't understand or agree with these Quranic verses, despite being aware of some of the more modern, revisionist interpretations that attempt to make them seem more benign. She felt she was able to disregard them, confident in her belief that Allah sees her as equal to her male counterparts.

"But isn't that disingenuous?" I asked. "Don't you believe the Quran is the perfect, unadulterated word of God?"

"Yes, of course. But everyone cherry-picks," she replied, with a shrug.

As cognitively dissonant as that sounds, my friend was right. Reconciling modernity and faith can only be made possible by a selective reading and following of Islam—by designating conflicting sets of values into separate, walled-off compartments in our brains. It has, of course, long been a phenomenon with other religious groups. Many of the world's Catholics ignore the Church's positions on birth control, fornication, and even abortion, while retaining their Catholic identities—so called "cafeteria Catholics." Similarly, many modern Jews expressly reject Judaism while selectively retaining some of its cultural elements and traditions.

Even those Muslims who believe the Quran is the perfect, infallible word of God tend to promote "moderation"—something I've always found curious. Whether you define moderation as committing to only parts of a doctrine that claims infallibility instead of the whole, or lowering the intensity of your commitment to a doctrine that commands complete submission, this approach to the faith stands in contradiction to the foundational precepts of the faith itself.

So who decides how far the cherry picking can go? If everyone cherry-picks, can one cherry-pick all the way to nonbelief status? If one can be a feminist Muslim, or an LGBT Muslim, can one not be a secular or even an atheist Muslim?

This question gets to the very heart of the idea that "Islam" does not necessarily equal "Muslims." In a popular blog post, an ex-Christian atheist who goes by the pseudonym "Re-Enlightenment" wonders, why not? "Would you only be prepared to grant someone a Christian identity if they successfully negotiated your questions on church attendance, the Old Testament, and attitudes to homosexuality?" he asks. "Why the different treatment for Islam?" Re-Enlightenment insists that Islam urgently needs to undergo the same process as Christianity and Judaism did long before it. It needs to be fed into the same "two-part grinder called 'Secularism and the Enlightenment'" in order to emerge as a diluted version of itself at the other end—one that can be dismembered, cherry-picked, or dismissed at the user's whim. And when we stop seeing the beer-drinking atheist Muslim as a walking contradiction, we'll know we're getting somewhere.[17]

The fact that we're having this conversation at all is evidence that we're already on the way. Every time a believer proclaiming to hold a holy book sacred reacts with shock when shown what's actually *in* the book—as with the above-described Quranic verses or the biblical words that began this chapter—this point is made.

The uncomfortable truth, however, is that the most dangerous are inevitably those who are most intimately familiar with these words, have studied them thoroughly, and actually take them seriously—whether in the Torah, Quran, or any other holy book they consider to be divinely sanctioned. Those who read these passages, thinking, "This is sacred and virtuous, this must be respected," are the ones to watch out for.

It's not "radicalization." It's increased faith. Faith is not a virtue. Faith means to believe outlandish things without any evidence, simply because someone centuries ago told us to. It fetters the intellect and taints the conscience.

People are much more than what they believe. Yet you hear it everywhere—the conflation of "Islam" and "Muslims." Are they really the same thing? The distinction can be challenging to navigate in practice, not least because of how strongly Islamic ideology is integrated into Muslim identity, as we've seen in the previous chapter. This integration makes leaving Islam not just an intellectual process, but also an emotionally fraught, full-blown identity crisis. Of course, Islam is just a religion—a collection of ideas in a book. But the experience of being Muslim—practicing or not—is much more nuanced and complex.

It is true that Muslims around the world are culturally heterogeneous. Pakistani Muslims, for instance, have more cultural similarities with Indian Hindus than with Arab Muslims. Arab Muslims, in turn, have more in common culturally with Arab Christians than with Indonesian Muslims, and so on. However, some elements of Muslim culture are universal. The festival of Eid is celebrated in all Muslim communities. The celebratory *iftar* (fast-breaking) feasts in Ramadan are common across all Muslim societies. These rituals are like any other: children are given gifts or money, people take days off work to travel, and families and friends come

together for food and conversation. During these holidays and celebrations, the focus shifts from *ideology* to *community*—and this is where a
key distinction comes in: Islam is an ideology. Muslims are a community.

Ideologies drive people apart. Community brings people together.

In an interview with Sam Harris, Phil Zuckerman, author of *Living the
Secular Life*, describes the process of "secularizing religion," and how
certain religious groups have achieved this, using Reform Judaism as an
example. From rituals and holidays, to charity and a sense of community and belonging, most American Jews have taken what they like
from Judaism, yet outgrown the supernatural fairy tales. In a sense, they
have divorced Judaism from the experience of being Jewish. They have
retained the identity and culture, while for many, the faith part is all but
scrapped. Zuckerman also gives the example of Nordic Lutherans, who
"observe traditional religious holidays and . . . congregate now and then
in church and they even 'feel' Christian—and yet they do all these
ostensibly religious things without a scintilla of actual faith in the
supernatural."[18]

Imagine that.

Imagine if, as a Muslim, you could keep your family and community
traditions, enjoy those Ramadan *iftar* parties, and celebrate the Eid holidays with your family and friends as always—but without the burden of
belief, or having to defend every line in your scripture.

Sounds contradictory, I know. And it's not going to happen overnight.
But as Zuckerman points out, there's precedent. It's been done with several other faiths, and they aren't so different from Islam. Rather, Islam is
largely derived from them.

To the young, questioning North American Muslim, I say this:

Remember, your religious beliefs aren't really *you*. They are simply
part of the medium you were cultured in when you were raised. You know,
deep down, that if you were born in a Hindu family, you'd probably be
Hindu; and in a Christian family, you'd be Christian. You know, deep
down, that your faith is really just an *accident of birth*.

So, logically speaking, it *can't* be about ideas, can it? Ideas don't come with birth. They need to be considered, explored, and evaluated. What does come with birth, however, is your sense of identity.

Many religious communities have now evolved past their religious beliefs. In effect, they've secularized their religions. Judeo-Christian scripture isn't vastly different from Islamic scripture. Yet many Jews and Christians are able to hold on to their cultural identities and customs without the burden of actually following every aspect of their faith, or even believing their holy books are necessarily immutable and perfect. Jews are typically accepted in their communities just fine even if they abandon their faith completely; and Catholics aren't being disowned, marginalized, or imprisoned en masse for using birth control in their premarital relationships.

You, as a Muslim, can still identify with the Muslim experience without feeling obligated to justify and defend every line in your book, especially when you know, deep down, you don't *really* agree with all of it. No rational, thinking person can agree with every single idea in *any* book of conjecture.

Yes, it's supposed to be the word of God, perfect and error-free. But you know, deep down, how reading some parts of it for the first time made you jump—they sent you scrambling to Google or to your parents' bookshelf. You couldn't believe God could ever say something like that, so you had to find some kind of explanation or "interpretation" that would make it all fit better with your *already present* sense of what's right and wrong.

Think about that for a second. Do you really think you need your religion in order to be good?

Or look at it another way: If the only thing keeping you from being bad or immoral is your religion, what does that say about you as a person?

You know, deep down, how it looks to others when you bend over backward just to make ancient verses about beating your wife or fighting non-Muslims sound somewhat palatable, just so you can defend your faith, and therefore, in your mind, your heritage and identity.

You know that you would never go to such an extent to justify the same ideas—expressed the same way—if I had written them in my book. You would've read them as they were and held me accountable for my words, instead of looking for "context," a "correct interpretation," or something else to make it sound better than it does.

You know, deep down, that it's becoming increasingly difficult and exhausting to keep telling others—and maybe even yourself—how your progressive, reasoned values are somehow completely compatible with those words written 1300 years ago.

Yes, loyalty to your loved ones and your people is a noble virtue. But being unwaveringly loyal to an ideology or a belief system both shackles the mind and corrupts the conscience. Critical thinking becomes blasphemy, curiosity leads to heresy, and your own sense of morality takes second place to the absolute morality of the divine creator. In effect, you're asked to abandon both your intellectual independence and your freedom to think and make your own choices just so you can stay in the club. And if you choose to free yourself, it too often means getting kicked out of it—which isn't easy when you've been in it since you were a child, and it's all you know. Does that sound fair to you?

You may have countless counterarguments and disagreements developing in your mind right now. That's okay. It's healthy, and it's actually the only way to go through this process. But please do think about it. When I was where you are, I resisted for years. This is not an easy thing to do.

But there needs to be a way—a way for Muslim youth to be able to think freely, question ideas, and come to different conclusions without fear, without having to lose their sense of identity or their connection to the life and people that they love. And in my experience, the one thing that helps most is knowing you're not alone, that there are others out here just like you.

It's time to let reformist Muslims, secular Muslims, questioning Muslims, agnostic/atheist Muslims, and ex-Muslims into the dialogue on Islam—so we can make it as diverse, varied, and complex as the Muslim world itself.

FIVE

Choosing Atheism

For the longest time, I didn't like the word *atheist* precisely for the same reason that I was one: I was deeply uncomfortable with any kind of absolute certainty in the absence of evidence. So I identified as an agnostic. My answer to whether or not I believed in God was always, "I don't know."

However, like many others, I was answering the wrong question. I had incorrectly defined both of these words. They aren't mutually preclusive. The distinction, in fact, is simple: atheism is *not believing*, and agnosticism is *not knowing*.

In my experience, most people—believers and nonbelievers alike—tend to be agnostic. Ask a theist if he believes in God, and he'll say yes. Then ask if he *knows for sure* that God exists. If he says yes, he is a *gnostic theist*. If he says no, he is an *agnostic theist*.

The same goes for atheists, commonly defined as those who *don't believe in God*. Ask them if they believe in God, and they will tell you that they don't. Then ask, "Do you *know for sure* that God doesn't exist?" Those who say yes are *gnostic atheists*. And those who say no are *agnostic atheists*.

Almost every atheist I know of is an agnostic atheist—as am I.

But first, how does one really define "atheism"? Is it really just the *lack of belief* in a god? Or is it the *belief* that there is no God? The simplest and most sensible approach would be to break it down into its root components. According to *The Oxford English Dictionary*, the word *atheist* comes from the Greek *atheos*, where the prefix, *a-*, means "without," and *theos* means "god." It therefore defines "atheism" as "disbelief or lack of belief in the existence of God or gods."[1] It is important to note here that atheism is not a *belief* that no God or gods exist, even though some dictionaries wrongly define it this way. It is precisely the opposite—it's a *lack* of belief. As Don Hirschberg has said, calling atheism a belief or a religion "is like calling bald a hair color."[2] And Bill Maher says, it's like calling abstinence "a sex position."[3]

But we're not done just yet. If "atheism" means "without theism," what is it that we mean by "theism"? *The Oxford English Dictionary* defines theism as "belief in the existence of a god or gods, especially belief in one god as creator of the universe, *intervening in it and sustaining a personal relation* to his creatures."[4] (Emphasis added.)

This is in contrast to the definition of "deism": "Belief in the existence of a supreme being, specifically of a creator who *does not intervene* in the universe."[5] (Emphasis added.)

Now, we can't fully understand the definition of "atheism" without having a definition of "theism." And we can't have a working definition of "theism" unless we first define God or a god. Indeed, we now have two types of god: the *theistic* god who intervenes and has a personal relationship with his subjects, that is, a "personal god"; and the *deistic* god who doesn't intervene in his creation, doesn't answer prayers, and doesn't bless your marriage.

In light of this, the word *atheism* no longer just means "without God or a god." It also means "without theism," or "without a *personal* god."

The implications of this are interesting. It means that deists—as were some of the Founding Fathers—are also atheists. So are pantheists, Buddhists, some Hindus, and those who define God as an abstract concept synonymous with awe, wonder, the laws of the universe, or—as Spinoza believed—nature itself.

Einstein was a proponent of Spinoza's idea of God. And despite being an atheist by definition, Einstein also disliked the word. (As it turns out, I wasn't in bad company.) In a letter to a correspondent in the 1940s, Albert Einstein wrote, "I have repeatedly said that in my opinion the *idea of a personal God is a childlike one* [emphasis added]," but also noted, "You may call me an agnostic, but I do not share the crusading spirit of the professional atheist . . . I prefer an attitude of humility corresponding to the weakness of our intellectual understanding of nature and of our own being."[6] Despite having declared his atheism by calling the idea of a personal god childlike, he still rejected the word "atheist" because of its connotations and associations.

However, in 1954, a year before his death, Einstein seemed to have become more definitive in his declaration of nonbelief. In a letter to the philosopher Erik Gutkind, he wrote:

> The word God is for me nothing more than the expression and product of human weakness, the Bible a collection of honorable, but still purely primitive, legends which are nevertheless pretty childish. No interpretation, no matter how subtle, can change this for me. For me the Jewish religion like all other religions is an incarnation of the most childish superstition. And the Jewish people to whom I gladly belong, and whose thinking I have a deep affinity for, have no different quality for me than all other people. As far as my experience goes, they are also no better than other human groups.[7]

Einstein's reluctance to embrace the word "atheist" seemed to originate from three key areas. First, he didn't want to be associated with the strident, "crusading spirit of the professional atheist," which implies a combative arrogance and certainty. Second, somewhat related to the first, he wanted to retain a sense of humility and awe, a sense that there is much about the wonders of the natural world and the universe that we as humans don't have the capacity to understand. And third, he wanted to preserve his identification with the community he was part of, avowing the kinship he felt with his fellow Jews, but without the "childish superstition" of Judaism, the faith.

Einstein's earlier statements about religion, however, had been confusing for those trying to pinpoint his actual beliefs. In 1941, he famously
wrote, "Science without religion is lame, religion without science is blind,"
an oft-quoted statement that appears to demonstrate his religiosity and
seems to stand in contradiction to his letter to Gutkind.[8] But if one looks
a little more closely, it doesn't. It's clear that Einstein defined "religion"
and "religious" in a completely different way than we traditionally do:

> It was, of course, a lie what you read about my religious convic-
> tions, a lie which is being systematically repeated. I do not be-
> lieve in a personal God and I have never denied this but have
> expressed it clearly. If something is in me which can be called
> religious then it is the unbounded admiration for the structure
> of the world so far as our science can reveal it.[9]

Another quote:

> I have never imputed to Nature a purpose or a goal, or anything
> that could be understood as anthropomorphic. What I see in
> Nature is a magnificent structure that we can comprehend only
> very imperfectly, and that must fill a thinking person with a
> feeling of humility. This is a genuinely religious feeling that has
> nothing to do with mysticism.[10]

And another:

> A knowledge of the existence of something we cannot pene-
> trate, of the manifestations of the profoundest reason and the
> most radiant beauty, which are only accessible to our reason in
> their most elementary forms—it is this knowledge and this
> emotion that constitute the truly religious attitude; in this
> sense, and in this alone, I am a deeply religious man. I cannot
> conceive of a God who rewards and punishes his creatures, or
> has a will of the type of which we are conscious in ourselves.
> An individual who should survive his physical death is also be-

yond my comprehension, nor do I wish it otherwise; such notions are for the fears or absurd egoism of feeble souls. Enough
for me the mystery of the eternity of life, and the inkling of the
marvellous structure of reality, together with the single-hearted
endeavour to comprehend a portion, be it never so tiny, of the
reason that manifests itself in nature.[11]

For Einstein, "religion" was an acknowledgment of the awe and wonder of the universe, a sense of humility in the face of *not* knowing the
truth—exactly the opposite of traditional religion. Like Einstein, there
are many atheists—that is, those without belief in a personal god—who
are uncomfortable with calling themselves "atheist." And like Einstein,
their reluctance often stems from the same three places that Einstein's
did—they do not want to be seen as arrogant; they reject religious belief
precisely because they want to embrace humility and reject the certainty
that many wrongly associate atheism with; and perhaps most importantly, they want to retain goodwill and a connection with the communities they feel part of. None of these reasons, of course, have much to do
with the actual definition of the word.

My own initial hesitation in embracing the "atheist" label came from an
aversion to absolute certainty. The stereotype of atheists was of strident,
aggressive, arrogant know-it-alls who wanted nothing but to tell other
people how to think and what to do. This is not how I wanted to identify.
I was humbled by everything I did not know, and everything I *could* not
know. It was later that I realized atheism *is* a position of humility, in contrast to theism, which claims to know the truth, and moreover, deems it
divine and absolute. *That* is arrogance.

Indeed, people arrive at atheism for a variety of reasons. Many of my
ex-Muslim friends grew up with stringent restrictions imposed by their
parents or communities on their behavior, thoughts, and capacity to
make independent, autonomous life decisions like marriage or choice of
career. These restrictions are almost always rooted in their religious beliefs, or in cultural beliefs endorsed by the religion. And because the

religion is ostensibly patriarchal in nature, they affect girls and women to a much greater extent than males. Enforcing hijab, imposing a double standard on modesty codes, shaming the expression of sexuality, and being taught submissiveness to their husbands (often the result of forced arranged marriages) are, sadly, common practices even among Muslim families living in Western countries. As I write these very words, I am in correspondence with a young woman in Canada who is a lesbian—unbeknownst to her strictly conservative Sunni Muslim family—and is about to be wed to her male cousin in a matter of weeks. There is little she can do about it, and there is little we can do to help her. This is not a one-off situation. And the few women who have found the courage to escape their oppressive circumstances—like Ayaan Hirsi Ali, the famous Somali ex-Muslim-turned-atheist who underwent genital mutilation at age five and escaped to the Netherlands to flee a forced marriage—are almost universally lambasted by mainstream Muslims, including American organizations like the Council on American-Islamic Relations (CAIR), for being traitors to their faith and their communities.[12] For these women and men who arrive at atheism by overcoming religious oppression, the opposition to religion is an impassioned fight for human rights and justice.

Growing up in Saudi Arabia and seeing the flagrant mistreatment of women and the egregious state-sanctioned human rights abuses there certainly fueled the doubt and skepticism seeded in me from a young age. As I described in chapter 2, this is what triggered my interest in studying Islam and the Quran in the first place. But my eventual transition to atheism didn't primarily come in the pursuit of justice. It came in the pursuit of truth.

My parents, both professors educated in the United States and Canada, always encouraged my siblings and me to engage in critical thinking. My mother in particular, with her doctorate focused on early childhood education, was passionate about raising us to be meticulously analytical and question everything for ourselves. While they were believers themselves, my parents were much more open to our questions doubting elements of the faith they were raising us with. Around the dinner table, we bounced ideas around and debated them, with all of us getting a chance to chime in, regardless of age. My parents didn't agree with us on every-thing, and at times even disagreed angrily—but we knew this would never translate to violence, disownment, or abandonment. We learned to disagree on ideas, yet still move on as family. In retrospect, this is the singular insight for which I am most grateful to them today.

There were, of course, limits—but these were largely due to reasons of security. As crazy as it sounds, if any of us had expressed views deemed even remotely "blasphemous" in front of outsiders who felt offended and reported us, my parents could have been whisked off to jail without ques-tion. And being Shia Muslims in Saudi Arabia, that may just have been the best-case scenario. This very fact, for me, further cemented the im-portance of questioning everything.

I first fell in love with science in the sixth grade, when my science teacher at the American International School showed us episodes of Carl Sagan's brilliant, beautifully written *Cosmos* series. Every episode left me with endless questions about the world and the universe that I would think and read about for days afterward. I learned about multiple spatial dimensions from Sagan's incredible "Flatland" segment, where he dem-onstrated what the third dimension would look like to people living in a two-dimensional world—and by extrapolation, how a fourth dimension would appear to us. I learned how time was integrated into the space-time fabric, and could slow down or speed up depending on how space-time is distorted by gravity. I learned about time dilation, the phenomenon of time slowing down when one travels near the speed of light, to the extent that a short ride at this speed for a few minutes would find one returning to a world where everyone else had aged by decades.

What impacted me most, though, was learning about the unfathom-able vastness of the universe—looking into the night sky at the stars with the surreal realization that I was looking millions, even billions of years back in time. I would wonder how many of those stars were still around, how many had already perished, and how many new ones had been born that we wouldn't see until their light reached us millions of years from now. I listened intently when Carl Sagan described how tiny our Earth was, utterly insignificant and inconsequential in the grand scheme of things—the "pale blue dot," as he would later describe it.[13] By the time

I started reading the Quran in English to understand my family's religion, I was already thoroughly taken by science, which not only made claims actually supported by mathematical and physical evidence, but also welcomed others to challenge and falsify them—without, I might add, the threat of being imprisoned or beheaded.

In *Surah* 45 of the Quran, Allah allegedly says, "Indeed, within the heavens and earth are signs for the believers." These signs include the "alternation of night and day," life on the earth from the "sky of provision," and the "directing of the winds." And verse 13:3 speaks of how Allah "spread the Earth and placed therein firmly set mountains and rivers," and then made "two mates" from "all of the fruits."

"Indeed in that there are signs," warns the verse, "for a people who give thought."

With my growing interest in science and my near-obsession with learning more about the world and the universe, I was avidly looking at these signs and amply giving thought, as per the Quranic recommendation. But the more I learned, the further I strayed from the faith. How could it be that the creator of this incredible, mysterious universe that Carl Sagan described so eloquently seemed so concerned with whether we eat pork or who we have sex with? The more my knowledge grew, the smaller God became. The Quran began to look petty, almost juvenile, with its melodramatic "Lo!"s and "Oh ye who believe!"s, instructing us to look for signs that confirm Allah's existence, yet promising eternal doom and hellfire if we remained unconvinced of it.

I would learn later that the god(s) of the Old and New Testament weren't all that different from the god of the Quran. They all seemed impossibly trivial and inconsequential compared to what Carl Sagan talked about. The sheer psychosis underlying the story of Abraham—the patriarch of the monotheisms, ready with sword raised to violently murder his own son and prove his loyalty to the supposed voice of God inside his head—made God seem more like a pathologically jealous and insecure significant other with attachment issues than an omnipotent deity who invented binary pulsars.

Sometimes, it takes the clarity of a child's mind to demonstrate how absurd an idea really is. On hearing the story of Abraham—or Ibrahim in the Quran—my four-year-old nephew was visibly shaken. His father told it to him on *Eid Al-Adha*, the Islamic holiday marking the end of the annual Hajj pilgrimage, where a lamb or goat is slaughtered to commemorate Abraham's sacrifice. Afterward, I asked him what he thought.

"It made me feel sad," he said. "God should have loved him more if he said he *wouldn't* kill his son."

So, which was it?

On one hand, there was the Big Bang—the creation of all matter and time—with a good amount of scientific evidence supporting it. On the other, there was the patronizingly boring "Let there be light!" with none. On one hand, there were the processes of random mutation and nonrandom natural selection working together for hundreds of millions of years to create the immeasurably rich diversity of life that graces our planet. On the other, there was a man fashioned from dust (Quran, 3:59) or a fluid ejected "from between the backbone and ribs" (Quran 86:5–7); and a woman fashioned from his soul (Quran 4:1) or his rib (*Sahih Bukhari hadith* 4:55:548); and both were responsible for our demotion to Earth from heaven. To any serious, rational person reflecting on any of this, the answers were obvious.

Despite all of this, I still wanted to try and give religion another chance. I was reluctant to completely let go of my personal God, and at this point, didn't feel the need to. Part of it was fear, but more than that, I simply couldn't wrap my head around the idea that billions of people around the world—including my parents, teachers, and even esteemed scientists like Newton—could be wrong. (Of course, if Newton had been alive today and aware of the facts of evolution and Einstein's revolutionary rethinking of his work, it's unlikely he would have remained a theist.) For every scientific argument I was presented with, there was always that last "How?" that remained unanswered: the "First Cause." I filled that void with God—albeit a loosely defined God—without paying much attention to the question of who created *him*. I was aware of the argument: if the universe is so magnificent that it must have a creator, that creator must be even *more* magnificent, requiring a creator *himself*. And if this creator doesn't need a creator, then neither does the universe. It was a good argument, and I reconciled it with my beliefs by adopting a somewhat pantheistic view of God, where he *was* the universe. I was doing everything I could to hold on to God in a way that was intellectually honest, and redefining him in this way made it easier. For instance, I accepted the theory of the Big Bang, but decided that God had started it. I embraced evolution, but didn't see it as contradictory to God either; I simply believed God set it in motion. I was happy to note that my position on this was similar to that of Dr. Francis Collins, the accomplished physician and scientist who led the Human Genome Project. He maintains that it was indeed God's plan to create moral creatures with souls and the gift of free will, and evolution was simply the mechanism by which he executed it.[14]

Even the extremely difficult question of why pain and suffering exist made sense to me. We only know about life here on Earth, I told myself. God knows about this side *and* the other side. This life is just a flash in the pan, and we humans look at pain and suffering in an almost negligibly narrow context compared to the eternity and magnificence of the hereafter. If life after death was truly eternal, pain and suffering in this life were virtually irrelevant. God knew that once we did get to the other side, we'd understand.

It's not something I struggled with intellectually. It was comforting: "Everything will be all right in the end." It brought a fatalistic meaning to everything: "I'm suffering for a reason. God is testing me." And though I didn't realize it at the time, it was also dangerous. This was the kind of thinking that makes people prioritize life after death over life *before* death.

I started to actually listen to those who would counter my questions about the Quran by saying I need to open my mind, that I was taking it too "literally." Today, I find it fascinating that so many Western Islamic scholars are genuinely terrified of anyone reading the Quran "literally"— that is, exactly the way Allah supposedly wrote (revealed) it. I think they have very good reasons to feel this way, as did I: if one reads the Quran as one reads any other book, taking its words at face value, it comes across exactly as the outmoded medieval document that it is. To sanitize it, one must move away from Allah's word choice and opt instead for the word choice of modern humans, who will often write entire books explaining why verses like 8:12–13, which endorse killing disbelievers, are somehow about *not* killing them. They will urge you to put down your Quran and listen to *them*—highlighting the good parts as they are, but using a wide array of intellectual acrobatics to explain away the more backward and violent verses as "out of context," "misinterpreted," or "metaphorical." Indeed, the more progress humanity has made over time—in everything from medical science to civil rights—the more "metaphorical" the scripture has become.

When I began to look at the Quran as a book of metaphors, faith suddenly became a whole lot easier. I discovered my creativity to be virtually limitless, and even impressed myself with my "interpretive" abilities—it was very convincing.

I was now in medical school in Karachi, Pakistan, where life was much different from Saudi Arabia. I attended the Aga Khan University in Karachi, regarded to be one of the best medical schools in the Indian subcontinent. The university was founded by the spiritual leader of the *Nizari Ismaili* sect of Shia Islam, Shah Karim al-Hussaini, who holds the title "Aga Khan," and is commonly referred to as "Prince Karim Aga Khan." The Swiss-born Aga Khan is believed by his followers to be a direct descendant of Muhammad, and to have infallible status—a representative of God on Earth—affording him a unique platform to directly reform and reinterpret Islam for Ismaili Muslims. A British citizen who lives in France, the Aga Khan is known to be very pro-West, and promotes gender equality, secular pluralism, and democracy, making the Nizari Ismailis one of the most theologically innovative and progressive sects in Islam today. (The Ismailis and other minority sects are discussed in greater detail in chapter 8.)

In Karachi, I had friends from a variety of religious backgrounds—Sunni, Shia, Ismaili, Ahmadi, even Christian and Hindu—from all over the world. They were still overwhelmingly Pakistani in origin, but many had grown up overseas, in the United States, Canada, Britain, the United

Arab Emirates, and so on. It was a great opportunity for overseas Pakistanis. You could start medical school immediately after high school. You finished in five years, at a fraction of the cost of medical school (and undergraduate studies) in the United States. And, importantly, a significant majority of the Aga Khan University's graduates performed very well on their U.S. medical licensing examinations, going on to secure competitive residency positions in the United States.

Religion was a very commonly discussed topic among students. Although publicly declaring oneself an atheist was still risky in Pakistan, we were comfortable confiding in close, like-minded friends, particularly in the relatively tolerant, secure environs of the university. It was here that I discovered secular, liberal Islam—and through much of my time there, this is the version of religion I identified with most.

In effect, my goal was to find a way to stay in the religion while doing exactly what I wanted to do. I read the scripture again, but differently. I used every interpretive tool I could dig up, and I got very good at it. Keep in mind that this is similar to the way a lot of moderate and liberal Muslims interpret scripture today.

First, I decided to look at the Quran like a textbook. You had your fundamental concepts, which were timeless and didn't change. Then you had examples, which changed depending on what time you were in. For example, basic concepts about motion in a physics textbook that might have been illustrated using trollies a century ago could be illustrated using space shuttles today. I would use the same approach to interpret concepts in the Quran such as modesty, the punishment for theft, and heaven and hell.

Modesty, for example, was one of the fundamental concepts. The examples used in the Quran to illustrate it at the time were in verse 24:31, which says that women should "wrap [a portion] of their head-covers over their bosoms"; and verse 33:59, which instructs Muhammad to tell his wives, daughters, and "the women of the believers" to "bring down over themselves [part] of their outer garments," because "that is more suitable that they will be known and not be abused." At the time the Quran was written, I told myself, this is how modesty was expressed. Today, however, a simple shirt and shorts—which would have been life-threateningly scandalous back then—are considered perfectly modest. The *concept* stays the same, but the *example* changes.

For those who commit theft, verse 5:38 in the Quran instructs Muslims to "amputate their hands in recompense for what they committed as a deterrent [punishment] from Allah." Hand amputation for theft, as mentioned previously, is still practiced as a punishment for theft in Saudi Arabia today. Here, I told myself, the fundamental concept was that theft is wrong and merited punishment. And the example prescribed for it at that time was hand amputation. Today, we would instead focus on the word "deterrent"; and "amputate their hands" could be interpreted as a metaphor for *restricting* them from stealing, by, for instance, putting them in jail for a prescribed term.

Many young Muslims like myself also struggled with the concepts of heaven and hell. Heaven, the reward for those who believed and did good deeds, would feature the *hūr*—stunningly beautiful women described in the Quran as being "virgins" (verse 56:36) who are "fair" and "full-breasted," (verse 78:33) with "large eyes" like "pearls, well-protected" (verses 56:22–23).[15] Other descriptions of heaven include "gardens beneath which rivers flow," "pleasant dwellings" (verse 9:72), a "flowing spring," "couches raised high," "cups put in place," "cushions lined up," and "carpets spread around" (verses 88:10–16). There would also be fruits of endless variety and rivers of milk, wine, and honey (verse 47:15).

Those who end up in hell, however, would encounter a "great fire" (verse 87:12), doomed to drink "scalding water that will sever their intestines" for eternity (verse 47:15).

These descriptions understandably brought up a lot of questions. If men are getting all of these things, what do the women get? And what exactly would we do with couches, cups, cushions, and carpets for eternity? Or, for that matter, a river of honey? One of my father's friends, a physician who was very religious, explained this to me.

"See, Ali, in this room where we are sitting, there are images and sounds of things happening all over the world right at this very moment. Can you see them? Hear them?"

"No," I replied.

"Now, what if I bring in a radio or TV and tune those waves and signals down to a frequency range that you can perceive? Will you be able to see them then?"

"Yes."

"This is how the Quran works! We won't have our physical bodies in Paradise. We will leave them here, buried under the ground, rotting away. What use can we possibly have for honey, women, and physical comfort when we aren't even in a physical state?"

Again, as he was pointing out, the fundamental concept here was simply that heaven is a reward and hell a punishment; but the *examples* used to describe them were metaphors—only relevant and appealing to an audience of Arabs in the seventh century that appreciated lush couches and carpets. Today, these examples would be different.

"After death, we will be in a spiritual state," he continued. "This isn't something we can even hope to comprehend as physical beings, so Allah has *tuned it down to our frequency*, using metaphorical language and descriptions we can understand. You see? It's not about the *hūr* or the honey. That would be silly. Muslims today look at these things too superficially."

This approach to interpreting the Quran is very common among educated, liberal Muslims, especially in the West, and I found it sophisticated and plausible at the time. "People are just too caught up in the dos and don'ts," my mother would tell me. "They don't look at the underlying philosophy behind it all."

All around me, I would hear examples of how wondrous our holy book was when it was read "metaphorically," ranging from genuinely thought-provoking to cryptically Deepak Chopra–like in their new-agey obscurantism. The latter was particularly evident when people tried to explain physical claims like the Prophet's *Meraj* journey to heaven on a winged horse—an event that even renowned journalists like Mehdi Hasan have admitted to believing in literally[16]—using Einstein's $E = mc^2$ equation. The explanation was that Muhammad flew at the speed of light, in the form of energy. The horse, of course, was a metaphor. And Allah himself declares in *Surah An-Nūr* ("The Light"), verse 35, that he is the "light of the universe" and "guides to His light whom He wills."

This metaphor thing was growing on me. And at times it could be very helpful. As a young man, I was perhaps disproportionately concerned about verses 24:2–5, which prescribed one hundred lashes each for the "[unmarried] woman or [unmarried] man found guilty of sexual intercourse." The verses say to "not be taken by pity for them," and to "let a group of the believers witness their punishment." To be sure, this was scary stuff. But, like always, there was a way around it.

"Look more closely at verse 24:4," I would tell my peers, who were equally intent on finding a loophole specifically in this particular set of divine commands. "It says that to prove the crime, you need four witnesses. Without producing them, the *accuser* gets eighty lashes, and the accused walks free. Presumably, these witnesses have to be Muslim. And we can assume from verse 2:282, which says one man's testimony is equivalent to that of two women, that these witnesses have to be men.

"Now, under what possible circumstances would you ever be in a position where someone could actually produce four male, adult Muslims—*all* of whom witnessed you having penetrative sex? How likely is that? You would have to be doing it in public, in a mosque, or on camera!

"And *that* is the point. The sin is not in fornication itself. It is in the *propagation* of it. As long as you don't have four witnesses, what you do is between you and God. And being beneficent and merciful as he says he is, you can bet that God understands that not all fornication is the same. I doubt sleeping a few times with your future spouse of fifty years before marriage would merit the same degree of punishment as lying to someone to get them into bed for a night. If God weren't okay with fornication, he would've prescribed more than just a worldly punishment for it, much less one that requires four male, adult Muslim witnesses before going into effect."

And just like that, we were able to use the very words of the Quran itself—although selectively—to show that Allah was perfectly fine with premarital sex. You could twist this stuff into anything you wanted. As you may well imagine, my friends were very happy about it. But their parents, having only the rudimentary understanding of the religion that most moderates do, weren't. Yet they had no compelling counterargument.

In this way, with a little bit of creativity, we could make the Quran (or any book, really) mean whatever we wanted it to. And today, when you add additional variables like Christoph Luxenberg's Syro-Aramaic reading of the text, which famously redefines *hūr* to mean "white raisins" instead of beautiful virginal women in Paradise, the interpretive possibilities become almost endless.[17]

However, those who actually knew the history and context behind these verses weren't buying my new age exegesis of the holy word. They would admonish me. "You have to look at the Quran in light of the *hadith* and historical context!"

Now, many of the *hadith* are quite clear in their prescription of punishments like the stoning of adulterers and execution of apostates, which would leave me with very little interpretive potential to play with. Fortunately, I was also prepared for this—I actually had Quranic justification to disregard the *hadith*, or anything external to the Quran. I was able to reference Quranic verses like 7:52, 10:37, and 6:114, which say the Quran is "detailed" or "fully explained"; verse 6:115, which calls the Quran "complete," "perfect," or "fulfilled"; verse 12:111, which says the Quran is a "detailed explanation of all things"; and verse 6:38, which declares straight up that nothing has been "omitted" or "neglected" in the book. To those of us who wanted to somehow make the words of the Quran fit with our secular lifestyles, these verses were, so to speak, a godsend. We would throw them in the faces of those who told us we needed to look at the *hadith* or read them in light of the circumstances under which they were revealed.

By its very nature, though, the Quran lends itself to cherry-picking. Verse 3:7 says there are two different kinds of verses in the Quran: the *muhkam* verses, which are clear and can only be interpreted in one way; and the *muttashabih* verses, which are "unspecific" and "allegorical." The clear verses "are the foundation of the Book," declares the verse. Of the allegorical verses, however, it says, "those in whose hearts is perversity follow the part thereof that is allegorical, seeking discord, and searching for its hidden meanings, but no one knows its hidden meanings except Allah." This is clearly not good news for those who try to interpret the allegorical verses their own way. Moreover, it actually seems to encourage taking the words of scripture at face value—that is, literally—without looking for "hidden meanings." But there is no consensus on which verses are clear and which are allegorical. One person's *muhkam* is the other's *muttashabih*. Scholars would tell me the verse was implying that the allegorical verses be interpreted *in light* of the clear verses. They claimed this proved that there were no contradictions in the Quran. To me, that sounded a lot like they were trying to "find hidden meanings" in the very verse that forbids doing exactly that. Nonetheless, there was no solution to this. To the man who believes without a doubt that the Quran is error-free, any critical reading of the book will always be wrong unless you come to the same conclusion he does.

Many modern, liberal Muslims approach the Quran in the ways described. I've seen the same to be true for those following other religions. For me, however, intellectual honesty eventually caught up to the denialism, and the search for truth overrode the desire to sanitize a scripture I was too afraid to let go. As fun as all the interpretive gymnastics were, this simply wasn't a sustainable system. Words *do* have meaning, these verses *did* have historical context, and in most cases, it wasn't pretty. There were still too many problematic aspects of the Quran that couldn't so easily be "interpreted away."

Besides, when anything can mean anything, everything becomes meaningless.

Ultimately, my rejection of religion as truth came through science. As I became better versed in science and medicine, I became increasingly wary of those who like to demonstrate the beauty of revelation by using science to support it. More often than not, their arguments are based on poor, biased, or incomplete scientific understanding. Nevertheless, it is still interesting to see that in using science to support scriptural claims, they unwittingly acknowledge the strength of the link between science and objective reality. Let's take a look at three key ways in which science and faith differ in their methods of arriving at the truth.

First, science relies on evidence. No matter how elegant or beautiful an idea might be, science will discard it mercilessly if it isn't backed up by nature and its laws: it simply must stand up to the scrutiny of experiment. On the other hand, faith—by definition—is belief in the *absence* of evidence. When there *is* evidence, it isn't called "faith"; it's called "knowledge." You don't have "faith" that the chair you're sitting on exists; you *know* it does, and you can physically demonstrate its existence. In this way, faith quite literally means to unquestioningly believe—and even *revere*—rumors and hearsay, usually from centuries past.

Second, any scientific inquiry must start with the assumption that it could be wrong. Falsifiability—the ability of a proposition to be proven false—is a necessary component of the scientific method, which begins with a hypothesis, tests it via experiment, and either verifies or nullifies it based on the evidence. Faith, in contrast, *begins* with a definitive conclusion believed to be correct—such as "Jesus is the son of God" or "Muhammad is Allah's messenger"—and then works *backward*, cherry picking pieces of evidence (or perceived evidence) in an attempt to support it. This preconceived conclusion is most often accepted on the authority of men who died over a thousand years ago, or the books they left behind. In essence, science poses questions before attempting to provide answers, whereas faith provides answers that it deems unquestionable.

Third, science is not only open to but also *thrives* on innovation and modification. Faith—particularly Abrahamic faith—is fundamentally characterized by infallibility, divinity, and the immutability of its holy texts. Those who challenge or modify these precepts are called blasphemers, heretics, or apostates, and have paid in horrific ways for their digressions throughout history. On the other hand, critical scrutiny and skepticism are key components that lie at the very heart of science. They are welcomed.

The language of scientific inquiry is deliberately conservative and humble. Evolution, for instance, is a fact now verified not only by paleontological evidence, but also by robust molecular genetic evidence. Yet it is still termed a "theory." This is understandably confusing to the science-naïve layman who may ask, "If it is proven, shouldn't it be called a law, like the laws of motion?" This deserves an explanation.

In science, a "law" is simply the *description* of a phenomenon. For example, Newton's law of gravity *describes* the attraction between two objects. It tells us *what* happens, but not *how* or *why* it happens. Specifically, it states that the force of attraction between two bodies is directly proportional to the product of their masses, and inversely proportional to the square of the distance between them. Using this law, one can calculate the gravitational force between two objects, like a bowling ball and the Earth it's being dropped on.

The "theory" of gravity, in contrast, explains *how* or *why* this attraction occurs. A scientific hypothesis only gains the status of a theory after it has been rigorously tested and demonstrated to be correct.

Theories, therefore, are works in progress. This doesn't mean they're not true; it means they are modified, added to, and constantly adapted as more evidence becomes available. For example, the theory of evolution was already widely accepted soon after Darwin first proposed it in 1859, based on evidence from biogeography, comparative anatomy, embryology, and other areas. But further discoveries over the next 150 years—notably from the fossil record and from DNA-sequencing technology—have strengthened the theory immensely. Today, DNA-sequencing has not only revealed to us the evolutionary relationships among living species, but also confirmed beyond a doubt that all living things arose from a single, common ancestor that lived about 4 billion years ago. The theory of gravity has followed a similar trajectory: The one we use today is Einstein's theory of general relativity, which too has been developed and strengthened extensively over the years.

Needless to say, faith—with its claims of absolute truth and its immutable texts—isn't inherently as adaptable or open to change. Moreover, science *works*. "If you base medicine on science, you cure people," says Richard Dawkins. "If you base the design of planes on science, they fly. If you base the design of rockets on science, they reach the moon."[18]

Obviously, this is not the kind of case one could make for, say, prayer—and most religious people I knew, who would easily choose medicine over prayer if told to pick just one, were well aware of this. They also valued evidence-based belief for everything else except their faith. As George Carlin never quite said, "Tell people there's an invisible man in the sky who created the universe, and the vast majority will believe you. Tell them the paint is wet, and they have to touch it to be sure."[19]

Many would mock others for believing in evolution and climate change, demanding evidence for these claims, yet themselves profess an unshakeable faith in the existence of angels, virgin births, or winged horses carrying prophets to heaven.

"Well, can you *disprove* the existence of God or his angels?" they would ask.

Of course not, I would tell them. I couldn't disprove the existence of Zeus or Santa Claus either—and neither could they. Not being able to disprove the existence of something—whether it's unicorns, fairies, or Bertrand Russell's famed celestial teapot[20]—doesn't mean you must believe in it. If it did, there would be no end to what we could all believe.

I was gradually beginning to see now that God was just a lazy answer to some very good questions—the "god of the gaps." For any scientific question that didn't yet have an answer, people chose to say, "God did it," instead of "I don't know." Before the discoveries of evolution, the Big Bang, heliocentrism, and the structure of DNA, these gaps were massive. Today, they are much more narrow. It was becoming readily apparent to me that God really was, as the science educator and astrophysicist Neil deGrasse Tyson so eloquently put it, an "ever-receding pocket of scientific ignorance that's getting smaller and smaller and smaller as time moves on."[21]

The problem with the "god of the gaps" approach is that it kills human curiosity. This is particularly concerning to science educators in the Muslim world like Pakistani physicist and professor Pervez Hoodbhoy, who has long lamented the correlation between Islamic fundamentalism and the dismal state of scientific progress in the Muslim world, a crisis he considers so dire that he risked his own security to write a book on the subject, entitled *Islam and Science: Religious Orthodoxy and the Battle for Rationality*, a job he said "simply had to be taken up."[22]

To me, this correlation was fast becoming obvious. If you were handed a book at birth with all the answers to everything, what incentive would you have to ask questions, especially if asking questions could land you in jail or get you killed for blasphemy? This goes back to what we discussed earlier: How can science and faith truly be compatible when merely *suggesting* that a claim can be falsified or rejected in the absence of evidence is at best taboo, and at worst, life-threatening?

On evolution, I could no longer share Francis Collins's comfort in reconciling faith with scientific reality as I once did. The idea that an ever-loving, merciful god would use a violent and unjust process like natural selection to create all life on Earth was beginning to look like a stretch.

I'd previously subscribed to Stephen Jay Gould's view of non-overlapping magisteria (NOMA). Gould wrote that science and religion dealt with different modes of inquiry: science dealt with facts, religion dealt with values and spiritual meaning, and there was no overlap. I could no longer support this view either, because it's clear that many of the claims made by religion—the creation of the universe, a virgin giving birth, Jesus being resurrected, animals being saved from worldwide floods via boat, and so on—are *scientific* claims.

And the one claim that is the deal-breaker—standing in direct conflict with evolution—is the claim that Adam was the first human being. Those who truly understand how evolution works know this can't be true, because they know Adam never existed; there was never any "first human."

How is this possible?

Say you take pictures of your growing child, one every single day from birth to age eighteen, and stack them up in order. If you pull out any two consecutive pictures representing two consecutive days, you won't notice much of a difference in your child's appearance, wherever in the pile you take them from. However, if you pull out pictures taken at six-month or one-year intervals, you will notice significant differences, and will better be able to appreciate her growth.

This is how evolution works on a much grander scale; it's a process that is so gradual that it is genuinely astounding. As Richard Dawkins has explained on several occasions, every organism to ever exist belonged to the same species as its parents. Despite the fact that our distant ancestors were fish, there has never been a time when, say, the last *Homo erectus* parents birthed the first *Homo sapiens* baby. To illustrate how this works, Dawkins uses another aging-related analogy. "At some point, we cease to think of ourselves as middle-aged, and we start to think of ourselves as old," he says. "But nobody ever goes to bed middle-aged and wakes up [old]."[23]

I have met several physicians—including one with a Ph.D. in molecular biology—who deny evolution. These are smart, educated people, fully aware of how, for instance, bacteria evolved to become resistant to penicillin before our very eyes. The only thing they all have in common is their deep religiosity. It is indeed unusual to find highly educated adults, particularly in the life sciences, who deny evolution, but it's not unheard of. Dr. Ben Carson, the former pediatric neurosurgeon and Republican presidential candidate, is also a vehement evolution denier who has said that evolution is the "work of the devil"[24] and the Earth's geological layers came about due to a large flood.[25] These creationists frequently claim that gaps in the fossil record are the "missing evidence" that disprove evolution (recall, again, that the people demanding "evidence" here sincerely believe the Virgin Birth and Noah's Ark to be irrefutable fact). Again, this is patent nonsense. To falsify evolution, all one would need, as J. B. S. Haldane once said, is the discovery of a rabbit in the Precambrian era, dating back to at least 541 million years ago. If God did in fact create every species individually, fossilized rabbits and other mammals would be happily found alongside the first hard-shelled animals that emerged in abundance at the time. As we all know, this is not the case.

Over in the Muslim world, we had our own Ben Carson–like figure: the award-winning, world-renowned Canadian anatomist and embryologist, Dr. Keith L. Moore. Moore is to the field of embryology what Carson is to pediatric neurosurgery. His textbook *The Developing Human* is read by medical students the world over, including many of us at the Aga Khan University. The book is excellent, and like Carson, Moore is undoubtedly an authority in his field.

In Pakistan, however, we were able to purchase two versions of the book—the original, and a second special edition sanctioned by Moore and his publisher, entitled *The Developing Human: Clinically Oriented Embryology with Islamic Additions*. This version of the book was coauthored by a Yemeni scholar named Abdul-Majeed Azzindani. The sections written by Moore were identical in both versions, but the second also featured Azzindani-penned pages with embryology-related Quranic verses and *hadith* interspersed within its text.

Islamic scholars—who usually have no real background in science—tend to tout the Quran's references to embryonic and fetal development as some kind of miracle due to their alleged prescience. And now, Azzindani was successfully able to gain the endorsement and platform of an internationally respected embryologist for this claim. In the foreword to the *Islamic Additions* edition, Moore wrote, "I was astonished by the accuracy of the statements that were recorded in the 7th century AD, before the science of embryology was established." And interestingly, the acknowledgments page listed a number of "distinguished scholars" who had helped support the project, including, at number 6, Azzindani's good friend, Osama bin Laden.[26]

Today, Moore simply doesn't talk about it. When the *Wall Street Journal* asked him about it a few months after 9/11, he had little to say. "It's been ten or eleven years since I was involved in the Quran," he told them.[27]

How did Moore land himself in this mess? It all started in 1980, when he was invited to lecture at the King Abdulaziz University in Jeddah, Saudi Arabia. While he was there, the university's embryology department approached him and proposed the idea of the book. Moore and his publisher agreed. The book was published in 1983 and widely read by medical students across the Muslim world. I was one of them—and even then, I was confused why Moore was so "astonished by" these vague Quranic verses about embryology that were not only unoriginal (Joseph Needham, another renowned embryologist, called them "a seventh-century echo of Aristotle and the *Ayur-veda*"[28]), but also explained easily by common sense.

Verse 39:6, for example, states that God creates us "in the wombs of your mothers, creation after creation, within three darknesses," or the "three veils of darkness," as translated by Yusuf Ali. These three veils are supposed to be the impressive part, and are thought to refer to the abdominal wall, the wall of the uterus, and the chorioamniotic membrane, which forms the fluid-filled sac that holds the fetus (and is really two membranes in one). Of course, there are several other layers that can be mentioned along the way, but let's give God the benefit of the doubt here.

So, how did they know this back then? Well, to start, the abdominal wall is a no-brainer, and cutting open a pregnant cow, goat, or any other mammal would easily reveal the fetus within the uterus, housed inside the membrane(s). Moreover, dissections of human cadavers by Greek scientists have been documented as early as the third century BCE.[29] And not to forget, the brutal practice of slicing open pregnant women in war is both referenced in the Hebrew Bible of millennia past (Hosea 13:16), and practiced by the Islamic State today.[30] What are the chances that none of these things had been done in Arabia prior to the seventh century?

The Quran also mentions a "sperm-drop" in verses like 23:13–14 and a "sperm-drop mixture" in verse 76:2 from which humans develop. The alleged miracle here is the phrase "sperm-drop mixture," or *nutfatin amshajin*, which some apologists reflexively interpret to mean the mixture of sperm and egg. But there is no evidence of this. Aristotle had proposed a mixture of sperm and menstrual blood, and Hippocrates mistakenly thought there was both male and female sperm. So the general term "mixture" is neither surprising nor original.

Verses 53:45–46 say that God created "both male and female" from the "sperm-drop." Some modern Islamic scholars say this points to the now-known fact that the sperm contributes the X or Y chromosome that determines biological sex. This is an ambitious interpretation. Well before Islam, again dating back to ancient Greece, the false idea that the male contributed all the genetic material for the embryo, and the female merely provided the uterine environment for its growth ("firm lodging," as described in verses 77:20–22), was commonplace. Considering that the Quran borrowed so much of its embryological claims from the Greeks, this is almost certainly what this verse means too, especially when looked at in light of verse 2:223, which says, "Your wives are a place of sowing of seed for you, so come to your place of cultivation however you wish and put forth [righteousness] for yourselves."

Next, we have the *alaqa*, mentioned in verses like 23:13–14 and translated as "blood clot," "clinging clot," "leech," or "leech-like," depending on who you read. The leech analogy can easily be dismissed outright, because the embryo/fetus undergoes so many conformational changes during its development from zygote to fully formed baby that the number of things it might resemble at any point is vast. Here, the apologist benefits from the "Texas sharpshooter fallacy," where a Texan shoots randomly at the side of a barn, draws a circle around the densest cluster of hits, and claims to be a skilled marksman. Thus, he presents the illusion of a pattern where there is none.

If anything, the leech comparison may connote the "clinging" aspect of *alaqa*, which again was described by Aristotle in the fourth century BCE. In his book *Generation of Animals*, Aristotle described how the embryo/fetus attached to the uterus via the umbilical cord for nourishment, the way a plant does to the ground via roots.[31]

The most popular translation, however, is "clot," or "blood clot." First off, the embryo does not look like a clot. However, thanks to chickens, it's understandable why people at the time almost certainly would have thought it did. Aristotle described the development of chick embryos in stages as early as the fourth century BCE in his book, *History of Animals*.[32] And even if he hadn't, any farmer at the time who raised chickens knew how it worked: eggs that were fertilized would develop into new chickens, and those that were not were okay to eat. In Pakistan, it wasn't uncommon for us to bring home eggs and find one or two that were fertilized. How did we know they were fertilized? Somewhere in or near the yolk, there would be a little red spot that looked exactly like—lo and behold—*a blood clot*. (If you haven't seen one, you can do a Google Images search for "fertilized chicken egg.") And if you cracked it a little later, you would find what looks very much like a small "lump of flesh," mentioned in the same verses to be the stage after the clot. In fact, you can crack open a chicken egg at any stage during the incubation period and study its embryonic and fetal development to your heart's content, as Aristotle did. All that's left then is to assume that something similar probably happens in humans. Only a serious deficiency in either eggs or curiosity would render the people of the seventh century ignorant of this easily discoverable phenomenon. Indeed, if no one ever did this in the Arabian Peninsula before Islam—*that* would be a miracle.

Of course, there's more. It's not remarkable to point out that bones are "covered with flesh" (verses 23:13–14) because this is a common-sense anatomical arrangement: we have a skeleton of bones inside us that is covered by flesh, and it's smart to build things starting with the support structure. This architecture would be apparent to anyone who ever prepared a meaty meal, broke a bone, or witnessed an amputation or beheading in battle—the odds of which weren't exactly low in seventh-century Arabia.

Verse 32:9 is admired for identifying the order of development of the ears first, then the eyes, and then the heart. Unfortunately for the claimant, this is not the order in which these organs develop. The heart actually begins to develop at about twenty days, and the ears and eyes begin to develop simultaneously in the fourth week.

Getting into the details of all the verses and claims on this topic is beyond the scope of this book, and they have already been countered thoroughly by many commentators. A number of good refutations are available online. Also, there are several obviously wrong verses that understandably go unaddressed, like 23:12, which says God fashioned humans from an "extract of clay" or "wet earth"; or 86:5–7, which say humans were created from a "fluid, ejected, emerging from between the backbone and the ribs." The area between the backbone and the ribs is the chest, and possibly the upper abdomen if we want to be generous. Of course, this isn't even close to where semen or sperm originates; but it still hasn't stopped the faithful from ardently defending it.

In my view, the most incriminating factor discrediting the Quran's claims about embryology is a glaring omission more than an error: *it never once mentions the ovum.* And any detailed account of embryology that neglects to mention the ovum—the source of more than half the genetic material in an embryo if you count the thirty-seven maternally derived mitochondrial genes—cannot be a miracle. It is merely a rehashing of earlier discoveries by Hippocrates, Aristotle, Galen, and others.

Learning about the sharp contrast between real embryology and Quranic embryology demonstrated to me how science illuminates and religion obscures. The clarity and transparency of science supported by experiment and evidence could be relied upon. Religion, with its use of reward, punishment, and fear to impose questionable yet unquestioned values or beliefs, couldn't.

"Science answers the 'how' questions. Religion answers the 'why' questions." Of all the attempts I've seen to reconcile science with religion, this is perhaps the most common—and not just among Muslims. It's often presented as a statement of fact rather than a claim to be argued, and it isn't difficult to see why. It's poetic, it's symmetrical, and it affords religion a status and platform alongside science, giving it room in a world where its influence steadily continues to decline. Like Gould's NOMA, it is also pleasantly conciliatory, as if to say, "There's space for everyone here. We can all get along."

The only problem is, it isn't true.

To start with, religion doesn't *provide* answers; it makes them up. The amount of evidence for the claim that Adam and Eve were banished from the Garden of Eden (or, in the Islamic account, sent down to Earth from Paradise) as punishment for eating forbidden fruit is the same as that for Earth being held up by a giant invisible turtle: *none*. If the statement said, "Religion *addresses* the 'why' questions," there would be some truth to it; but as it stands today, if there's something that science can't answer, you can bet religion can't answer it either.

It also isn't true that religion only speaks to the "why" questions. Religion makes strong "how" claims as well—like how the Earth came to exist, how humans came into being, and how woman was created: from a man's rib. Today, we know these claims are false, and we have much more comprehensive, evidence-backed answers for these questions, thanks to science.

Moreover, science answers plenty of "why" questions correctly. Why does a supernova occur? Why do the planets revolve around the sun? Why does nature select some species to survive and not others? TV host Bill O'Reilly once famously told atheist author David Silverman, "Tide goes in, tide goes out. You can't explain that."[33] *But we can.* High and low tides occur due to the moon's gravitational pull, and to a lesser extent, the sun's.

There is a good reason, however, that people like to draw on both sci- ence and religion, as per the initial quote. As curious human beings, we seek answers and like to solve mysteries. Suppose you're watching a mys- tery or suspense movie that builds up a brilliant murder case, keeping you at the edge of your seat in anticipation. And then—at its peak—it ends without explaining who did it, how they did it, and why. Imagine the frus- tration. Well, life isn't a movie, the mysteries of our world and the universe are as brilliant as ever, and many of them are yet unsolved. Some people are more impatient than others, and will take any answer they can get. Others would rather ask questions. And the most persistent, never-ending question, as anyone with an inquisitive preschooler probably knows, is, "Why?"

"God did it," was indeed the answer to that final "why" *and* "how" for most of us. When they told us the universe started with the Big Bang, it wasn't satisfying. Who created the Big Bang in the first place? There had to be a First Cause, right? Where did all of this come from?

As with evolution, I could no longer tell myself that the Big Bang hap- pened because God did it. That would be too lazy. Once you believe a supernatural God created the Big Bang, you can believe in anything— angels, talking snakes, winged horses, ghosts, goblins—and it can trans- form an otherwise sound adult mind into a cesspool of irrationality. As CNN columnist Haroon Moghul admits, "If I can believe a Being [created the universe], out of nothing, then yes, I can handle a winged horse."[34] Again, if the Big Bang required a creator, then by that same logic, this creator would require its own creator. And if the creator didn't require a creator, why would the Big Bang require one? If the First Cause argument can be applied to God, why can't it be applied to the Big Bang?

In his book *Possible Worlds and Other Essays*, J. B. S. Haldane said, "The universe is not only queerer than we suppose, but queerer than we *can* suppose."[35] To my physics-naïve mind, the Big Bang theory seemed so much crazier than the relatively easy-to-comprehend idea of a creator creating his creation; yet it was supported by evidence, unlike God's sup- posed accounts in both the Judeo-Christian and Islamic creation stories. I wanted to learn more about this bizarre idea that seemed to claim that the entire universe came into existence from what seemed like an explosion that arose out of nothing. So I started reading. Already having some footing from watching *Cosmos* as a child, I started with Stephen Hawking's *A Brief History of Time*, and read anything and everything else I could get my hands on. I wanted to know what happened before the Big Bang.

And this—*this* is when I let go of religion completely, and haven't turned back since.

It was when I first learned that the Big Bang wasn't just the beginning of the universe, but the beginning of time itself. This is an incredibly strange and beautiful idea. Even the phrase "beginning of time" is somewhat strange, because words like *beginning* and *end* can only exist if time *itself* exists. In fact, many of the words we use every day—*before, after, when, then, now, later, first, last, start, finish, today, tomorrow,* and so on—only make sense if time exists. Time is so inextricably ingrained into nature that it is impossible for us to imagine existence without it. But according to this theory, there really was a "time" *when time itself didn't exist*: at the Big Bang.

Not only queerer than we suppose, but queerer than we can *suppose.*

Without time, there is no "before" or "after"—and therefore, no cause or effect, because cause comes *before* effect. And when there is no cause and effect, there is no creator or creation. As some physicists point out, asking, "What happened before the Big Bang?" is like asking someone standing right at the North Pole to walk north. The question itself doesn't make sense. There is no such thing as "before the Big Bang" because there *was* no "before." Stephen Hawking says that asking this question is like looking for the edge of the Earth—a fruitless endeavor, considering the Earth is a sphere. "You can't get to a time before the Big Bang, because there was no 'before the Big Bang,'" says Hawking. "Since time itself began at the moment of the Big Bang, it was an event that could not have been caused or created by anyone or anything."[36]

This idea is complex, bizarre, and yet elegantly simple at the same time. It is nearly impossible for the human mind to imagine time itself slowing down, speeding up, or stopping altogether. Yet we know time ticks at different rates depending on where we are in the universe, and see proof of this every day with GPS technology. In space, where there is less gravity, time moves slightly faster. And on Earth, where there is more gravity, time moves slower. If our GPS systems didn't continuously correct for this tiny difference between the locations of our satellites and our cars, our GPS would be off by about 10 kilometers a day, accumulating to about 300 kilometers in a month.[37]

Some respond to all of this by arguing that God created the universe "outside of time." This again doesn't make sense. Space and time are both integral parts of the fabric of the universe, and without the existence of time, all the laws of nature would collapse. There is no universe without time.

Unlike the Abrahamic creation myths, there is strong mathematical and physical evidence to support this theory. Also unlike the Abrahamic creation myths, this theory is subject to falsification as any other would be. There are also other fascinating ideas and theories about how the universe—or many universes composing the "multiverse"—began, and we don't know yet which of them will turn out to be correct. And there's the chaotic beauty of the subatomic universe, which I am exceedingly unqualified to comment on.

But all of that's beside the point. What moved me the most about all of this were the *possibilities*. The idea alone that time can speed up or slow down—a proven, demonstrated fact—was enough to fill me with awe and send me daydreaming for days.

These ideas made the holy books I'd read growing up seem small, narrow, and so . . . *human*. Why was the supposed creator of this unfathomable universe advising us on how much our daughters should inherit compared to our sons? Why was he so concerned about punishing those who opposed his authority? What creator of nebulae, time-distorting black holes, and hundreds of billions of stars and galaxies would be so insecure to consider it an absolute requirement that the inhabitants of this infinitesimally tiny speck of a planet regularly kiss his ass in gratitude for the infinitesimally tiny fragment of time they're here, or suffer an eternity of fire and torture? What creator of the inanimate double-helix DNA molecule that codes for a single-cell zygote to multiply and differentiate into a mind-bogglingly complex human being within forty weeks would fill up his handful of books to humanity with imbecilic fables about men living in the bellies of fish (verses 37:139–144), or men delivering two hundred foreskins to a king in order to marry his daughter (1 Samuel 18:27)?

At this point, I was somewhat open to the possibility of a higher power, the god of Spinoza, or something abstract that was synonymous with the laws of nature. But I knew that no god of any religion could possibly be any more real than Santa Claus or the Tooth Fairy (you can't disprove their existence either). These holy books that I had read several times by that point seemed like nothing more than ancient collections of fairy tales—and I couldn't understand how so many grown, educated adults around the world didn't see through them and were even *willing to kill or die for them*. I had read and heard countless apologetic interpretations and explanations of these books, and none could ever supersede for me the sheer wonder of reality—the most effective antidote to faith.

To the believer, I say only this: Even if you do believe that a god created the universe, why go to a messiah or a book from thousands of years ago to get closer to him? Why not study his creation that is all around you? This "creation" is called nature—and the study of it is called science. And the language of science isn't Hebrew, Aramaic, or Arabic. It's mathematics—which stays the same whether you're in Israel, the West Bank, or on the moon. Why rely on faith without evidence when the evidence is so much more breathtaking?

To me, the beauty lies in real questions, not false answers.

SIX

Islamophobia-Phobia
and the "Regressive Left"

F reedom of speech does not mean the freedom to offend!" a born-
and-raised American Muslim friend says to me, in reference to the
Charlie Hebdo attacks, protesting my telling him that I'm a free speech
absolutist. We're at a small party, and I am ideologically outnumbered by
a group of young, bright, and inebriated American Muslims, all of whom
have condemned the shootings but have taken issue with the content of
the satirical French magazine, articulating some version of an argument
beginning with the words, "I believe in freedom of speech, *but . . .*"

"On the contrary," I reply, making an argument I sadly have to make
too often. "Freedom of speech *is* the freedom to offend. Without the freedom to offend, what is the point of free speech?" Indeed, the most trans-
formative revolutionaries throughout history could not have achieved
what they did without offending a lot of people. This doesn't just include
scientists like Darwin and Galileo, or visionaries like Susan B. Anthony
and Martin Luther King Jr.—it includes Jesus Christ himself, not to mention Muhammad, who was chased out of Mecca for gravely offending the
Quraysh, the merchant tribe that ran the city.

The conversation now veers toward hate speech. "Doesn't hate speech
cross the line? Or do you think that should be protected too?" I under-

stand why my friend is asking this. Even France, where the attacks happened, has laws against hate speech. Shortly after the attacks, the French comedian Dieudonné was arrested for Facebook posts sympathetic to the views of the terrorists. And in 2011, fashion designer John Galliano was famously arrested, tried, and fined for anti-Semitic hate speech. Is France right to criminalize hate speech?

I don't think so.

In the United States, you can deny the Holocaust all you want. You can join the Ku Klux Klan and hold white supremacist rallies with police protection. You can print cartoons of Muhammad (the self-censoring of some American media outlets being a separate matter) and not be prosecuted for it. You can buy *Mein Kampf* or borrow it from a library. You can join the Westboro Baptist Church and picket the funerals of slain soldiers with signs reading, "God hates fags," backed by the full support of an eight-to-one Supreme Court decision in your favor.[1]

In the United States, hate speech is protected as free speech, and for good reason.

France, like many other European countries, does not understand free speech. It enforces secularism by banning the wearing of religious symbols. It arrests people like Dieudonné for nonthreatening Facebook posts, as vile as they may be. To me, this feels like more of a Saudi Arabia / Iran thing, and really shouldn't be a France thing. France is inconsistent—an inevitable consequence when you get into the business of legislating what is and isn't hateful. There is a legitimate (though flawed) debate about why anti-Semitic cartoons are a crime while cartoons offensive to Muslims and other minority groups are considered fair game under "free expression."[2] Here, the apologists who say France has double standards on free speech may have a point. France should be consistent. To Islamists, this means France should ban all hate speech. To me, it means France should allow all of it.

In case you're wondering why I'm standing up so vehemently for hate speech, I'm not. What I'm standing up for is not letting your government define "hate speech" *for* you. That should be *your* decision, not theirs. The cartoonists at *Charlie Hebdo* were frequently targeted by the French government itself, which used its hate speech laws to justify telling them what to do. Islamists in the West who denounce infidels and spout jihadist rhetoric in their Friday mosque sermons invoke these hate speech laws to silence any criticism of their beliefs by calling it "bigotry" or "Islamophobia." The supposed parameters of where free speech ends and hate speech begins (an imaginary distinction) are too important for you to let someone else define them.

Criminalizing hate speech like France does infantilizes people. It doesn't just take away someone's right to speak; it takes away *your* right to form your own opinions and response to them. By supporting a ban on hate speech, you're allowing your government to regulate not just what someone can say, but what *you* can *hear*.

Moreover, banning hate speech is a slippery slope. Consider the following.

Deuteronomy 22:20–21 says that nonvirginal brides should be stoned to death on their fathers' doorsteps. Leviticus 20:13 says that any two men having sex with each other should be killed. Verses 5:72–73 in the Quran say that anyone who believes in the Trinity or that Jesus is the Son of God is a blasphemer or disbeliever doomed to eternal hellfire. Verse 5:51 says not to take Jews and Christians for friends. Verse 9:5 endorses the slaying of polytheists.

Is there a doubt in anyone's mind that these ideas would be considered hate speech if voiced by someone today? Yet these words appear in holy books considered sacred by *billions* around the world.

"From a hate-speech perspective, which would you say is more offensive?" I ask my friend. "Those verses? Or a *Charlie Hebdo* cartoon?"

The uncomfortable truth is this: if you really wanted to ban all hate speech, the Bible and Quran would be the first to go. Next would be the preachers who read from them and quote them in their sermons. Without hate speech, freedom of religion can't really exist.

I grew up in countries where simply speaking your mind could get you sent to prison, flogged, or even executed. Early on, I promised myself that when I got to a place where I had the freedom to speak, I would. And I wouldn't take my freedom of speech for granted, not even for a day. But when I finally arrived in North America, I saw that things weren't that simple.

In countries where Muslims are a minority, Islam is an identity. In countries where Muslims are a majority, Islam is a religion. This dichotomy has consequences for liberals on either side.

For the liberal in North America, Islam is the faith of a small minority of Muslims who are often discriminated against and whose rights must be protected, as with any minority group. But for the liberal in a Muslim-majority country, Islam is a tool the government uses to justify censorship, oppression, and other *illiberal* values, like forcing women to wear the hijab, persecuting homosexuals, and publicly lashing bloggers. The same holy book that Muslims in the United States and elsewhere revere as divine and peaceful is used by the governments of Muslim-majority countries to endorse everything from domestic violence to the execution of apostates. The hijab—worn proudly by Muslim-American women who choose it as a symbol of their identity—is forced on women in many Muslim-majority countries by their governments, imams, or husbands. And many criticisms of Islamic doctrine made by liberal reformers and dissidents in Muslim-majority countries are labeled "Islamophobic" when voiced here.

It's easy to see how this can get very confusing very fast. In their well-intentioned effort to protect what they see as a targeted minority, Western liberals unwittingly find themselves fighting to guard and protect the same backward values that their counterparts in Muslim-majority countries are fighting *against*. My friend Faisal Saeed Al-Mutar, an Iraqi refugee, writer, and human rights activist, puts it best: "Many [Western liberals] have betrayed us liberals in the Middle East and other Muslim countries, and sided with the Islamists against us."[3] As blunt as it sounds, this is a common sentiment among liberals in the Arab and Muslim world, and understandably so.

Things become even more complicated when people like Faisal or I come to North America from places like Iraq or Pakistan. There are millions of people like us living in the Muslim world that you will never hear from.[4] Even if they want to speak up, they can't because they don't want to put their lives and families at risk. Then, there are those who do dare to speak up, but their voices are too often silenced before even reaching us. Consider the case of my friend Raif Badawi, the liberal Saudi blogger who is currently serving a ten-year prison term with a sentence of one thousand lashes; or all the Bangladeshi bloggers who have been hacked to death for writing critically about Islam.[5]

Finally, there's the group that Faisal and I belong to; it includes those who have left their countries of birth and now live in societies where free speech is a right, not a crime. We speak out as often as we can for all those back home who can't. My resolve is enormously strengthened by the incalculable number of messages I have received from closeted secularists in Egypt, Saudi Arabia, Pakistan, Syria, Malaysia, Bangladesh, and more—asking me to "tell the world" about something or another that they cannot speak openly about.

As well intentioned as they may be, Western liberals like Noam Chomsky and journalist Glenn Greenwald have conflated protecting the *right* of Muslims to believe as they want with protecting the beliefs *themselves*. This has the inadvertent effect of empowering despots and dictators who are brutally oppressing sizeable dissident minorities *within* the Muslim world—the very people who carry the most promise for reform.

Today, the Muslim world is undergoing its own Age of Enlightenment. Like the courageous revolutionaries of eighteenth-century Europe who rose up against theocracy, irrationality, and superstition, many in the Muslim world today are standing up for freedom of speech, challenging religious authority, criticizing and satirizing age-old dogma with no relevance in the modern age, embracing science and reason, and risking their lives just to lead their children and their communities to a more rational world. You don't hear of it, but it's happening.

To be sure, Greenwald-style apologists were present during Europe's Enlightenment as well, perhaps upset at men like Voltaire for not being "respectful" in their criticisms of religion, suggesting that Christendom might have something to do with Christianity, or inflaming the sentiments of the peaceful majority of citizens whose beliefs were being challenged. The names of these apologists aren't so quick to appear in our memories, though—and for good reason: they were on the wrong side of history.

It is more important now than ever to challenge and criticize the doctrine of Islam.

And it is more important now than ever to protect and defend the rights of Muslims.

Both of these must go together. Doing the first without the second would be grossly unfair to millions of good Muslim people who are not only the most frequent victims of Islamic terrorism, but also maligned due to the actions of violent jihadists who actually take their faith and holy book seriously. And doing the second without the first would be grossly unfair to the innumerable victims of "Allahu Akbar"–yelling militants who chop off heads, take sex slaves, and accurately quote Quranic verses supporting their actions. The only rational position between Islamic apologism and anti-Muslim bigotry is one espousing secular and liberal values. This is the only position that allows both the right to criticize bad ideas and the right to believe in them—both of which must be protected in order to set the stage for meaningful dialogue.

This approach isn't contradictory. It's a manifestation of the famous words of Evelyn Beatrice Hall (widely misattributed to Voltaire himself): *I disapprove of what you say, but I will defend to the death your right to say it.*[6]

I was in my twenties when I first moved to North America. Two years after I settled in Toronto with my family, the September 11 attacks happened. Suddenly, the conversations I'd had with myself for years were out in the open. Everyone knew there was a problem, including my Muslim family and friends. But no one could agree on what it was, much less how to approach it. Back home in Pakistan, everyone was convinced the Jews did it, and a ludicrous rumor about four hundred Jews staying home the morning of the attacks spread online like herpes. President Bush, on the other hand, decided to go after Saddam Hussein, reportedly unaware of the history of sectarian conflict between Sunnis and Shias (he didn't even know the two sects *existed*).[7] Either way, Islam and Muslims were suddenly front and center in world politics like never before, and no one knew how to navigate this. Every jihadist terrorist who had carried out an attack, or tried to, was a Muslim who did it in the name of Islam, praising Allah and saying something or another about "infidels" or America being in "Muslim lands." Whatever the other case-specific circumstances, this was the single common denominator. Yet, as he started up the wars in Afghanistan and Iraq, Bush emphatically and repeatedly declared that this wasn't a war against Islam. On the one hand, terrorists would quote passages from the Quran and *hadith* that clearly seemed to support their actions. On the other, a non-Muslim Bush would say they didn't represent the Islamic faith. As one would expect, all of this was very mystifying to a lot of people. Soon, the social media revolution exploded onto the Internet, giving everyone a voice. From the din, two starkly different narratives began to emerge—and I was caught right in the middle.

The first was driven by anti-Muslim bigotry: all Muslims were closeted terrorist sympathizers, moderate Muslims were just extremists in waiting, stricter immigration policies were needed to keep Muslims out, and people with brown skin would have to start being profiled. Of course, these brown-skinned people included much of my family, friends, and me—never mind that the underwear bomber was black, Jose Padilla was Hispanic, and the Boston marathon bombers came from the Caucasus, literally the place Caucasians are *named* for. Sikhs and Hindus were targeted because some people thought they were Muslims. Women with hijabs were harassed. Born-and-raised Americans with dark skin reported being told to "get out of our country." And most of those spewing out this prejudice happened to be far right, religious Christians and Jews themselves, which didn't give them much credibility in my eyes. I had read their holy books as well, and they weren't all that different.

The second narrative, more disappointing to me personally, was from the liberal left that I consider myself a part of. This narrative was one of apologism, where any criticism of Islam was conflated with bigotry against Muslims. Criticizing Islamic beliefs or the contents of the Quran would promptly earn one the label of "racist," "Islamophobe," or in my case, "sellout" or "Uncle Tom." Many liberals also seemed to excuse any atrocity committed in the name of Islam as some kind of reaction to Western imperialism or U.S. foreign policy. Of course, they weren't completely wrong. The causes of unrest in the Muslim world are complicated and varied. But I also knew firsthand that claiming that these deeply held religious beliefs were completely unrelated to the behavior they clearly drove was at best disingenuous, and at worst, dangerous. Islamic fundamentalist governments and militant groups alike use this far-left narrative of victimization to deflect criticism and further justify oppressing their own people. They thrive on it.

This was my conflict. I wanted to be able to criticize Islam as one should be able to criticize any set of ideas, but I didn't want to be seen to demonize an entire group of people—the very people I was raised by and grew up with. Neither narrative made this distinction between *ideas* and *people*.

Again, it's crucial to emphasize the difference between criticism of Islam and anti-Muslim bigotry. The first targets an ideology. The second targets human beings. This is an obvious, significant distinction, yet both are frequently lumped together under the unfortunate, reductive umbrella term "Islamophobia." Again, human beings have rights and are entitled to respect. Ideas, beliefs, and books don't and aren't. The right to believe what one wants to believe is sacred. The beliefs themselves aren't. Challenging ideas moves societies forward. Demonizing people rips societies apart. If anything, it's precisely *because* of how I'd seen ordinary Muslims suffer under theocratic policies and Sharia law that I wanted to start a dialogue to help shatter the taboo of criticizing religion. Luckily, I wasn't alone.

Three years after 9/11, a book entitled *The End of Faith: Religion, Terror, and the Future of Reason* hit the shelves. Authored by Sam Harris, then a little-known Californian graduate student, the book was a no-holds-barred attack on Abrahamic religions that went on to win the PEN/Martha Albrand Award for First Nonfiction, and become an international best seller. In 2006, Richard Dawkins's *The God Delusion* came out, which went on to sell millions of copies, has been translated into thirty-five languages, and is possibly one of the most pirated English books I've seen making the rounds in the Middle East.[8] Add to that the success of Daniel Dennett's *Breaking the Spell*, Ayaan Hirsi Ali's *Infidel*, and Christopher Hitchens's *God Is Not Great*, and it was clear that a full-fledged movement was taking shape. Almost all of the authors cited 9/11 as the catalyst that drove them to attack and expose religion as a destructive force that must be countered. Moreover, atheists were encouraged to "come out" and speak about their nonbelief without shame or intimidation. "People are always going on about, 'How did September the 11th change you?'" said Dawkins in his now-classic TED talk, "Militant Atheism," given a few months after 9/11. "Well, here's how it changed me: let's all stop being so damned *respectful*."[9]

Here, finally, was a group of liberals who were true to their values. They used reason and rational argument to attack bad *ideas*. And these bad ideas didn't suddenly become worthy of "respect" just because they happened to be in a holy book. In *The God Delusion*, Dawkins focused largely on Judaism and Christianity, which he tore to shreds. The most famous quote from the book is inarguably his description of the God of the Old Testament: "the most unpleasant character in all fiction: jealous and proud of it; a petty, unjust, unforgiving control-freak; a vindictive, bloodthirsty ethnic cleanser; a misogynistic, homophobic, racist, infanticidal, genocidal, filicidal, pestilential, megalomaniacal, sadomasochistic, capriciously malevolent bully."[10] After *The End of Faith*, Harris wrote *Letter to a Christian Nation*, an entire book dedicated to demolishing Christianity. Christopher Hitchens too had been an equal opportunity offender, targeting religion in general as a particularly sinister form of totalitarianism—a "celestial North Korea," but worse because it continued for eternity after death. Religion was "the wish to be a slave," said Hitchens, ". . . the desire that there be an unalterable, unchallengeable, tyrannical authority who can convict you of thought crime while you are asleep, who . . . must subject you to total surveillance around the clock every waking and sleeping minute . . . of your life, before you're born and, even worse—and where the real fun begins—after you're dead. Who wants this to be true? Who but a slave desires such a ghastly fate? . . . This is evil. This is a wicked preachment."[11]

These were powerful, persuasive, and provocative arguments, badly needed in Bush's America, a country that was increasingly turning to God as a reaction to being attacked in God's name. These writers didn't just single out Islam or Muslims—they attacked all religions, and the very idea of faith being a "virtue."

But here's the thing: while they didn't single out Islam, they didn't *spare* Islam either. This is something no one was used to, especially Muslims. The conventional wisdom was that Islam is a religion of peace, and it's the people distorting it that are the problem. However, to the "new atheists"—as they came to be known—it was the other way around. Islam *itself* was a problem; most Muslims around the world were moderate, but the author of the Quran clearly wasn't.

The last time anyone had so egregiously targeted Islam was when Salman Rushdie wrote *The Satanic Verses* and got himself a death fatwa for it. That worked out well for many aggrieved Muslims. Rushdie was forced into hiding, and even to declare that he'd accepted Islam, just so the fatwa could be revoked and he could get his life back. The media and his own fellow liberals openly admonished Rushdie for writing the offensive novel and provoking the murderous reaction against him. Even former president Jimmy Carter jumped on the blame-the-victim train with his angry *New York Times* missive, "Rushdie's Book Is an Insult," published less than a month after the fatwa.[12] So it's easy to understand why so few wanted to poke at this hornet's nest again. Until now.

As I mentioned in chapter 3, the aggressive approach of new atheist writers seems to resonate much better with nonbelievers living in the Muslim world. They are censored, persecuted, and angry. They find the polite, tiptoe-around-taboos approach to criticizing religion in the West frustrating, a privilege of open societies where the right to free speech is taken for granted. But unlike Rushdie's time, new atheism happened in the Internet age. From Turkey and Egypt to Saudi Arabia and Palestine, these books became wildly popular, often hidden and shared underground in their pirated, unofficially translated bootleg forms, because those governments didn't like them one bit. Even in Turkey, a secular democracy and one of the most progressive Muslim-majority countries in the world, the translators of *The God Delusion* were threatened with jail and the official website of Richard Dawkins was banned.[13]

At last, here were liberal thinkers who didn't have double standards.

The far left would slam misogyny and homophobia when it came from Tea Party Republicans, but label you "Islamophobic" if you criticized them as part of Islamic doctrine. And the far right would direct its hostility toward Muslims themselves, by proposing immigration bans or linking all of them with terrorism.

But the new atheist writers knew the difference between saying "Smoking is a filthy habit" and "All smokers are filthy people." They criticized religious *ideas*. They promoted science and secularism using rational, logical arguments, consistent with liberal values. Most importantly, their criticism of Islam was driven by a *compassion* for Muslims—Muslims who were being beheaded for sorcery, stoned to death for adultery, married off in childhood, flogged for speaking their minds, massacred in sectarian warfare, and killed in terrorist attacks; indeed, the majority of the victims of Islamic terrorism are Muslims themselves.

Needless to say, these authors provoked a diverse range of reactions, from people saying their books had changed their lives, to those charging them with bigotry for ridiculing the beliefs of billions. Now, it isn't completely baseless to say there was ridicule. But one must recognize that undertaking to criticize (1) supernatural claims, that are (2) believed passionately by a majority of all human beings in existence, is almost necessarily going to sound like provocative ridicule no matter how it's done. But what if the intention *is* to mock, satirize, or ridicule? Is doing that okay? Or is it a form of bigotry?

Let's try something.

In 2007, Al-Fayhaa TV in Iraq held a debate entitled, "Is the Earth Flat?" One of the guests was Fadhel Al-Sa'd, an Iraqi "researcher on astronomy." Read how this grown, literate, adult man uses verses from the Quran to support his beliefs that (1) the Earth is flat, not round; and (2) the sun is smaller than the Earth, and revolves around it:

> The Quranic verse that I have just recited—"The breadth of Paradise is as the breadth of the heavens and earth"—attests to the fact that the Earth is flat . . . In 1999, there was a full solar eclipse. We went to Mosul, and over there we climbed to Mar Matti Monastery, the altitude of which is 3,600 feet. The sun began to

disappear slowly behind the moon. This is because the moon is half the size of the sun. The moon's diameter is 1,200,000 kilometers, while that of the sun is 2,400,000 kilometers.[14]

At this point, his opponent, physicist Aboud Al-Taei, protests his claims, prompting the interviewer to ask, "Lunar and solar eclipses, sunset and sunrise, and the changing of seasons—how would you explain all these phenomena if the Earth is not round as you claim?"

Answers Al-Sa'd:

> The sun circles the Earth because it is smaller than the Earth, as is evident in Quranic verses. Have you ever seen how the sun moves? I have seen the sun moving. The sun makes one move every twenty-four hours. What I say is based on Quranic science. [My opponent] bases his arguments on the kind of science that I reject categorically—the modern science that they teach in schools. This science is a heretic innovation that has no confirmation in the Quran. No verse in the Quran indicates that the Earth is round or that it rotates. Anything that has no indication in the Quran is false.

What goes through your mind as you read or watch this? Remember, these are the man's sincerely held religious beliefs. I showed the video clip to a handful of my family and friends, of varying degrees of religiosity. All of their responses, whether they were religious or not, were similar. They ranged from laughter and shaking their heads in disbelief, to statements like, "How could someone seriously believe this?," and even, "Wow, what an idiot."

Take a moment to record your own reaction to Al-Sa'd's flat-earth claims in your mind. Got it? Good. Now, consider beliefs like:

- a virgin giving birth;
- a man flying to heaven on a winged horse;
- the first-ever man and woman to exist being successfully persuaded by a snake to eat a fruit;

- the existence of angels;
- the existence of *djinns*;
- a nine-hundred-year-old man building a wooden boat and loading it with animals to survive a worldwide flood;
- Jesus being either resurrected from the dead (as Christians believe) or lifted up to heaven directly (as Muslims believe).

How are these beliefs—held by billions of adults worldwide—any less laughable or worthy of ridicule than the Iraqi astronomer's belief that the Earth is flat?

How can Christians mock Scientologists when their own beliefs are just as irrational, if not more? How can a Muslim who actually believes Muhammad rode a winged horse to heaven think that the man claiming the Earth is flat is the crazy one?

Think about your reaction to this man's astronomy claims, and you may better understand why mockery and ridicule—as much as they may sting—aren't bigotry. They simply come with the territory. Your right to believe what you want must be respected, yes; but the beliefs themselves need not be. If you do happen to hold any of these beliefs, recall how you reacted to what Al-Sa'd said about the Earth, and understand that those who ridicule *your* beliefs are simply reacting the same way to *you*. As Thomas Jefferson wrote in 1810 regarding the Trinity, "Ridicule is the only weapon which can be used against unintelligible propositions. Ideas must be distinct before reason can act upon them; and no man ever had a distinct idea of the Trinity."[15]

To be sure, there are many other irrational ideas that I'm not railing against or writing a book about. Some people sincerely believe in astrology, for example. But imagine a state government officially sanctioning imprisonment or death for those who say astrology is nonsense, or terrorists killing dozens of civilians as a condition of the moon being in Leo. Would we not then have a moral obligation to openly discredit these clearly irrational beliefs? And how do you "respectfully" argue against, say, a belief prescribing mutilation of your newborn baby's genitals in order to please the North Star? If these hypotheticals sound completely ridiculous to you, it's only because you haven't grown up hearing them repeatedly, or seen most of the adults around you living their lives according to them. Rest assured, the story of Jonah and the fish, Noah and the flood, and Muhammad and the flying horse are just as ridiculous to someone unfamiliar with them or encountering them for the first time as an adult.

Criticizing, satirizing, and even mocking any belief system is never bigoted or racist. Criticizing capitalism does not make you an anticapitalist bigot, and satirizing communism does not make you a "Communophobe." Criticizing religious ideology is no different. It's merely a bunch of ideas in a book. Moreover, Islam is not a race. You can't convert in or out of being black or white—but you *can* convert in or out of a religion. No one is born precircumcised or prebaptized, or with a hijab or a yarmulke fused to his or her head. It is clear now, as it always has been, that race, ethnicity, gender, age, nationality, educational status, financial status, citizenship status, marital status, or family background have very little to do with Islamic fundamentalism or jihadism. There is only one requisite common denominator: a sincere belief in and submission to the ideology.

It isn't just the Muslim world where being a nonbeliever is looked down upon. In 2011, psychologist Will Gervais and his colleagues at the University of British Columbia conducted a study that looked at public perception of atheists. They provided study participants with the hypothetical scenario of a man who hits a parked car and flees without leaving any insurance information, and later the same day, steals money from a wallet he finds on the sidewalk. Participants were asked if this man was most likely to be a Christian, a Muslim, a rapist, or an atheist. Most chose rapist and atheist in approximately equal numbers. Surprisingly, this wasn't just the majority response of religious participants, but also of the religiously unaffiliated.[16]

Other surveys have shown that atheists are the least-trusted group in a variety of scenarios. From those who disapprove of an atheist marrying their child to those who say they'd never vote an atheist into the presidency, atheists always hover close to the bottom of the list.[17]

Why is this?

Gervais's team found that people generally believe that human beings behave better when they think God is watching them. For obvious but mistaken reasons, words like *atheist, non-believer,* and *godless* are considered synonymous with lapsed or deficient morality.

This, of course, is inaccurate. There is now a solid body of evidence to demonstrate that morality and religion are distinctly separate kinds of value systems. Primatologist and ethologist Frans de Waal says that morality most likely predates religion, and religion isn't the *source* of morality as much as a secondary element that might help *fortify* it.[18]

The reality is, for most ex-Muslims who were raised in Islam, leaving the religion is a *moral* choice, as became readily apparent in the #ExMuslimBecause social media campaign described in chapter 3. This isn't unique to Islam. Atheists from all kinds of backgrounds frequently say they broke from their religious upbringing because they found these religious "values" to be unacceptable. They consider the secondary status of women, the often-violent discrimination against gays, and the tribalistic exclusion and "otherization" of those deemed "infidels" and "kuffar"—or those who aren't "chosen" or "saved"—to be divisive and morally abhorrent.

Why is it that rejecting illiberal ideas like misogyny and homophobia is a hallmark of liberalism, but when the exact same ideas are part of a religion like Islam, criticizing them becomes bigotry or Islamophobia? Why is it that domestic violence is considered unacceptable in any civil society, but truthfully stating the Quran endorses beating your wife (verse 4:34) is seen as an offense to an aggrieved minority? Why is it that homophobic rhetoric from the Ku Klux Klan or evangelical Christians is widely denounced by liberals, but correctly stating that the deplorable treatment of gays by Saudi Arabia, Iran, or the Islamic State has basis in the Quran and *hadith* is considered anti-Muslim bigotry? Why is it that men who marry children are universally lambasted, but speaking critically of the Prophet Muhammad's marriage to his best friend's nine-year-old daughter is "disrespectful"?

On October 3, 2014, liberal talk show host Bill Maher brought this up to his guest and fellow liberal, Sam Harris. Why is it, he asked, that liberals become upset when it is pointed out that the same values that they otherwise applaud—free speech, freedom of religion, equality for women, gays, and minorities—are lacking in the Muslim world? Harris expanded on this, pointing out how liberals openly criticize Christians, referencing abortion clinic bombings in the 1980s, but somehow cower when one brings up the inhumane treatment of women, homosexuals, and secularists in the Muslim world. Notably, he denounced the term "Islamophobia" for conflating any legitimate criticism of Islamic doctrine with bigotry toward Muslims, calling it "intellectually ridiculous."[19]

Also present as a guest on the show was actor Ben Affleck, who was growing visibly agitated. He angrily interrupted the interview to tell Maher and Harris that what they were saying was "gross" and "racist." By the time Harris tried to clarify that he was pointing out the *difference* between criticism of Islam (an idea) and bigotry against Muslims (a people), Affleck had become too emotional to listen clearly, accusing Maher and Harris of "stereotyping" and "painting the whole religion" with the same brush. In essence, Affleck proved Harris's point—that liberals too often miss the crucial distinction between criticizing ideas and demonizing people, and end up conflating the two.

I will grant that Affleck's heart was in a good place, even if his mind may have been too overwhelmed to understand Harris's argument. It is part of the liberal moral fabric to look out for minorities and ensure their rights and freedoms are protected. In the United States, Muslims are a minority group that finds itself under ever-increasing scrutiny and pressure with every new terrorist incident. In 2015, we even saw the unprecedented development where a leading presidential candidate of the Republican Party, Donald Trump, called for a complete ban on all Muslims entering the United States, and subsequently went on to win the nomination.

Anti-Muslim hate is a real thing, and is no longer limited to just white supremacists, nationalists, or far-right bigots. On November 19, 2015, a fourteen-year-old schoolgirl in New York City was placed in a headlock by three boys in her class who punched her repeatedly and called her "ISIS" while trying to yank off her hijab.[20] Just imagining something like this happening to my own beloved niece is heartbreaking to me. As a man with a similar name, heritage, and look as the Muslims I grew up with, I am as much a potential target for these thugs as my Muslim family and friends. So, again, let me be clear: anti-Muslim bigotry is real, it exists, and it is wrong.

This is all the more reason why umbrella terms like "Islamophobia"—which conflate criticism of Islam with anti-Muslim bigotry—are so sinister. Semantics matter. When legitimately criticizing illiberal elements of Islam—as we might do any other religion or political ideology—elicits accusations of bigotry and racism, it abruptly ends an important conversation that needs to be had. Calling someone a bigot, racist, or Islamophobe isn't a counterargument. It's a lazy substitute for one. Yet we all fall for it. Liberals—particularly conscientious white liberals well informed about history—don't want to be called bigots or racists. And they certainly don't want to be seen as beating up on a minority. I can tell you firsthand that many religious minorities know how this works. They know they can deflect criticism against their cultural or religious beliefs simply by accusing white liberals of bigotry or racism, guilting them not only into silence but also, on occasion, a near-unconditional advocacy for everything good or bad the minority group does.

I can also tell you firsthand that many white Western liberals privately acknowledge holding back their opinions on Islam for fear of being seen as Islamophobic—what I call "Islamophobia-phobia"—or in the interest of supporting moderates within the Muslim community who share their goals of fighting jihad and fundamentalism. This is not to say they are not sincere: they do believe the vast majority of Muslims are good people, and that the only real hope of eradicating the scourge of jihad is to bolster them. Still, many have reservations about Islam, the religion, as they do about Christianity, which is easier to publicly criticize. They'll talk to me about it because they know how I think, but won't bring it up in front of our Muslim friends out of respect. It's also much more difficult for a white person to make those arguments the way a person with my looks can, without accusations of racism or bigotry. Bill Maher and Sam Harris dared to do it, and that was exactly the response they got.

More problematic is what former Islamist turned reformer Maajid Nawaz has dubbed the "regressive left"—the Affleck-style apologist liberals who are not only reluctant to challenge illiberal attitudes like misogyny or homophobia in minority communities, but also denounce those who do as racist or bigoted. The regressive left, however, engages in its own brand of racism, borne of particularly dangerous cultural relativist attitudes, namely, the *racism of lowered expectations*.

As a brown-skinned man with a Muslim name, I can get away with a lot more than you'd think. I can publicly parade my wife or daughters around in head-to-toe burkas and be excused out of respect for my "culture," while a white, non-Muslim man doing the same would rightly be universally excoriated for it. I can redefine "racism" as something non-whites can never harbor against whites, citing historical colonialism and imperialism as justification for my prejudice. And in an increasingly effective move that has fast become something of an epidemic, I can shame you into silence for criticizing my beliefs and ideas simply by calling you an Islamophobe.

For decades, Muslims around the world have rightly complained about the Israeli government labeling even legitimate criticism of its policies anti-Semitic, effectively shielding itself from accountability. Today, many of the same Muslims and their regressive left allies have borrowed a page from that playbook with the "Islamophobia" label, and taken it even further.

Let's take a look at what this term means. "Islam" is a religion—a set of ideas and beliefs in a book. A "phobia" is defined by most dictionaries as "an irrational fear." So we're dealing with a term that translates to "an irrational fear of Islam." Note the contrast between the words "Islamophobia" and "anti-Semitism." "Semite" literally refers to descendants of the biblical Shem, Noah's son. Today, it is most commonly used to refer to Jews, although it is technically a collective term for both Jews and Arabs. The term targets people: it's "anti-Semitism," not "Judaism-phobia."

Again, bloggers are being flogged, imprisoned, and hacked to death in Muslim-majority countries for speaking their minds. Women and gays are being persecuted simply for being who they are. And I could be jailed or executed in my country of birth, the country I grew up in, and a host of other Muslim countries around the world merely for writing this book. All of these things can be justified using a plausible interpretation of the

Quran and *hadith*. For those in the line of fire, they can be scary and un-settling. But is this fear "irrational"? No—it is very rational and very real. It is for these reasons that I use the term "anti-Muslim bigotry" in-stead of "Islamophobia." This allows us to challenge both anti-Muslim prejudice and the doctrine of Islam.

But is this really that big a deal or are we splitting hairs here? What's the harm in using these two terms interchangeably? Let's dig deeper.

Shortly after the Maher/Harris/Affleck dustup, the Iranian-American scholar of religions Reza Aslan was interviewed by *New York* magazine to discuss what new atheists were getting wrong about Islam. He said, "People don't derive their values from their religion—they bring their values to their religion . . . Two individuals can look at the exact same text and come away with radically different interpretations. Those interpretations have nothing to do with the text, which is, after all, just words on a page, and everything to do with the cultural, nationalistic, ethnic, political preju-dices and preconceived notions that the individual brings to the text."[21]

Now, what Aslan is saying here is pretty extraordinary. He is assert-ing that Muslims around the world—a significant number of whom have said that they support practices like killing apostates[22] and stoning adulterers to death[23]—don't get these views from their religion, but their attitudes are somehow *inherent* in them as people.

Think about that for a second. Aslan isn't being equivocal here. He is using absolute terms. He's saying that interpretations of the Quran have "nothing"—*nothing*—"to do with the text," and "everything"—*every-thing*—to do with people's "prejudices and preconceived notions." In a *New York Times* op-ed published around the same time, Aslan wrote, "If you are a violent misogynist, you will find plenty in your scriptures to justify your beliefs."[24] The fault, according to Aslan, lies not with the scriptures, but with the people.

As my friend Christopher Massie has pointed out, "The conclusion that disproportionate numbers of intrinsically violent and misogynistic people reside in a certain region of the world could not be more bigoted or racist."[25]

Of course, there is good reason to believe that Aslan is neither racist nor bigoted. Why, then, would he make such a statement, demonizing large groups of people in order to defend a religion?

This is the consequence of conflating criticism of ideas with bigotry against a people.

Aslan says these "prejudices and preconceived notions" can be "cultural, nationalistic, ethnic, [or] political"—but, somehow, never religious. How does this logically make sense? Why go out of your way to indict every etiology but one—especially when it shares indistinguishable characteristics with the others—if there isn't some kind of compulsion or bias to protect it? Because it's taboo to criticize religion? Because it's revered by billions and criticizing it would give offense? Are these really good reasons to compromise your intellectual honesty, letting the fear of unfavorable consequences retrospectively color how you perceive reality, in effect letting the tail wag the dog? So, every time a jihadist yells "Allahu Akbar!" and severs an infidel's head from his body with a knife, citing verses like 47:4 and 8:12–13 from the Quran, you would blame every possible factor for his actions *except* the one that literally contains the words, "Smite the disbelievers upon their necks"? And then claim these words have nothing—*nothing*—to do with an action that is the exact physical manifestation of them?

There is one thing Aslan is partially right about: thankfully, the majority of Muslims don't derive all of their morality from the Quran. But he is dangerously wrong to disregard those who *don't* simply dismiss scriptural passages as "words on a page," but take them seriously. The truth is, words *do* have power. Aslan acknowledges this when it comes to the role of politics, culture, and nationalism in shaping people's "prejudices" and "preconceived notions"—but strangely doesn't when it comes to religion. This doesn't make any rational sense, considering the potent, binding influence these holy books have held over billions of people for millennia, despite a plethora of scientific discoveries and advancements that have successfully countered virtually all of their claims.

The apologists of the regressive left will often go to unreasonable lengths to protect inhuman ideas at the expense of living, breathing human beings. They will also frequently label criticisms of ideas, books, and beliefs "bigotry" or "racism" in the absence of any substantive counter-argument.

It is an injustice and an insult to genuine victims of anti-Muslim bigotry to exploit their pain for the political purpose of stifling criticism of Islam. And that is precisely what umbrella terms like "Islamophobia" do.

In 2014, a white American man was able to successfully convince the Massachusetts liberal arts school Brandeis University that he was being victimized and oppressed by a black African woman from Somalia—a woman who underwent genital mutilation at age five, narrowly escaped a forced marriage, and travels with armed security at risk of being assassinated by terrorists. The man, Ibrahim Hooper, is a Muslim convert and a founding member and spokesman for the Council on American-Islamic Relations (CAIR). The woman, Ayaan Hirsi Ali, is a renowned, unapologetic, ex-Muslim activist for the rights of girls and women worldwide, and a harsh, no-holds-barred critic of the religious ideologies (particularly the Islamic ideology in Muslim-majority countries that she experienced firsthand) that perpetuate and maintain their abuse. Not only was Hooper's organization successful in convincing Brandeis to rescind its offer of an honorary degree to Ayaan—he was also victorious in getting the University of Illinois and the University of Michigan to cancel their screenings of *Honor Diaries*, her award-winning documentary film exploring violence against women in honor-based societies, featuring stories and commentary from several activist Muslim women. The reason? CAIR thought it was "Islamophobic."

That is the power of this term.

Ayaan Hirsi Ali is a controversial figure who disproportionately draws the ire of countless Muslims, as well as many liberals. Now, suppose she was an ex-Mormon fighting against child brides, an ex-Catholic fighting for reproductive choice and abortion rights, or even an ex–Orthodox Jew fighting gender segregation. Secular women who fit these descriptions are almost always embraced and bolstered by liberals. Why, then, is the liberal reaction so different when it comes to Ayaan and Islam?

One reason might be her connection with the American Enterprise Institute (AEI). Ayaan openly describes herself as a liberal, so her association with the conservative Washington think tank is viewed with suspicion. The background of her connection, however, shows that it's more the *effect* of her being shunned by American liberals on first arriving in the United States than the cause. She describes how she asked Cynthia Schneider, former U.S. ambassador to the Netherlands under Bill Clinton, to introduce her to different think tanks on her arrival in New York. After getting no response from liberal-leaning institutions—which she sensed were uncomfortable with her statements on Islam—she went to join the conservative (but nonreligious) AEI as her only real option.[26]

Ayaan is now vilified by many liberals for joining a conservative institution that took her in after all of the liberal institutions refused to. This abandonment of ex-Muslim or Muslim reformist liberals by their Western counterparts, as we've also seen in the case of Salman Rushdie, isn't new. The Islamophobia smear fear is an effective deterrent that really functions as a covert form of terrorism: it's how perfectly intelligent, well-read writers, commentators, and broadcasters can not only be silenced, but also shamed into opposing the very same liberal principles they value. Consider how, in the aftermath of the *Charlie Hebdo* attacks, CNN, NBC, ABC, and CBS all made a conscious decision not to show the cartoons of Muhammad that drew such murderous wrath from the terrorists. The policy of the BBC at the time read, "Due care and consideration must be made regarding the use of religious symbols in images which may cause offence. The Prophet Mohammed must not be represented in any shape or form."[27] Thankfully, in the immediate aftermath of the shootings, it was revised.

Whether they fear a terrorist attack on their offices, or the accusation of being Islamophobic, the effect is the same: censorship, capitulation, and an assault on free expression. They think they are helping curb terrorism, but all the while, they have become unknowing victims of it.

In Pakistan, there are blasphemy laws to force us into silence. Here, there are accusations of Islamophobia to shame us into it. And a particularly pernicious use of the word is on the occasion that someone dares to link terrorism to Islamic doctrine.

"This has nothing to do with Islam," the mantra goes, "but the Islamophobes will continue to tell you it did!"

This is unsurprisingly effective, but flat-out wrong. The number-one reason that terrorism is linked with Islam is not "Islamophobes" or the media. It is that jihadi terrorists link *themselves* with Islam. They quote scripture and yell "Allahu Akbar!" as they do what they do. It's in every slogan, every pre-suicide video, and every statement of responsibility. Timothy McVeigh (a terrorist by any definition of the word) didn't yell, "Jesus is great!" before blowing up that building in Oklahoma City. His brand of terrorism wasn't linked to Christianity, because it wasn't carried out in the *name* of it. In contrast, the bombing of abortion clinics is universally acknowledged as terrorism linked with Christian fundamentalism. Islamic terrorism is more analogous to the latter.

Critics of Islam are also frequently *blamed* for bigotry against Muslims. As we saw in chapter 2, both Reza Aslan and Glenn Greenwald have attempted to hold atheist writers like Richard Dawkins responsible for increasing Islamophobia in Western societies. But this is not how bigotry spreads; it increases with the frequency of Islamic terrorist attacks, not Dawkins's book releases. And unfortunately, well-intentioned attempts by moderate Muslims and their Western liberal allies to curb anti-Muslim sentiment inadvertently perpetuate it further. This is how it works:

- Radical Islamic terrorists around the world behead or blow up any number of innocent people who believe differently from them. These terrorists don't just "happen" to be Muslim—they commit these atrocities in the very *name* of their faith, quoting passages from the Quran and *hadith* word-for-word that clearly support their actions and can be confirmed by anyone with an Internet connection.
- Moderate Muslims react by condemning the violence, but fiercely defending the same book and faith that the terrorists cite to justify killing people.
- Ordinary people—especially non-Muslims—become confused, and start to fear not just the terrorists, but also the faith that drives them.

This is a difficult problem to solve. But denying any link between the religious doctrine and the violence only makes matters worse. Maajid Nawaz has called this the "Voldemort Effect," based on the villain in J. K. Rowling's *Harry Potter* series, who is referred to by the other characters as "He Who Must Not Be Named" because they are so terrified of him. Aside from not naming him, they deny that he even exists—which, in turn, worsens the situation, causes more fear and panic, and further glorifies the myth of his immense power. "Refusing to name a problem, and failing to recognize it, is never a good way to solve it," writes Maajid.[28]

The Obama administration has certainly been guilty of this, refusing to name radical Islam or Islamism, instead opting for the diluted "violent extremism." The most egregious example of this obfuscation was after the Orlando shooting, when the administration released heavily redacted transcripts of the shooter's conversation with 911 dispatchers to the public. His pledge of allegiance to ISIS and its caliph Abu Bakr Al Baghdadi, his self-description as an "Islamic soldier," and his praise and blessings for "the prophet of God," were censored from the transcripts. Thankfully, the ensuing backlash compelled the FBI to release the unedited transcripts soon thereafter.[29]

It isn't that Obama isn't aware of the real threat. He famously angered apologist Muslims and non-Muslims alike by correctly stating in his 2016 State of the Union address that the conflicts in the Middle East "date back millennia."[30] In a comprehensive interview with *The Atlantic*, he lamented to Jeffrey Goldberg that "some currents" of Islam "have not gone through a reformation" that could help its adherents adjust to modernity. He also described the increase of hijab-wearing women in Indonesia as a reflection of a "fundamentalist, unforgiving" interpretation of Islam. And Goldberg reports that privately, Obama has told other world leaders that the problem of Islamic terrorism cannot be resolved unless Islam itself undergoes the kinds of reforms that changed Christianity.[31]

As a politician, it is understandable why Obama doesn't openly refer to Islamic terrorism by name. But not naming a problem makes it harder to fight and, importantly, fails to differentiate peaceful, moderate American Muslims from radical jihadists. This is dangerous. If liberals had taken on this problem honestly from a position of moral strength, the likes of Donald Trump and Marine Le Pen (of France's far-right National Front) would have been less able to jump in and channel it from a position of xenophobic bigotry.

Another prototypical example of a regressive left apologist is John Kerry. As secretary of state, he has said that the best way to fight the Islamic State is to "put real Islam out there."[32] He has said that the November 2015 Paris attacks didn't have a "rationale" behind them the way the *Charlie Hebdo* attack did.[33] And astonishingly, he has denounced ISIS as being not just killers and thugs, but "above all apostates . . . who have hijacked a great religion and lie about its real meaning and . . . deceive people in order to fight for their purposes."[34]

This is somewhat reminiscent of George W. Bush starting a war with Iraq without knowing what Sunnis and Shias were.

In Islam, an apostate is someone who has left or renounced his religion, a crime punishable by death according to the majority of Sunni and Shia scholars. This, in fact, is what the Islamic State widely uses to justify killing other Muslims, saying they have apostasized and betrayed their faith. The governments of Muslim-majority countries like Saudi Arabia and Iran frequently sentence their most liberal, progressive minds— scientists, artists, writers, and poets—to death, or imprisonment, for apostasy. Moreover, activists like Ayaan Hirsi Ali and Maryam Namazie are apostates. Salman Rushdie is an apostate. So am I. Kerry's demonization of apostasy not only plays right into ISIS rhetoric, but is also fundamentally against freedom of religion. Again, I'm sure his heart's in the right place, but his rhetoric supporting the idea that choosing to leave one's religion is a *bad* thing does more harm than good.

In late 2014, I had the honor of consulting on an early draft of *Islam and the Future of Tolerance*, a short book that is essentially a conversation between Sam Harris, an atheist, and Maajid Nawaz, a Muslim reformer. The book was praised not just for the considered, thought-provoking dialogue between the authors, but also for the very fact that an atheist known to be vocally critical of Islam could actually sit down with a committed Muslim and have a reasoned conversation that both they and their readers learned something from (Harris noted that their first meeting was "inauspicious," yet now they're good friends).

Not everyone was pleased, and some liberals were especially incensed. During a Harvard event marking the release of the book, Murtaza Hussain, a writer at Glenn Greenwald's *The Intercept*, tweeted out a picture of the authors at the event with the caption, "Nice shot of Sam Harris with his well-coiffed talking monkey." When readers called him out for the racism-tinged comment, he doubled down: "His pitiful whining aside accurately calling him a 'monkey,' as in a porch monkey, is not a slur."[35]

Nathan Lean, a researcher at Georgetown University's Prince Alwaleed bin Talal Center for Muslim-Christian Understanding (developed and supported by a generous $20 million donation from the Saudi royal[36]) and contributor to *Salon* and the *New Republic*, joined the anti-Maajid chorus once the book was released, referring to him as Sam Harris's "Muslim validator" and "lapdog."[37] CJ Werleman, a writer for *Middle East Eye* and *Salon* who once referred to me as a "brown faced, white masked water carrier for Empire,"[38] called Maajid a "House Muslim,"[39] playing off the despicable racist term "House Negro."

There's more where this came from. Like many of my fellow progressive Muslims and ex-Muslims, I have been referred to as a "sellout," an "Uncle Tom," and an "Oreo" (implying I'm brown on the outside and white on the inside—a relatively appetizing slur compared to the others). I have been accused of "cozying up to the imperialist agenda" and being a "native informant," a term used by Deepa Kumar, a journalism and media studies professor at Rutgers University, to describe ex-Muslims.[40]

Keep in mind, these are all well-educated liberals who are dedicated to fighting "Islamophobia." This is a key research interest of Professor Kumar, and Lean has even written a book entitled *The Islamophobia Industry*. There is an underlying narrative powering all of their work—that the West is oppressive and Islamism is somehow the third-world reaction to this oppression. As one would expect, the growing influence and audience of reformers, ex-Muslims, and liberals who recognize the problem of Islamism like Bill Maher and Sam Harris, pose a very inconvenient challenge to their narrative.

All of this begs several questions. What exactly is this "imperialist agenda"? And what does "cozying up" to it look like? And why is it that when a brown-skinned person rejects his ancestors' religion to embrace secularism and liberal values, he is called a "sellout"?

What would a regressive leftist call the dissidents of Christian Europe centuries ago who stood up, fought, and died for the same secular values and liberty that today allow him or her to call dissidents in the Muslim world—who are trying to achieve the exact same thing in *their* societies— "sellouts"? Must all good brown boys think alike and have the same beliefs, lest they be "sellouts" to that well-oiled imperialist machine? Again, religion is not determined by skin color. How is it that Western, non-Muslim men like Greenwald, Lean, and Werleman are discrediting the narrative of people like Ayaan, who grew up in Somalia in a strict Muslim household, or Maajid, a former Islamist who spent five years in an Egyptian prison, demanding that they should conform to *their* narrative, and then demonizing them as "House Muslims" if they don't?

The topic of imperialism is also a sore spot among my peers in Pakistan. There's a pervasive sense that renouncing the Islamic religion somehow translates to abandoning your people. Even believing Muslims who merely adopt values *seen* as Western—free speech, secularism, liberalism, and so on—are thought of this way. Indeed, many South Asian Muslims have a glaring blind spot when it comes to imperialism.

"Why do you speak against Islam?" they ask me. "This is our heritage, our identity. You are betraying your community by selling your soul to the imperialists and colonialists." As dramatic as that sounds, it is a very close paraphrasing of what relatives, friends, and strangers alike have told me. If you still feel that it may be an exaggeration, consider that leaving Islam is considered a form of treason in Pakistan, and according to a 2013 Pew research poll, 62 percent of Pakistanis believe this apostasy should be punishable by death.[41] Note also that by telling me I'm selling my soul to the imperialists, they are simply talking about my advocacy for secularism (which isn't antireligion, but separation of religion and state) and liberal values like free speech, gender equality, and gay rights. Criticizing the monotheisms, including Islam, is an inextricable component of standing up for liberal values. Misogyny, for instance, doesn't suddenly get a pass the moment it appears in a holy book. If you want to fight patriarchy but won't fight religion, you're not fighting patriarchy.

The notion that people from Muslim backgrounds who embrace progressive values or a critical approach toward their ancestors' ancient beliefs are somehow "betraying" their identity and heritage suggests that *the only true Muslim is a conservative Muslim*. It also suggests that progress, freedom, and liberalism are somehow Western ideas that no self-respecting Muslim should adopt. And by labeling a Muslim reformer or ex-Muslim dissident a "lapdog," "House Muslim," or "native informant," Western non-Muslim liberals, astoundingly, join the chorus and perpetuate this toxic idea.

Muhammad Syed, president of EXMNA, is often asked why he remains optimistic despite being smeared by far-left paternalistic apologists, far-right anti-Muslim bigots, and Islamists alike. "The fact of the matter is that our ideas—free speech, freedom of conscience, secularism, the idea that the civil liberties of even our enemies guarantee our own; in short, the ideals of the Enlightenment—resonate around the world," he says. "I'm increasingly confident that if we continue pushing for our ideas, we can pave the way for liberalism and secularism far beyond the West."[42] My interactions with ordinary people in the Muslim world reveal the same: the desire to speak and live freely, as one chooses, is a universal value. In my experience, even those who wish to restrict the freedoms of others—such as those who tell pollsters that apostates should be punished by death—often still want these freedoms for themselves. It may not sound rational, but in instances such as these, human beings are nothing if not irrational. As any marketing expert will tell you, what people say they want isn't always what they really want; and people don't always know what they want until it's shown to them.

As for my Pakistani Muslim friends who accuse me of betraying my heritage and being blindly obsequious to Western imperialism, I say only this:

Islam is an Arab religion. Consider that you are a person of South Asian heritage who:

- follows an Arab religion;
- reads and reveres an Arabic holy book;

- prays in Arabic;
- greets others in Arabic;
- reveres and emulates an Arab prophet; and
- bows in the direction of Arabia five times a day in prayer.

In light of this, how can you possibly accuse *me* of being part of an "imperialist agenda" with a straight face? Western imperialism (which I'm not a fan of either) isn't the only imperialism out there. Read the history of your religion and how it was spread. Consider the Arab-Islamic imperialism of seventh-century Mecca, which spread as far west as Spain and east as India in a matter of decades, and to this day has an intractable chokehold on the lives and minds of over a billion people. From the language that you pray in, to the headscarves worn by your women, to meeting loved ones with the Arabic greeting *As-salaam-u-alaikum*, to your people showing more solidarity with Palestinians than Kashmiris, to a majority of your people believing that apostates from this Arab faith must be killed—this foreign ideology has transformed your heritage and history in a way that you can hardly recognize it. How is Western imperialism any different? If you oppose Western imperialism but not the Arab-Islamic imperialism of the seventh century, you're not anti-imperialism—you're just anti-West.

Often in his speeches and writings, Christopher Hitchens would issue a challenge to his audience: "Name me a moral action committed by a believer, or moral statement uttered by [a believer], that could not be made or uttered by a non-believer."[43] To this day, no one has been able to successfully name such an action or statement.

Then, he would ask his audience to name an evil or immoral statement or act, made or performed by a believer, that can only be attributed to his or her religious faith. This part of the challenge was easy—there are numerous bad things that believers do as a direct result of their faith that nonbelievers don't.

And for the sake of completeness, let's acknowledge that all bad things done by nonbelievers can be (and have been) done by believers as well.

Taken together, these insights logically lead us to deduce that faith is at the very least unnecessary, and at most, a net negative for humanity. And glamorizing faith as a virtue is precisely the opposite of what we should be doing.

Hitchens described himself as an anti-theist, which I suspect would be an appropriate description for a number of new atheists, including myself. His challenge gets to the heart of what drives many of us. Our rejection of religion is a *moral* choice—and it is one that has precedent.

The most revolutionary human rights struggles in history have drawn violent opposition, ostracism, alienation, abuse, injury, and even death for those engaged in them. The fight for women's rights took much more courage for the women of the 1800s—who became pariahs in pursuit of their cause—than for those born in the late twentieth century. Civil rights activists who spoke up at a time when lynching blacks was publicly accepted and commonplace took on a much more dangerous task than those born in the America of Barack Obama. Countless LGBT activists have faced violent discrimination, cruelty, and death merely for demanding acceptance in the last few decades; today, marriage equality is the law of the land in both the United States and Canada, no matter the unspeakable things the Bible tells us to do to homosexuals.

New atheists and anti-theists think of religion the same way. Today, it is considered sacred and untouchable, just as racial segregation or state-sanctioned gender discrimination were in the United States less than a century ago. The consequences for speaking out against religion today—especially Islam—are often as dire as they were for those who spoke out against white or male authority back then.

To us, the fight against religious ideology isn't a struggle *against* human rights, but a struggle *for* them. To us, a simple reading of the Abrahamic holy books reveals endorsements of virtually all the oppressive and discriminatory systems that civil and human rights movements have tried to dismantle over time: patriarchy, misogyny, slavery, tribalism, xenophobia, homophobia, and totalitarianism, all rolled into one. Our criticisms of religion aren't an attack on people, but a challenge to what we consider bad *ideas* that drive bad behavior, and the sacred status afforded to them. Our opposition to religion isn't a demonstration of bigotry; it is a demonstration against it.

Bigotry against bigotry isn't bigotry, and tolerance of intolerance isn't tolerance. Intolerant attitudes that are unacceptable in general life shouldn't suddenly become acceptable when presented under the guise of religion. The statement "This is my faith" should not automatically confer immunity on the faithful for misogyny, bigotry, discrimination, or the irreversible mutilation of the genitals of completely healthy babies unable to give consent.

Liberalism isn't just about tolerance of dissent. It is also about an intolerance of those that *don't* tolerate dissent. While many of us accept the first, we fall short on the second. This oversight can unwittingly have the devastating effect of empowering the very fundamentalists who are persecuting our own liberal counterparts in the Muslim world. This must stop. The most important battle raging within the Muslim world today is not between Sunni and Shia, conservative and liberal, or West and East. It is between the past and the future. And we must pick a side. In order to be true to our values, we must first be true to ourselves.

SEVEN

The Quran:
Misinterpretation, Metaphor,
and Misunderstanding

Some time ago, I posted the following statement on one of my social media timelines:

> The worst of living creatures, in our view, are the followers of Allah—those who believe in Islam. They're the ones you make treaties with, but they break those treaties every time because they have no fear of the law.

As is obvious, this statement is blatantly bigoted hate speech against Muslims. But it is not something I have written. It is a modified passage from the Quran, verses 8:55–56, with references to disbelievers replaced by "followers of Allah" and "those who believe in Islam." The original verses read:

> Indeed, the worst of living creatures in the sight of Allah are those who have disbelieved, and they will not [ever] believe. The ones with whom you made a treaty but then they break their pledge every time, and they do not fear Allah.

Several commenters jumped on this, accusing me of taking these verses "out of context."

"It's a warfare verse," said one. "It's like taking a sentence out of a military book. If you are at war, then I think it's fair that you can say it. But it is only applied in self-defense. You have to have a just reason for it."

Okay, I told him. Let's change the context then. Suppose the United States is at war with ISIS or Al Qaeda, and the president says:

> The worst of living creatures, in our view, are the followers of Allah—those who believe in Islam. They're the ones you make treaties with, but they break those treaties every time because they have no fear of the law.

Does that read any better?

"It does if the fight is on the land of the one being attacked," he replied. "The aggressor can be identified easily by where the war takes place. What if the attacked people are fighting in self-defense?"

Fine. Let's suppose ISIS or Al Qaeda has attacked New York City, and the president of the United States says, in response:

> The worst of living creatures, in our view, are the followers of Allah—those who believe in Islam. They're the ones you make treaties with, but they break those treaties every time because they have no fear of the law.

Better now?

The commenter persisted. "But the verse wasn't for the general public! It was for the soldiers fighting in the war. It is only talking about people who break treaties!" And so on.

I won't repeat the passage again. The point was obvious: however you paint the modified passage, it still reads as hate speech against all Muslims. There is no context—historical or otherwise—that justifies labeling an entire people "the worst of living creatures."

And herein lies the problem: if there were a book that talked about

Muslims the way the Quran talks about disbelievers, heads would roll. Literally.

Religious scripture is a fascinating thing. Whether you're religious or not, there's an unwritten rule that it can never be *bad*. It has to be *good*. If you read the Bible, you are a "good, God-fearing" Christian. This is the book on which court witnesses swear to tell the truth, the whole truth, and nothing but the truth. It's what presidents are inaugurated on. The Quran cannot be read or recited unless an ablution ritual is first performed to cleanse both the body and the soul. Purity. Chastity. Honesty. The moral good. When the words of scripture inspire good things, all credit goes to them and their author. When they inspire atrocities, all association between them and the perpetrator is denied.

The sacred scriptures of religion are approached uniquely—very differently from other books. Criticizing the content of the Quran, for instance, can be construed as a blanket statement of bigotry against all Muslims, and you can get hit from all directions for doing it. The most pious of extremists might kill you for it, while some leftist liberals will shame you for prejudice against an aggrieved minority. Some of the support that you *do* get—from far-right ideologues like Pamela Geller with her genuinely bigoted views, or the anti-Muslim Quran-burning pastor Terry Jones—you want absolutely nothing to do with. All you want to say is that the Quran is wrong about many things, from its claims about science to the status it gives women and polytheists. You don't want to ban Muslims any more than you'd want to ban Christians for revering their holy book, which similarly endorses terrible things like slavery and homophobia. But you don't want to encourage hate against Muslims either. That would be despicable. You simply want to comment on the Quran as you would comment on *The Wealth of Nations*, *The Communist Manifesto*, or any other book of global significance and consequence. (As I said earlier, it is exceedingly unlikely that criticizing these texts would get you shamed as an anticapitalist bigot or a "Communophobe.") You're simply pointing out what you think are bad *ideas*. You may attract debate and impassioned argument, but you won't have to hire armed security to help ensure your anatomical integrity.

You know very well that if you wrote a book speaking of Muslims as "the worst of living creatures," advocating beating one's wife (even if lightly), or instructing readers to fight Muslims until they adopt your beliefs or pay a special tax, you would be heavily criticized and shamed from all ends of the political spectrum. You might even have to go into hiding. No one would buy your pleas for nuance, metaphorical interpretation, or context. Yet the Quran, which says precisely these things in plain language, somehow gets a pass.

This can lead to a somewhat conflicted existence for many Muslims, one recently illustrated all too well by an online interaction between Richard Dawkins and Fatima Bhutto, a liberal Muslim and niece of the late Pakistani prime minister Benazir Bhutto.

"Islam needs a feminist revolution," tweeted Dawkins. "It will be hard. How can we help?"

The backlash to these words was swift, furious—and immensely confusing. In a year rife with stories and media images of horrific sex slavery, stoning to death of rape victims for adultery, and honor killings, committed in the name of Islam by the Islamic State and others, Dawkins expressed what countless women and men around the world—not discounting those in the areas affected—were thinking. However, Dawkins has a history of upsetting Muslims on his Twitter account; like Bill Maher and *Charlie Hebdo*, he is an equal opportunity critic of all three Abrahamic religions, and at times has also made religious Jews and Christians very angry. But the moment he turns his attention to Islam, the accusations of hate and bigotry pile on like nothing else.

Fatima Bhutto responded to Dawkins with a series of tweets, starting with, "How many Muslim women does it take to tell Richard Dawkins he's not needed?" and then, "It should be perfectly obvious that only Muslim women are qualified to speak/act on the changes they need."

The exchange was documented and reported on the website of Pakistan's English daily, *Dawn*, under the headline, "Richard Dawkins Mansplains Feminism to Women, Bhutto Hits Back."[1] Now, it is indeed problematic when men condescendingly explain to women how to dress, speak, act, and live. I grew up in societies where this "mansplaining" was the norm. Seeing the women in my family and community having to put up with it was infuriating, and became a strong impetus for my writing this book.

This, however, felt different. For one, Dawkins's message was one of solidarity, along with an earnest offer to help. And second, it wasn't about—or directed to—privileged members of Pakistan's elite like Bhutto, who probably doesn't have to worry about face-to-face interactions with the Taliban or ISIS like countless other women do. But let's set that aside.

Here's the thing: like virtually all religions, *the entire religion of Islam is founded on "mansplaining."* Islam came to Muslims through Muhammad, a male prophet who had eleven wives. For Sunnis, Muhammad's legacy was perpetuated by four polygamous, male caliphs. For Shias, by twelve male imams. Even in minority sects like Ahmadis and Ismailis, every single caliph and imam has been a man.

There certainly were strong women in Muhammad's household. His first wife, Khadijah, was an accomplished businesswoman fifteen years his senior. She was his only wife until her death, ten years after Muhammad began preaching. Their daughter Fatima, the only biological child of Muhammad to survive his death and whom Bhutto was named after, is also documented as a strong, accomplished woman. Still, the successorship went to men: for Shias, it was her husband and Muhammad's cousin, Ali. For Sunnis, Muhammad's close friend, Abu Bakr.

So, in effect, what Fatima Bhutto was saying was that she didn't want to be mansplained to, unless it was by seventh-century tribal men from the Arabian Desert, whose communications to humanity were to be believed as the word of Allah himself.

It's easy to see how this can be confusing.

However, there is a counterargument to this, and it goes thus: these men merely *conveyed* Allah's message; they didn't *generate* it. Allah is genderless, it claims, even if every single one of his messengers—from Adam and Noah to Moses, Jesus, and Muhammad—were men, along with their associates. Now, to the rational mind, this counterargument is weak for obvious reasons. But to those raised in the religion—or any of the other patriarchal monotheisms, for that matter—it carries heft and must be addressed.

Evolutionary biologists aren't entirely sure why the human male lost his *baculum*, the penile bone responsible for erection in most mammals, including some of our closest primate cousins—the orangutans, chimpanzees, and bonobos. Dr. Paula Stockley, an evolutionary biologist at the University of Liverpool, finds the disappearance of the baculum in the hominid lineage "enigmatic."[2] And Richard Dawkins suspects it may have served as a diagnostic tool to aid women in their mate selection. "Anybody can grow a bone in the penis," he writes in the thirtieth anniversary edition of his 1975 classic, *The Selfish Gene*. "You don't have to be particularly healthy or tough." But in humans, he points out, the erection is achieved and maintained by blood pressure alone, indicating the strength of a suitor's health.[3]

Some biblical scholars, though, have generated their own controversies in trying to explain the loss of the baculum. In 2001, Ziony Zevit and Scott Gilbert sent a letter to the *American Journal of Medical Genetics* on this pointed topic. They felt the Bible had actually attempted to explain humanity's bonelessness, in Genesis. Noting that there is an equal number of ribs in men and women, and that ribs "lack any intrinsic generative capacity," the authors concluded that Adam did not actually lose a rib when Eve was created; rather, it was "far more probable" that Eve was created from Adam's baculum—which is missing to this day from human males, but not from their male primate cousins.[4]

In 2015, Zevit again brought up the proposal, this time in the *Biblical Archaeology Review*.[5] The article, entitled "Was Eve Made from Adam's Rib—or His Baculum?," aroused global discussion and rebuttals from linguists and theologians alike. But Zevit stood firm in his argument that the Hebrew noun *tzela* was possibly mistranslated as "rib," and really had a broader definition that could conceivably be taken to mean penile bone.

Seeing this debate play out in the world media would be amusing if it wasn't so consequential. Here in the twenty-first century, less than two months prior to the monumental discovery of Einstein's predicted gravitational waves, grown adults, including Ph.D. professors, were seriously discussing whether woman was created from a man's rib or his penis.

This is how woman was introduced into the world of the Abrahamic faiths, now comprising billions and as patriarchal as ever: created from the bone of a man, with a naïve partiality to the persuasive charms of a talking snake. Eve took us all down when she tasted that fruit—and the three or so millennia between the loss of our bacula and the advent of Viagra have provided ample time for the bitterness to build further.

And build it has. In my own personal experience, as well as that of the majority of ex-religious people I have spoken with, the abhorrent treatment of women in religion is by far the most common reason cited for abandoning it. My own mother is a university professor with a doctorate in education. My younger sister, now a specialist physician, professor, and talented musician, was an honor student throughout school. To watch both of them have to put on their black *abayas* (body cloaks) every time they stepped out of the house to be driven to work or school in Riyadh, where they were banned from driving, was infuriating. I was repeatedly told that religion isn't responsible for the cultural misogyny I saw all around me in any of the Muslim-majority countries I grew up in. Of course, a careful reading of the holy religious texts dispelled that notion instantaneously. And it wasn't just Islam.

In the Old Testament, the misogyny is overt and straightforward. If a woman is found not to be a virgin on her wedding night, for instance, she must be brought to her father's doorstep where men of the town must stone her to death for "playing the whore" in her father's house (Deuteronomy 22:20–21). And if a man rapes a woman, the victim must marry her rapist after being remunerated with fifty shekels of silver (Deuteronomy 22:28–29).

The New Testament appears milder: 1 Timothy 2:11–15 simply tells women to stay quiet in submission to men, saying that they may not exercise authority over men because it was Eve, not Adam, who sinned in the Garden and got us all into this mess. Ephesians 5:22–24 tells women to obey their husbands as the church obeys Christ. And 1 Corinthians 11:3–9 reminds believers that the woman is not only made *of* the man, but *for* him.

But the most catastrophic display of misogyny in all religion lies at the very heart of Christianity—in the story of the Virgin Mary. That

Jesus was born of a virgin is a fundamental narrative upon which all Christianity is based. It is one that is carried through to Islam, where the Quran holds Mary in great esteem.

The implications of this have historically been devastating to women.

Remember that Jesus certainly wasn't the first historical figure believed to have been born to a virgin. The emergence of a number of divine (and semidivine) figures over the millennia has been via asexual means. Buddha was born from a slit in his mother's side. The virgin Isis gave birth to Horus. The virgin Maia gave birth to Mercury. The virgin Rhea Silvia gave birth to Romulus and Remus. The virgin Devaki birthed Krishna. And even Genghis Khan is believed to have been born of a virgin in whom a "great light" suddenly induced labor one night. "For some reason," wrote Christopher Hitchens, "many religions force themselves to think of the birth canal as a one-way street."[6]

Mary gave birth to Jesus Christ as a virgin, with no man ever having touched her. She is therefore described as pure, chaste, undefiled, innocent—being the product of an "immaculate conception" herself (as per Catholic doctrine), and now hosting God's immaculate son in her unblemished womb.

What does this mean for women who *are* touched by men? Are their conceptions corrupted? Are their characters and bodies now *im*pure or *un*chaste? Have they been "defiled"? Think about the words we use to describe our first experience of sexual intimacy. "Losing my virginity." What exactly has been "lost"? Every time we begin a new phase in our lives—starting up a career, buying our first home, having our first child—we feel a sense of achievement, a sense that we're *gaining* something, starting a new chapter, making progress. Why is the exploration of one's sexuality, the beginning of one's sexual life, an almost universally cherished feature of human existence, registered as a "loss"? "Losing my innocence." How does one become less innocent after experiencing a sexual connection for the first time? "Deflowering." Another word that implies removal of beauty or sanctity. Was all of Mary's beauty, sanctity, chastity, and innocence confined to her vagina?

Fetishizing Mary's virginity—as Christians and Muslims both do—is a sickness that directly leads to a dangerous, unnatural glamorization of celibacy and sexual repression. Demonizing female sexuality is seen as a virtue, and slut-shaming and victim-blaming accepted norms. When you really think about it, this is the kind of mentality that leads to millions of young girls around the world, mostly in Muslim-majority countries, having to undergo violent mutilation of their genitals. There is only one organ in the entire human body—male or female—that is responsible *solely* for sexual pleasure: the clitoris. The vagina has a reproductive function, and the penis has both reproductive and excretory functions. The clitoris, however, has no reproductive, excretory, or other physiological function except for sexual pleasure—a function not required for women to reproduce. If God chose to afford this privilege uniquely and solely to women, isn't demonizing it a blasphemous undermining of his divine plan?

The control of women for the benefit of men has always been a hallmark of the great monotheisms. Islam is certainly no exception, yet claims abound in moderate and liberal Muslim circles that it was Islam that somehow brought feminism and gender equality to the world 1300 years ago. The young Muslim reader might be familiar with these claims; they were repeatedly told to many of us growing up. And rebutting them with verses from the Quran was a fruitless endeavor. You would simply be met with an eye-roll, and condescendingly pitied for your naïveté. "Oh, come on, Ali. You know those verses have been mistranslated and misinterpreted. People have twisted the words of the Quran to suit their agenda."

But this is not the case. It is the less-informed moderate and liberal Muslims who seem to have misinterpreted many of these verses to represent something much tamer and palatable than their actual meaning. An excellent example to illustrate this is found in the most famous and contentious verse in the Quran about women—verse 4:34.

Verse 34 of *Surah An-Nisa* (The Women) is one of the most widely debated Quranic verses there is. It establishes a hierarchy of authority, where men are deemed to be "in charge" of women. It also asks wives to be obedient to their husbands, and allows their husbands—in the most controversial part of the verse—to beat them if they fear disobedience. The translation of the verse is as follows:

> Men are in charge of women by [right of] what Allah has given one over the other and what they spend [for maintenance] from their wealth. So righteous women are devoutly obedient, guarding in [the husband's] absence what Allah would have them guard. But those [wives] from whom you fear arrogance—[first] advise them; [then if they persist], forsake them in bed; *and [finally], strike them*. But if they obey you [once more], seek no means against them. Indeed, Allah is ever Exalted and Grand. (Emphasis added.)

This is the *Sahih International* translation, which most widely accepted translations are consistent with. Yusuf Ali, M. H. Shakir, Muhsin Khan, Muhammad Sarwar, and N. J. Dawood all translate the problematic phrase—*adhribu hunna* in Arabic—to mean "beat them," or "strike them." Marmaduke Pickthall translates it as "scourge them."

There are other translators, almost all recent and contemporary, who interpret the phrase differently. The Pakistani-Canadian Ahmad Shafaat translates it as "beat or separate them from you." Muhammad Tahir-ul-Qadri, another Pakistani-Canadian scholar, translates it as "turn away from them, striking a temporary parting."

So, which one is it?

Religious scholar Reza Aslan believes that the prime reason *adhribu hunna* is translated to mean "beat them" is the "traditionalist, male-dominated, and often misogynistic" interpreters who got it all wrong. He instead favors a more modern, gender-equal approach to the Quran, which he thinks might resolve this scriptural inconvenience. Claiming that *adhribu hunna* has been noted by some female Quranic scholars to mean "turn away from them" or even "have sexual intercourse with them" (an absurd take, considering the penalty immediately prior to this is to "forsake them in bed"), Aslan says it really just comes down to the translator's "preconceived notions" about a husband's authority.[7]

What Aslan is talking about is a relatively recent interpretation that has been put forward by largely non-Arabic-speaking Muslim scholars, regarding the word that *adhribu* is derived from: *daraba*. *Daraba*, they say, does not just mean "beat." Later in the very same *surah*, verse 4:101, the same root word, used as *darabtum*, means "to go forth." Verse 3:156 also uses the word *darabu* to mean "travel through." In verse 2:61, the word *waduribat*, also derived from *daraba*, means "to be humiliated." Therefore, say these modern scholars, the phrase *adhribu* in verse 4:34 doesn't necessarily mean "beat" your wife, but could mean a variety of things: to move away from, to separate, to chastise or humiliate, or, as Aslan says, to "go forth" and have intercourse (again, a rather bizarre final-straw punishment when you look at the context of the verse).

On the surface, this sounds reasonable. However, as anyone who is actually familiar with the Arabic language will tell you, these new age interpreters couldn't be more wrong—and you don't even need to know Arabic to understand why.

Take a look at the word *hit* in the following phrases:

- Hit the road
- Hit the lights
- Hit the goal
- Hit the bottle
- Hit me up
- Hit up a bar
- Hit the woman

Now look at the word *strike* in these phrases:

- Strike a deal
- Strike a balance
- Strike up a conversation
- Go on strike
- Strike a woman

You may see now where I'm going with this. What defines the verbs *hit* or *strike* in all of these cases is the *object* of the verb. In the phrase "hit the goal," the word *hit* means to "reach" or "achieve" the goal. Would it make sense to apply the same definition to the phrase "hit the woman"? It wouldn't, would it? None of us would say, "'Hit the goal' means 'reach the goal,' so 'hit the woman' must mean 'reach the woman.'"

Similarly, "strike up a conversation" means to start a conversation. This obviously does not mean that "strike a woman" implies starting a conversation with a woman.

In the verses described above, the same principle applies. Each form of the verb *daraba* is defined by its object. In verse 4:101, the full phrase used is *darabtum fil ardi*, or "hit the earth," implying travel. In 3:156, it's *darabu fil ardi*, again meaning "hit the earth," or travel. And in 2:61, the full phrase is *waduribat alayhimuz-zillatu*, which literally means, "they were hit with humiliation." These are just three examples of many. In each case, the verb *daraba* and its derivatives mean "hit," "strike," or "smite." And this punishment isn't just for arrogant or disobedient spouses according to the verse; it's for those from whom one merely *fears* arrogance or disobedience. As many Arabic speakers will tell you, if the verse was intended to instruct men merely to separate from their spouses or abandon/boycott them, the phrase used wouldn't have been *adhribu hunna*, but *adhribu* an*hunna* (emphasis added), which literally means to "smite their will."[8]

The "misinterpretation" in cases like this isn't on the part of the original translators of the Quran, but of modern exegetes attempting to soften and egalitarianize the harshness of this ancient book.

In other cases, one doesn't require any knowledge of the Arabic language to see through attempts at sanitization. The most illustrative case here is of verse 4:24, also in *Surah An-Nisa*. This verse deals with slaves, or captives of war, referred to in the Quran in several places as *ma malakat aymanukum*, or "those your right hands possess." According to the Quran, sex with slaves is permissible outside wedlock. Verse 33:50 says that Allah has "made lawful to you your wives" and "those your right hand possesses from what Allah has returned to you [of captives]," or, as translated by Pickthall, "those whom Allah hath given thee as spoils of war." Verses 23:5–6 and 70:29–30 are virtually identical, saying that those who "guard their private parts" from anyone "except from their wives or those their right hands possess . . . will not be blamed." Muhammad himself had slaves; he took Rayhana bint Zayd after executing the male members of the Jewish *Banu Qurayza* tribe for treason following the Battle of the Trench (*Ghazwah Al-Khandak*), where Meccan Arabs conspired with the Jewish tribe in an attempt to take control of the city of Yathrib, or modern-day Medina. Rayhana was the widow of one of the executed men. Another of Muhammad's concubines was Maria the Copt, gifted to him by Egypt's ruler at the time. With Maria, he had a son named Ibrahim, who died in infancy. Some say Muhammad ultimately married Rayhana and Maria, which would mean he had thirteen wives instead of eleven. However, this claim is disputed by most.

The first part of verse 4:24 reads as follows:

> And [also prohibited to you are all] married women except those your right hands possess. [This is] the decree of Allah upon you. And lawful to you are [all others] beyond these, [provided] that you seek them [in marriage] with [gifts from] your property, desiring chastity, not unlawful sexual intercourse.

The verse is a continuation of the previous verse (4:23), outlining which women are prohibited for Muslim men to marry or have sex with, such as blood relatives, wet nurses, daughters-in-law, and others. Then, the first line of 4:24 says that all married women are also prohibited—with the exception of "those your right hands possess." As is obvious, this means that women captured and enslaved in war are permissible for Muslim men *even if they are already married.*

This is not a *hadith.* It is a very clear verse in the Quran. Of course, there's context, which can be found in the *hadith*; but believers seeking context might do well to be careful what they wish for. Going by the Quran only, it's open to interpretation whether the verse is permitting Muslim men to marry these already-married captives, or have sex with them without wedlock. Neither is a good option for the slave, I gather—but several *ahadith* seem to indicate that it is the latter. The verse was allegedly revealed after the Battle of Hunain, when Muhammad's companions brought back female prisoners of war, but were reluctant to have sex with them because their husbands were still alive. Soon after they expressed this to Muhammad, he received the verse giving them permission: yes, married women were indeed prohibited, but not those captured in battle—these were fair game.[9] Now, these *ahadith* are considered quite authentic by Sunni Muslims—they corroborate each other and appear separately in three of the six great *hadith* collections for Sunnis, including *Sahih Bukhari* and *Sahih Muslim*, the largest ones. But even if they are disregarded completely by non-Sunnis, the Quranic verse alone endorses either marrying or having sex with female captives of war whose husbands are still alive. However you look at it, this doesn't change. The rationale given by some is that the captive women were now separated from their husbands, so their marriages had become null and void. Others say that the prisoners gave consent. But how can a *slave* possibly give consent? Would a "yes" register as genuine consent from someone under duress and captivity? Wouldn't this be rape either way?

And this brings us to our next question. What does the Quran say about rape?

Rape doesn't exist in the Quran.

The concept of sex without consent isn't even acknowledged as an entity.

There isn't even a word for "rape." The word used for a sex crime is *zinaa*, defined as "unlawful sexual intercourse." According to the Quran, there are only two types of unlawful sexual intercourse:

- fornication (premarital sex)
- adultery (extramarital sex)

Consent is simply not a factor.

This only makes sense in a book written from the point of view of men. The concept of consent was much more important to women, for obvious reasons, and sex crimes violating consent—that is, rape—are simply not acknowledged.

Some South Asian Islamic scholars use the phrase *zinaa bil jabr* to refer to rape, but this phrase never appears in the Quran. In the Quran, sex is classified into only two categories:

- lawful sex (with wives or slave girls)
- unlawful sex (fornication or adultery)

That is the only distinction, and those are the only classifications.

The word *zinaa* causes a lot of confusion. In the absence of a pregnancy or confession, the Quran requires four male witnesses (verses 4:15 and 24:4) to prove that *zinaa* occurred. This makes fornication and adultery extremely difficult to prove, which actually protects the perpetrators from punishment. But some Islamic societies use *zinaa* to also mean rape—again, because there is no word for rape in the Quran—and this ends up making rape extremely difficult to prove, placing the responsibility of providing four male witnesses on the rape victim. If she is unable to produce four male witnesses who saw the rape, she is subject—according to this version of Sharia law—to a hundred lashes, the punishment for *zinaa* (fornication or adultery) in the Quran (verse 24:2); or death by stoning, the punishment for *zinaa* (adultery) in the *hadith*.[10]

We see this unfortunate outcome in the form of the *Hudood* ordinance in Pakistani law or the rules of the Supreme Judicial Council in Saudi Arabia, where victims are often blamed and punished for their own rapes.[11] If they can't produce four male witnesses, they automatically become guilty of making a false accusation, or are asked to marry their attackers. Reporting that they have been raped, in this case, is seen as confessing to sexual intercourse.

There are people who say the Quran forbids rape. This is not true. There are others who say it explicitly allows rape—also not true. *The Quran simply doesn't recognize or mention rape as an entity.*

As discussed above, slaves can't give consent. So verses like 4:24, that make slaves and captives of war legal for men, can actually be seen as encouraging rape; but they aren't described as such in the Quran, because the very concept of female consent simply doesn't exist.

Back then, the male point of view was primarily concerned with establishing lineage and paternity. Men wanted to ensure that their children were indeed their own, and their heirs were genuine. Consent doesn't interfere with this. But fornication and adultery do. This is also one of the main reasons men are allowed to have up to four wives[12] (verse 4:3), while women can only have one husband.

Feel free to ask Islamic scholars or experts about rape in the Quran. Ask them to give you any verse that mentions it. They will give you verses like 4:19, which says one cannot inherit a woman against her will; or 5:33, prescribing punishments for general crimes like spreading "corruption," a broad term thought to refer more to vocal blasphemy or apostasy than rape; or verses dealing with adultery and/or fornication. They will never be able to provide you with a single verse that even acknowledges the concept of rape or female consent. Some will tell you that these more general verses prohibiting bad behavior essentially cover rape as well. They are wrong about this. For one, the Quran allows sex with slaves and captives of war, even married ones, which is rape. And second, why was it so difficult for the omnipotent, infallible creator of the universe, sending out his final book to humanity via his final prophet, to simply include in it the words, "Don't rape"?

This is something that has consistently amazed me. The Ten Commandments made room to condemn taking God's name in vain, keeping the Sabbath holy, and prohibiting graven images; but there is no "Thou shalt not rape." The Quran places great priority on not eating pork and on gathering wives and slave girls; but this horrific, devastating crime that has been committed rampantly throughout history against half of humanity doesn't even get an acknowledgment of *existence*.

It therefore makes sense that every transmitter of Islamic doctrine— from Muhammad himself to the caliphs and imams—were men. They weren't merely conveying the word of a genderless Allah. With all due respect and sensitivity to the views of Fatima Bhutto and other believing Muslim women who rail against "mansplaining," Islam—like nearly every other religion out there—is the ultimate form of it, in the guise of divinity.

A common counterargument from the Islamic apologist is, "What about all of the good things in the Quran? Why are you ignoring those?"

This would be a fair question were it not for the claim of divine authorship. If we do away with the idea that the Quran is the perfect word of God, we can select the good and ignore the bad, as we do with any other historical literature. But we'll get to that later. For now, let's take a look at the two Quranic verses most often cited to demonstrate that Islam is peaceful and tolerant.

"There is no compulsion."

The first is the beginning of verse 2:256, which Pickthall translates simply as "There is no compulsion in religion." The *Sahih International* translation says, "There shall be no compulsion in [acceptance of] the religion." Either way, this statement establishes plainly that no one can be forced to accept the religion, and is seen by religious moderates to be emblematic of the tolerant nature of Islam.

What you don't hear, however—and this is often because those quoting the verse don't know it themselves—is the very next verse, 2:257, which says:

> Allah is the ally of those who believe. He brings them out from
> darknesses into the light. And those who disbelieve—their allies
> are Taghut. They take them out of the light into darknesses. Those
> are the companions of the Fire; they will abide eternally therein.

Taghut refers to idolaters or those who believe in any deity other than Allah. And while verse 2:256 says there is no compulsion for anyone to believe, 2:257 adds that those who choose not to are doomed to eternal torture in hell. In effect, this is saying, "You're under no obligation to accept my proposal. But if you reject it, I will torture you for eternity."

In verse 18:29–30, this strange duality is repeated:

> And say, "The truth is from your Lord, so whoever wills—let
> him believe; and whoever wills—let him disbelieve." Indeed,

We have prepared for the wrongdoers a fire whose walls will surround them. And if they call for relief, they will be relieved with water like murky oil, which scalds [their] faces. Wretched is the drink, and evil is the resting place.

Indeed, those who have believed and done righteous deeds—indeed, We will not allow to be lost the reward of any who did well in deeds.

In other words, it's up to you if you want to believe or disbelieve. But if you are one who has not believed or "done righteous deeds," you'll forever be drinking viscous water that will burn your face.

As always, though, there is a counterargument.

"But if you're not a believer, you don't even *believe* in hell," says the apologist. "So why would this even matter to you?"

This is a frequent last-resort argument that apologists default to when faced with contradictions like these. Another instance where I've come across it is in the case of verses 5:72–73, which read as follows:

They have certainly disbelieved who say, "Allah is the Messiah, the son of Mary" while the Messiah has said, "O Children of Israel, worship Allah, my Lord and your Lord." Indeed, he who associates others with Allah—Allah has forbidden him Paradise, and his refuge is the Fire. And there are not for the wrongdoers any helpers.

They have certainly disbelieved who say, "Allah is the third of three." And there is no god except one God. And if they do not desist from what they are saying, there will surely afflict the disbelievers among them a painful punishment.

These verses are pretty straightforward: those who believe Mary gave birth to the son of God (Islam acknowledges Jesus to be a prophet born of the virginal Mary, but not the son of God), or those who believe in the

Trinity ("the third of three"), will be forbidden from Paradise, have refuge in the fire, and be afflicted with a painful punishment.

Essentially, these verses condemn all believing Christians to permanent, eternal doom. Moreover, some translations of these verses, such as the one by Yusuf Ali, refer to Christians not as those who have "disbelieved," but those who "blaspheme." Verse 5:69, preceding these verses, says that those who were previously Christians or Jews will suffer no penalty (as does 2:62), as long as they accept Allah and his prophet now.

Here again comes the last-resort default argument. "These verses aren't telling anyone to kill Christians. They're just promising punishment in the hereafter. If you're not a believer anyway, why care?"

Now, consider that over a billion people in the world believe the words of this book to be the words of Allah himself. And in verses 5:72–73, Allah makes clear his disdain for those who believe Jesus to be his son, or him to be part of the Trinity—so much so that he declares them deserving of eternal hellfire. He also calls them "disbelievers" or "blasphemers" who are "forbidden from Paradise." How, then, would you expect believers of Allah and his words to approach the Christians in their midst? The answer is, pretty much the same way that Christians themselves approached disbelievers and blasphemers several centuries ago, which wasn't pretty. Add to this the fact that verses 9:29–30 *do* say (as mentioned earlier in this book) that Christians and Jews *should* be fought until they willingly pay a non-Muslim *jizyah* tax or convert to Islam. In light of all this, it's clear how these verses do matter, even if they don't prescribe earthly punishments.

The same goes for verse 2:256. You could repeat "There's no compulsion in religion" a hundred times, but combined with the idea in the very next verse that disbelievers will go to hell—and verses endorsing fighting disbelievers (9:29–30), slaying them (9:5), beheading them (8:12–13), and more—the statement becomes meaningless.

"Killing one person is like killing all mankind."

Another verse frequently quoted by the Islam-is-a-religion-of-peace crowd is verse 5:32. President Obama himself referenced the verse in his famous 2009 Cairo speech, where he told his audience, "The Holy Quran teaches that whoever kills an innocent, it is as if he has killed all mankind; and whoever saves a person, it is as if he has saved all mankind."

The full verse reads as follows:

> Because of that, We decreed upon the Children of Israel that whoever kills a soul *unless for a soul or for corruption [done] in the land*—it is as if he had slain mankind entirely. And whoever saves one—it is as if he had saved mankind entirely. And our messengers had certainly come to them with clear proofs. Then indeed many of them, [even] after that, throughout the land, were transgressors. (Emphasis added.)

In its entirety, the verse is confusing because it is badly written. The contextual background is the story of Adam's sons, Cain and Abel (Qabil and Habil for Muslims), where one brother killed the other. Based on this incident, the Children of Israel—that is, the Jews—were later told that killing a person is like killing all people, and saving one is like saving all of them. (This statement is also found in the Mishnah [Oral Torah], Sanhedrin, 4.5: "anyone who destroys a life is considered by Scripture to have destroyed an entire world; and anyone who saves a life is as if he saved an entire world.")

The verse, however, makes an exception—emphasized above—for the person killed in retaliation for killing someone else, and the person causing "corruption" in the land; that person, according to the verse, is still legal to kill. And yet again, what you don't usually hear when this verse is quoted are the next two verses immediately following it, 5:33–34, which double down on exactly what should be done with the person who causes this "corruption":

> Indeed, the penalty for those who wage war against Allah and His Messenger and strive upon earth [to cause] corruption is none but that they be killed or crucified or that their hands and feet be cut off from opposite sides or that they be exiled from the land. That is for them a disgrace in this world; and for them

in the Hereafter is a great punishment, [e]xcept for those who return [repenting] before you apprehend them. And know that Allah is Forgiving and Merciful.

"But it says this is only for those who wage war and cause corruption," protests the apologist. "It's specific."

Actually, it's not.

What constitutes "corruption" or "waging war against Allah and His Messenger" varies according to perspective. There is no doubt that a large number of Muslims see the drawing of cartoons of their prophet as an act of war. Seeing that U.S. bombs have fallen in seven Muslim-majority countries in just a decade[13] may plausibly lead even moderate Muslims in these countries to believe the United States is "waging war" in their lands and therefore hold its government and the population that elected it into office responsible. Vocally apostasizing and writing articles, books, or even Facebook posts criticizing Islamic doctrine and promoting atheism are widely seen as "spreading corruption." And the Islamic State, which strictly follows *ahadith* that prescribe brutal punishments for blasphemers and homosexuals, clearly sees blasphemy and homosexuality as corrupt and sinful; it believes that killing those who commit these acts is the legally permitted exception to the 5:32 rule, and therefore endorsed by Allah himself. This is a very slippery slope. If "spreading corruption" is punishable by execution and/or crucifixion, imagine the number of "crimes" that might fall into this broad category. Just as moderate Muslims use verse 5:32 to legitimately support their argument that Allah frowns on killing people, ISIS uses the very next verse, 5:33, to legitimately support murdering thousands.

The apologist's claim is that taking unfavorable-sounding verses out of context makes them sound worse; it seems, however, that putting favorable-sounding verses *in* context often has the same effect.

Interpretation of the Quran, called *tafsir* in Arabic, is no simple feat. Yet without it, modern Islamic exegetes run into a lot of problems. The worst nightmare of virtually every Western Islamic scholar is that the Quran be read "literally"—that is, the way it's actually written. As discussed in chapter 2, there is a good reason for this. Going by all that we see done in the world in the *name* of Islam—the murder of disbelievers, the stoning to death of adulterers, beheading of blasphemers and apostates, child marriage, polygyny, domestic abuse, jihadist terrorism, sex slavery, persecution of gays, and more—you would think Islam is the most misunderstood religion in the world, especially in light of its claims to be the religion of peace. It would seem from the apologist's lamentations that the meaning of the scripture's words is not merely misinterpreted, but often taken to mean the *opposite* of peaceful. From average Muslims to renowned historical scholars and exegetes, almost everyone seems to have misinterpreted the scripture in one way or another. How could this happen? If any other book was this widely misunderstood or misinterpreted, what would you think of the author? You might think he is either exceedingly inarticulate or incompetent. Indeed, a Venn diagram of the two descriptors would be indistinguishable from a circle to the naked eye.

It is true that many verses have certain contexts under which they were allegedly revealed. But that doesn't necessarily render them obsolete. A good example is verse 8:12:

> [Remember] when your Lord inspired to the angels, "I am with you, so strengthen those who have believed. I will cast terror into the hearts of those who disbelieved, so strike [them] upon the necks and strike from them every fingertip."

This verse originates from the Battle of Badr, the first battle between the Meccan pagans ("those who disbelieved") and Muhammad's fledgling army of new Muslims ("those who have believed"). The verse claims that Allah himself sent angels to help strengthen the Muslims, who were outnumbered three to one, and "cast terror" in the hearts of the Meccans, enabling the Muslims to behead enemy fighters and cut off their fingertips. (For those who followed the earlier discussion on the word *adhribu*, it again appears in this verse, twice, meaning "strike.")

The argument from moderates is that this verse is not applicable anymore because it's another verse of war, and is only to be implemented in that context. But even if we set aside the fact that many Muslims around the world actually do think they're at war with the United States and other Western powers, this explanation falls short. The very next verse, 8:13, states:

> That is because they opposed Allah and His Messenger. And whoever opposes Allah and His Messenger—indeed, Allah is severe in penalty.

The Badr verse isn't just a one-off. The example of the battle is used to illustrate the fate of "*whoever* opposes Allah and His Messenger," removing any contextual qualifiers. And this time, it isn't just those who "wage war" or "spread corruption," as in 5:33. It's those who "oppose" Allah and Muhammad. What does this entail? Would it include, say, questioning the Quran, or drawing satirical cartoons?

You decide.

As with any other holy book, there are also many good things in the Quran. And fortunately, it is these good parts that are taught to most young Muslim children growing up, as was the case with me. Like most human beings, Muslims want nothing more than to be happy, secure, and provide their families with the best lives possible. My parents were certainly no exception. The fact that moderate Muslims will often bend over backward to try and prove somehow that their faith and scripture are peaceful is a testament to their utter distaste and disapproval for violence.

As jihadist attacks around the world increase and the resulting anti-Muslim sentiment in Western countries rises, there seems to be this growing rhetoric that any Muslim who reveres the Quran endorses by default the violence and misogyny within it. But this is simply not how human beings work. Many Christians revere the Bible, and Jews the Torah. Yet it is nearly impossible today to find anyone who would actually carry out or even endorse the biblical commands of putting gay men to death, killing one's neighbor for working on the Sabbath, endorsing slavery, or telling women to be silent and submit to men's authority—all of which are clearly written in their holy book. Most religious people derive their beliefs and practices very broadly from their families and culture. Few even know the contents of their scripture, and many who do dismiss it as inconsequential. This is a good thing. Religion—or this broad perception of religion—*can* inspire people to do good things. But as we saw with Hitchens's challenge in the last chapter, religion certainly isn't required for this. There is no good deed done by a believer that cannot be done by a nonbeliever; but there are numerous wicked deeds done by believers that are attributable only to their religious beliefs.

There are elements in the Quran that were a significant improvement over the status quo at its time of writing. Remember, the verses of the Quran were allegedly revealed to Muhammad gradually over the course of many years, and some of the earlier ones seem notably idealistic. For instance, pre-Islamic Arabia was not known to be kind to women; and as problematic as many Quranic verses about women are, the earliest verses actually sought to better their treatment in Mecca, which included the burying alive of newborn girls and not allowing women to even inherit property, much less own it. The trajectory of Muhammad's life shows a classic pattern found in many young revolutionaries who are rebellious and idealistic when young outcasts, but embrace some level of conformity as they gain power and influence and grow a following, ultimately becoming statesmen susceptible to the same corruption as those they dethroned.

Muhammad's father died while his mother was pregnant with him. So his earliest years were spent primarily with two women: his wet nurse, Halimah, and his mother, Aamina. At the age of six, Muhammad's mother died, and he became an orphan. He was then placed under the guardianship of his paternal grandfather, Abdul Muttalib, who also died just two years later, when Muhammad was eight. Obviously, this is a lot for a young boy to handle. Muhammad then moved into the home of his uncle, Abu Talib, and under his tutelage grew up to be a successful and reputable merchant who regularly engaged in trade with his counterparts up north in Syria.

In his twenties, he met Khadijah, a widow who was also a successful businesswoman. She hired him for one of her jobs, and his performance brought her enormous profit, significantly exceeding her expectations. It wasn't long before her admiration for him began to transcend professional bounds. She proposed to him when he was twenty-five years old. She was forty.

Khadijah and Muhammad stayed married for the next twenty-five years, until her death. During this entire time, Muhammad was married only to her, never taking a second wife. Together, they had six children—four daughters and two sons. Both sons died in infancy, but all four of Muhammad's daughters grew to adulthood. Three predeceased him, and one, Fatima, survived him. (Shias believe that Fatima was Muhammad's only biological daughter, and the other three—Zaynab, Umm Kulthoom, and Ruqaiyyah—were either the daughters of Khadijah's late sister, or Khadijah's daughters from a previous marriage; Sunnis believe all four were biological.) Muhammad's only other biological child, Ibrahim, was born later in his life to his concubine, Maria the Copt. Like his sons with Khadijah, Ibrahim died early, before age two.

What is remarkable about Muhammad's first marriage is how progressive it was. Not only was Khadijah fifteen years older and a successful businesswoman, but also Muhammad's employer, financial supporter, and a nonvirginal widow who took it upon herself to initiate the marriage proposal that he was on the receiving end of. She was also his best friend and confidante. When he allegedly received his first revelation while meditating in the *Hira* cave in Mecca, Khadijah was the first person he told— and by believing him, she became the first ever Muslim in history.

Between his mother, wet nurse, first wife, and daughters, Muhammad was always surrounded and influenced by strong women. The earlier, Meccan *surahs* of the Quran—largely from the time that Muhammad was happily married to Khadijah—reflected this. These verses were relatively broad, idealistic, and somewhat philosophical. They dealt with the prayer and worship of Allah, life after death, the concepts of heaven and hell, treating the needy and the orphans (like Muhammad himself) with kindness, and stories of prophets past. They would often start with the address, *Yaa ayyuhan-naas*, or "O, mankind," in contrast to the verses that came after his migration to Medina, which began with *Yaa ayyuhal-lathzeena aamanu*, or "O ye who believe." In her book *Heretic: Why*

Islam Needs a Reformation Now, Ayaan Hirsi Ali characterizes the large majority of the world's peaceful Muslims as "Mecca Muslims" for precisely these reasons. During his time in Mecca, Muhammad was a young man disgruntled with what he saw around him, and earnestly wanted to change it for the better.

Shortly after Khadijah's death, Muhammad migrated to Medina and soon found himself no longer an outcast, but a statesman and military leader in command of a small but powerful, fast-growing army. The Medinan *surahs* became longer and more political, legalistic, and militaristic. This is also the time that Muhammad became polygamous. He married several wives, allowed the taking of concubines and slaves, and became much harsher with disbelievers.

These disparate approaches are naturally reflected as contradictions in the Quran, although many Muslims who hold the book to be divinely authored and free of error deny that these contradictions exist. Their reasoning is predictably circular: "The Quran has no contradictions because the Quran says so."

Which it does. Verse 4:82 states plainly, "Do they not reflect upon the Quran? If it had been from [any] other than Allah, they would have found within it much contradiction." Well, there *are* contradictions. In verse 4:15, those engaged in unlawful (premarital/extramarital) intercourse proven by the testimony of four witnesses are to be confined in their home until "death takes them or Allah ordains for them [another] way." But in 24:2, as we've seen earlier, the punishment is one hundred lashes. Another example: verse 3:20 instructs believers to ask others to submit to Allah, but if they don't, "then upon you is only the [duty of] notification. And Allah is Seeing of [His] servants"; that is, no force, no compulsion, just like 2:256. But in 8:38–39, believers are instructed to fight those who don't submit to Allah "until there is no *fitnah* and [until] the religion, all of it, is for Allah" (*fitnah* in this context means hostility or oppression).

One method used to resolve these contradictions is called *naskh*, or "abrogation." The premise is fairly simple at first glance. If two verses are in conflict, look at the time of revelation, discard the earlier verse, and go with the one that came later. The abrogating, or newer, verse is referred to as *al-nasikh* and the abrogated, or discarded, verse *al-mansookh*. This exegetic technique has robust support in the Quran itself. Verse 2:106 asserts that older verses can indeed be replaced by newer ones. "We do not abrogate a verse or cause it to be forgotten except that We bring forth [one] better than it or similar to it," reads the verse. Another verse, 16:101, protects Muhammad from accusations of lying when he presents conflicting verses. "And when We substitute a verse in place of a verse—and Allah is most knowing of what He sends down—they say, 'You [O Muhammad], are but an inventor [of lies].' But most of them do not know."

As you may well imagine, *naskh* can easily lend itself to a more political and violent version of Islam. For example, *Surah Al-Kafiroun* is a Meccan surah explaining that one should tell non-Muslims unswayed by the message of Islam, "For you is your religion, and for me is my religion"—a combination of "agree to disagree" and "live and let live." However, the later Medinan verses 8:38–39 and 9:29–30, as mentioned earlier, instruct believers to fight disbelievers until they either embrace Allah or pay a tax. In this case, the earlier Meccan verse is abrogated by the newer, much less tolerant Medinan one.

It gets more complicated. There are three types of abrogation. In the first, both the verse and its ruling are discarded. In the second, the verse is discarded but the ruling stands. The most commonly given example of this second type of abrogation are the verses of *rajm*, prescribing stoning as a punishment for adultery. These are believed to have been real verses that didn't make it to the Quran (according to some Sunni *ahadith*, the paper they were written on was eaten by a sheep[14]), but their ruling, according to many scholars, still stands. The third type of abrogation is the most common, the one we've been focusing on here—the abrogated verse stays in the Quran, but the ruling is discarded in favor of the abrogating verse.

The problem, of course, is that the average Muslim reading her Quran will have no way of telling which of the verses she's reading have been abrogated. There is nothing in the Quran that indicates this, and there is no indication in the *hadith* either. Even the scholars are split. Some claim that the number of abrogations is in the hundreds, while others say they're in the single digits. The reality is, no one knows for sure.

There are also many scholars who don't buy the abrogation concept at all. They believe verse 4:82 is correct in saying the Quran has no contradictions, and these seemingly conflicting verses merely serve to complement each other. Take the example, again, of the above-quoted verse 4:15 saying that fornicators are to be bound to their homes either until death or until "Allah ordains for them [another] way." Scholars who reject the idea of abrogation say that the punishment of one hundred lashes decreed in verse 24:2 *is* the "other way" that Allah asked believers to hold off for. Therefore, these verses aren't in conflict; rather, they complement each other. Abrogation skeptics also explain the contradictions between peaceful and violent verses similarly. There is a time for peace, and a time for fighting, they say. Depending on the time and place we're living in, the appropriate verses apply. None are abrogated.

But then, what about the verses 2:106 and 16:101, which clearly state that Allah indeed replaces older verses with newer ones? Scholars who reject abrogation believe these verses are referring to the replacement of previous *scriptures* like the Torah and Gospels in their entirety by the Quran.

Either way, though, the violent passages cannot be ignored. Being mostly Medinan verses, those who interpret the Quran using *naskh* favor them; and those who don't use *naskh* still have to recognize their legitimacy as part of the word of God.

When he was a presidential candidate in 2016, Donald Trump stoked outrage for retweeting the Mussolini quote, "It is better to live one day as a lion than 100 years as a sheep."[15] On NBC's *Meet the Press*, host Chuck Todd asked Trump if he had known the quote was from Mussolini.

"Sure, it's okay to know it's Mussolini," replied Trump. "It's a very good quote, it's a very interesting quote, and I know it . . . I know who said it. But what difference does it make whether it's Mussolini or somebody else? It's certainly a very interesting quote."[16]

He wasn't wrong—but this brings up a good question. When do you disregard a good quote from a questionable source? A friend once tweeted the quote, "To learn who rules over you, simply find out who you are not allowed to criticize." He attributed it to Voltaire, as most people do. It's a good quote (even relevant to this book), and garnered the usual likes and retweets. Barely a few minutes had gone by before people started pointing out that Voltaire had never said it, although it is frequently misattributed to him. To my friend's horror, the quote was a slightly modified version of the words of a white supremacist, Holocaust-denying neo-Nazi named Kevin Strom.[17] The difference here, of course, is that my friend wasn't aware in the slightest that the quote was from a reprehensible source—unlike Trump and his Mussolini retweet. What to do? A commenter informed my friend that if he quoted Hitler in Germany, he would be locked up. "Dude," my friend replied. "That's totalitarianism."

Good things can often come from bad sources. One can easily imagine many good, conscientious people tapping "like" on Internet quotes like, "A man does not die for something which he himself does not believe in," or, "To change a thing means to recognize it first." As a quasi-experiment, I once posted both of these quotes on my own social media timelines, attributing them to Ali ibn Abu Talib, Muhammad's cousin and son-in-law who went on to become the fourth caliph of the Sunnis and the first Imam of the Shias. The likes went through the roof, and understandably so: none of my readers recognized that both of these quotes were actually from Hitler's *Mein Kampf*.[18]

In some ways, this is where my experience reading the Abrahamic holy books as a young boy fits in. A few good ideas in *Mein Kampf* don't make the whole book good. Conversely, a few bad ideas in an otherwise good book don't necessarily make the whole book bad. This dynamic, however, changes dramatically with books that claim divine authorship or even divine inspiration. If one is to believe that a book is the infallible word of a flawless god, there is no latitude for error. Yes, I did come across some really good things in all of the scriptures, even if they were largely derivative. But the bad things, especially in the Old Testament and Quran, were too much for me to embrace the entire text as somehow virtuous— much less inerrant.

Infallibility changes everything. If there were even a single, small fly in a glass of otherwise pristine water, would you drink it?

EIGHT

Reformation and Secularism

The belief that the Quran is perfect, infallible, and divine—not "divinely inspired," but *divine*—is central to the Islamic faith. And whenever you have a concept like infallibility, any kind of innovation or reform is bound, by definition, to have very limited breathing room before venturing into the territory of heresy, blasphemy, or apostasy—all of which, as we've seen, carry grievous penalties.

In chapter 2, I spent some pages discussing Thomas Jefferson's contribution to secularism in the United States. Jefferson, not unlike the other Founding Fathers, is a widely admired historical figure with an arguably unparalleled legacy, perhaps characterized most notably by his penning of the words "all men are created equal" in the Declaration of Independence. Yet, like some of the other Founding Fathers, Jefferson was also a slave owner. After his wife died, Jefferson, in his forties at the time, had a sexual relationship with her teenage half-sister, Sally Hemings, a slave at his Monticello plantation. Hemings had six children, and DNA testing in 1998 all but confirmed that Jefferson had fathered them all.[1]

This is clearly a stain on Jefferson's legacy that makes him appear hypocritical. However, in light of all the good things he did, as well as a consideration of what was thought to be accepted practice at the time, many of us give him a pass for these disturbing indiscretions. But imagine if Jefferson had claimed God-given infallibility, and had followers to this day who defended his owning of slaves and his sexual relationship with a child because they believed he could do no wrong. Would we give him a pass then? Likely not. Even Jefferson's most ardent admirers today acknowledge that on these counts, Jefferson was wrong. Indeed, if they defended his bad actions, it would cast them as much less credible in their defense of his good actions.

Infallibility changes everything.

Devout Muslims think Muhammad to be a perfect human being to be emulated for all time. And as his biography shows, his intentions as the founder (or messenger, depending on what you believe) of Islam, at least initially, were to improve the milieu of pre-Islamic Meccan society. He was passionate about protecting the well-being of orphans, having been one himself. He established obligatory almsgiving, called *zakah*, as one of the five pillars of (Sunni) Islam, to help the poor. And while he took slaves, mostly later in his life, he also freed many, even adopting as a son one, named Zayd bin Harithah, given to him as a wedding present by his wife Khadijah.

But according to numerous *ahadith* from the books of *Sahih Bukhari*, *Sahih Muslim*, and others, he also married his best friend Abu Bakr's daughter, Aisha, when she was just six years old, consummating the marriage when she was nine.[2] He enslaved female prisoners of war. He prescribed harsh punishments for adulterers and nonbelievers. And like most other historical military statesmen, he killed hundreds in battle.

Muhammad's followers, however, defend and justify all of his actions even today. His marriage to Aisha, for example, is justified by saying he waited three years to consummate the marriage because he was waiting for her to reach puberty, which they say happened when she was nine. Many Shias deny she was that young at all; some accounts say she was fifteen, and others say she was eighteen or nineteen. They all maintain, however, that Muhammad was fifty-three, and Aisha was his eleventh wife. None of these scenarios are particularly comforting. Whatever the case, not being able to burden Muhammad with any error creates barriers not only to open debate, but to justice. Suppose you are in front of the

Supreme Judicial Council in Saudi Arabia, the country's equivalent to the Supreme Court (excepting the Saudi council's Sharia-based rulings). You are making the argument to raise the age of female marital consent to eighteen, or even sixteen. Then, after hearing your arguments, one of the judges reminds you that the Prophet himself married his eleventh wife when she was a child. Was he wrong in doing so?

And this, right here, is the wall of infallibility that you cannot get past. How do you answer the judge? You could either say, yes, the Prophet was wrong, but you know the consequences of that would be dire. Or, you could make the case that the Prophet was right to marry a six-year-old, but *today's* men should not be allowed to. But if Muhammad is to be emulated as a timeless example of perfection, this is a challenging argument to make. The judge would tell you that banning a legitimate practice of Sunnah would be against Islam.

This is not a hypothetical situation. Saudi Arabia does legally allow child marriage on this basis. And in Pakistan, a proposed bill to ban child marriage was struck down twice by the Council of Islamic Ideology—a committee that advises parliament on the compatibility of legislation with Sharia—first in 2014, and again in 2016, for being "un-Islamic" and "blasphemous."[3] This stuff is real, and for moderate, liberal, and progressive Muslims, it presents a real dilemma, one I grappled with myself for some years.

Assuming default inerrancy of scripture almost necessitates confirmation bias. The process is always the same. You read something in the holy book that clashes with your conscience and makes you jump. Knowing that this is the inerrant word of God, you decide there must be some justification. You begin by thinking the verse can't *really* mean what it says. It must be a mistake in translation or interpretation. So you look up several translations. Here, you may either find one or two that you can settle on because they say something relatively palatable; or you're unable to find a translation that convincingly dilutes the problematic part. So you go back and study the context. You dig into the *hadith* and read the scholars. You select one or two that agree with what you hoped the verse really meant, if you're lucky enough to find them. Otherwise, you decide that the verse must be read "metaphor-ically."

But if any kind of literature is to be interpreted metaphorically, it has to at least represent the original idea. Metaphors are intended to illustrate and clarify ideas, not twist and obscure them. When the literal words speak of blatant violence but are claimed to really mean peace and unity, we're not in interpretation/metaphor zone anymore; we're heading into distortion/misrepresentation territory. If this disconnect was limited to one or two verses, I would consider your argument. If your interpretation were accepted by all of the world's Muslims, I would consider your argu-ment. Unfortunately, neither of these is the case.

Your metaphorical explanations are very convincing to your fellow be-lievers. That's expected. When people are caught between their faith and their conscience, they'll jump on anything they can find to reconcile the two. Outside the echo chamber, though, all of this is very confusing. It can eat away at your credibility. This is what makes otherwise rational moder-ate Muslims look remarkably inconsistent. Despite your best intentions, you may even unwittingly embolden anti-Muslim bigots by effectively narrowing the differences between yourself and the fundamentalists. You condemn all kinds of terrible things being done in the name of your religion—but when the same things appear as verses in your book, you use all your faculties to defend them. This comes across as either denial or disingenuousness, both of which make an honest conversation impossible.

But what choice do you have? The belief that the Quran is divine and inerrant is central to the Islamic faith, and held by the vast majority of Muslims worldwide, fundamentalist or progressive. You believe that let-ting it go is as good as calling yourself non-Muslim. But is this really the case? Suppose you still believed in Allah and Muhammad, and still em-braced the basic philosophical principles of the Islamic faith, but consid-ered the Quran to be divinely *inspired* instead of divine and inerrant—as most Christians and Jews believe their holy books to be. Would that make you less of a Muslim? Can Islam survive a rejection of scriptural iner-rancy and remain intact?

The answer is a tried-and-tested yes.

During a Republican presidential debate in 2008 hosted by CNN and YouTube, one of the more memorable questions came from a young man from Dallas.

"How you answer this question will tell us everything we need to know about you. Do you believe every word of this book?" he asked, holding up the King James Version of the Bible. "And I mean specifically this book that I am holding in my hand. Do you believe this book?"[4]

All the candidates who answered said yes, they believe the whole book, but they differed as to how. Rudy Giuliani said he believes all of it, but not literally—some of it, he said, was "allegorical." Mike Huckabee was less equivocal, but granted that it was "complicated." And Mitt Romney, a Mormon who lost the nomination that year but did win it four years later in 2012, was more straightforward: "Yes, I believe it's the word of God. The Bible is the word of God . . . I might interpret the word differently than you interpret the word, but . . . I believe the Bible is the word of God."

What Romney was talking about is what Christians had believed for centuries—that the Bible is the word of God and must be followed as such. But how many Americans today agree with him? According to a 2011 Gallup poll that put the question to the test, three out of ten Americans said they interpreted the Bible literally as the word of God. Broken down into groups, 46 percent of Protestants said the Bible was the actual word of God, while 41 percent said it was the inspired word of God. Among Catholics, 21 percent said it was the actual word, and 65 percent said it was inspired.[5] What the poll also showed was that a majority of Americans *don't* believe the Bible is the actual, literal word of God. While many may still think of the Bible as divinely inspired, the majority of Christians in America have, in effect, rejected the notion of scriptural inerrancy.

Yet Christianity is alive and well today.

Rabbi David Wolpe, named America's Top Rabbi by *Newsweek / The Daily Beast* in 2012,[6] writes that despite there being no claims of divine authorship in the Old Testament, "due to various interpretations and doctrines, the belief has grown up in Judaism that the whole Torah . . . is divine." For this, he credits the "slippery slope" argument: if so much as a single word in the holy text is claimed to be written by man, there's no telling how much more of the book's alleged divinity one can defend. Therefore, it has to be all or nothing. This way, says Wolpe, "it is intellectually neater to hew to a hard line. If it is all from God, then that's the end of it. For centuries, Jewish exegetes . . . argued that this was the simple truth." But this thinking was not to last. Eventually, reality caught up to belief, and with a host of developments in "literary criticism, comparative religion, archaeology, and so forth—the divinity of the Bible seemed less secure."[7] Indeed, only a minority of U.S. Jews today believe the Torah to be divinely scribed; the majority believes it is the work of man.[8]

Yet Judaism is alive and well today.

Can Islam undergo this sort of evolution? Even questioning the inerrancy of the Quran in most Muslim-majority societies could get you into serious trouble. Even in the United States and Canada, doing away with scriptural inerrancy is seen as an incendiary proposition to most Muslims: "You can't be serious. Your solution to reforming Islam is to tell Muslims to abandon Islam? If you don't believe the Quran is the word of God, you are not a Muslim."

This is admittedly a well-founded response. For most Muslims, rejecting scriptural inerrancy is synonymous with abandoning Islam. The Quran itself says in several places that it is the word of Allah; and in verse 15:9, Allah even says he himself will guard it: "Indeed, it is We who sent down the Qur'an and indeed, We will be its guardian."

There haven't been many polls conducted to tell us exactly how many Muslims truly do believe in the divine origin of scripture, but the ones that do paint an interesting picture. A 2012 Pew research poll asked people in fifteen Muslim-majority sub-Saharan African countries if they believed the Quran was the word of God and should be "read literally, word for word." Over 90 percent of all questioned Muslims agreed it was the word of God, with over three-fourths on average saying it should be read literally.[9] American Muslims were asked the same question in another Pew poll in 2014; 82 percent said they believed the Quran was the word of God, with only 12 percent saying they thought the Quran was "written by men." However, American Muslims did differ somewhat: of those that believed the Quran was divine, only 42 percent said the Quran was Allah's "literal" word.[10]

Simply observing how North American Muslims live indicates that this number may be even lower. When it comes to regular day-to-day activities, my observations are admittedly anecdotal. Only on occasion have I seen Muslims break from work or their daily routine to complete all five obligatory prayers, the first of which is to be offered at the crack of dawn. Muslim women in the United States and Canada seem to dress almost indistinguishably from most of their American non-Muslim counterparts, with only a minority wearing hijab. Most North American Muslim families of my generation here are dual-income households, where the man does not have any particular authority over the woman; and even nonanecdotal evidence shows that in the United States, Muslim women tend to be at least as professionally qualified as, if not more than, their male counterparts.[11] I would wager that many non-Muslim readers might have had a drink or two with their Muslim friend or coworker, despite the Quran's ban on alcohol. I would also wager that very few of the large number of Western Muslims who drink alcohol would also eat pork, banned too by the Quran. This is a selective practice I always found intriguing growing up; many Muslims would drink alcohol, but very few would go near pork.

But it is the bigger stuff that is more telling. Read literally, the Quran tells Muslims not to take Jews and Christians as friends (verse 5:51), but most Western Muslims dismiss this as a mistranslation or specific to a particular time and context that doesn't apply now. Of course, other verses say the same thing—verses 3:118 and 4:144 tell believers not to have close friends who are nonbelievers, and 9:23 even tells believers to break alliances with "your fathers or your brothers if they have preferred disbelief over belief." Yet Western Muslims continue to have friendships and alliances with non-Muslims. Most Western Muslims also reject—and often have very unfavorable views of—a host of other Quran-endorsed ideas, such as permission to beat one's wife (even lightly or as a last resort), the word of two women being equal to one man, polygamy, and the idea that fornicators must be lashed, or thieves must have their hands amputated.

Although they do say they consider the Quran to be the word of God, they don't necessarily live their lives as if it were. Their selectivity of the components of scripture more commensurate with the secular society they are part of is evidence of this. The *hadith* seem to hold even less sway, because there is always disagreement about which ones are authentic. In my interactions, the unwritten rule seems to be: those *ahadith* we like that are compatible with modern society are authentic, and those we don't like are not. Interestingly, while the Quranic verses mentioned above are largely disregarded, there are certain practices, like the hijab and circumcision, that aren't even mentioned in the Quran, appearing only in the *hadith*.[12] Male circumcision, however, is a near-universal practice among Western Muslims.

Among Western Muslims, Islam is more of an identity than a religion. I remember growing up hearing my female relatives defend Muhammad's polygamy, but they would never accept their own husbands taking a second wife. They would defend wife-beating in verse 4:34 as reasonable ("You can only do it lightly, and as a last resort! The Prophet actually helped *prevent* wife-beating as a first response this way!"), but vow to walk out if their husbands ever tried to discipline them this way. They would treat death as a finality, mourning the deaths of their loved ones as a permanent loss rather than a transition to a much better world where they would soon be reunited. It is on this last point that I decided that the cognitive dissonance of the moderate believer might just be a good thing. Let me tell you why.

I never truly grasped what it would be like to really believe in life after death—and I mean *really* believe in it—until shortly after the Taliban's attack on the Army Public School in Peshawar, Pakistan, in December 2014. These murderers stormed into the school and shot dead 141 people, including 132 children, chanting, "Allahu Akbar!" as they shot each child.

After the attack, I had a conversation with a Taliban supporter online who was protesting my posts condemning the massacre; he defended it. He seemed sincere. Instead of brushing him off, I decided to engage him and ask him questions just to understand how his mind worked. I started by asking the obvious—why was he defending the killing of innocent people? His answer:

Human life only has value among you worldly materialist thinkers. For us, this human life is only a tiny meaningless fragment of our existence. Our real destination is the Hereafter. We don't just believe it exists, we know it does. Death is not the end of life. It is the beginning of existence, in a world much more beautiful than this. As you know, the [Urdu] word for death is "intiqaal." It means "transfer," not "end."[13]

I asked him what right he had to decide that. Why was he making that decision for others? Shouldn't they have the right to make that decision for themselves? And why *children*? They haven't even had a chance to process what they've been taught, or make their own decisions. He justified it by saying these were children of army officers, who he believed were treasonous for fighting against the Taliban, Allah's soldiers:

Paradise is for those of pure hearts. All children have pure hearts. They have not sinned yet . . . They have not yet been corrupted [by their apostate parents]. We did not end their lives. We gave them new ones, in Paradise, where they will be loved more than you can imagine . . .

They will be rewarded for their martyrdom. After all, we also martyr ourselves with them. The last words they heard were the slogan of Takbeer [Allahu Akbar]. Allah Almighty says Himself in *Surah Al-Imran* [3:169–170] that they are not dead.

The man was quoting verses from the Quran that state, "And never think of those who have been killed in the cause of Allah as dead. Rather, they are alive with their Lord, receiving provision, rejoicing in what Allah has bestowed upon them of His bounty, and they receive good tidings about those [to be martyred] after them who have not yet joined them— that there will be no fear concerning them, nor will they grieve." There is another verse in the Quran, 2:154, that drives home the same point: "And do not say about those who are killed in the way of Allah, 'They are dead.' Rather, they are alive, but you perceive [it] not."

This is where it hit me. I could not argue with this man unless I challenged the Quran. And if I challenged the Quran, I knew exactly how he would respond. It was a true deadlock, maybe even worse, considering one side genuinely believed it had divine endorsement on its side. There was absolutely no way to get through. He was quoting verses from a book that over a billion people in the world claim to be infallible, and this man took it very, very seriously.

I went back to talking about the fact that these were children. They didn't choose to die in the way of Allah, and the jihadists had simply robbed them of the opportunity to make that decision. He didn't think this seemed to matter, and indeed, the verses cited don't seem to make the distinction either—they only speak of those "killed in the way of Allah," irrespective of consent.

> You will never understand this. If your faith is pure, you will not mourn them, but celebrate their birth into Paradise. But most of the people who call themselves Muslims do not believe this. They believe death is an end. This is because their faith is not pure.

The most chilling aspect of all of this was that everything he was talking about was what I had been taught growing up as a child: this life is temporary, just a test, heaven is infinitely preferable to life here and lasts forever, and death is not the end, but a transition to the afterlife. A lot of this doesn't just apply to Muslims. When faced with the death of a fellow human being, it is almost cliché to hear consolers say, "She's smiling and looking down at us from above," or, "He's in a better place now." The difference between us saying this and the Taliban supporter saying it is that *he really, really believes it*. If death really gets us to a better place, why do we treat it as such a permanent thing? Why does our mourning have an intensity that is so far beyond a temporary separation after which we would be reunited? Why do we speak of our dead in the past tense? Why is death treated as a finality instead of a transition to something much better?

One could protest the man's stance on killing children, of course, but is his view of death not identical to what we're drumming into the heads

of our children at Sunday school and the Friday mosque sermon? I remember asking my Islamic Studies teacher as a child, "What if children
die? Do we also go to hell?" I was assured that we don't, because we are
yet too young to assume responsibility for our actions. But we did grow
up celebrating our martyrs. The story of the martyrdom of Muhammad's
grandson Husayn (see chapter 2) is central to Shia Islam, similar to how
the martyrdom of Christ is central to Christianity. My friends and I
would talk about it. "When you die, how do you want to die?" The answer was clear.

"I want to be *shaheed*." A word that means martyr, or one who dies
in the way of Allah. And we weren't even fundamentalists. We were regular, everyday kids from moderate to liberal Muslim families whose parents would ground us and commit us to psychiatric therapy if we so much
as thought of joining a jihadist group. But this concept of being *shaheed*
was never treated with anything less than great reverence.

This glorification of life after death isn't just done by the Taliban, but
by any Muslim who uses the words *shaheed* or *martyrdom* in a positive
sense. When Muslims glorify the *shaheed* or the martyrs, they celebrate
death over life, and they should be aware of how toxic this idea is when
people *really* believe it, like my Taliban-supporting correspondent. The
notion that this life on Earth is secondary to the afterlife—a fundamental tenet of many religious faiths—is deadly when it is genuinely and sincerely believed from the heart. I also believe this to be true of many other
elements of religious belief.

As I've mentioned before, most moderately religious people, especially here in the West, approach their religious scriptures very differently from how they would read, say, *Alice in Wonderland*, or this book
that you're reading right now. As I write this, I am making a conscious,
deliberate effort to be as clear as I possibly can and minimize any potential
ambiguity. I know I will not be given the luxury of generous "interpretation" beyond what these words say at face value. I will literally be held to a
much higher standard as a writer than God himself. It isn't uncommon for
critics of Richard Dawkins or Sam Harris to quote decontextualized
excerpts from their writing to accuse them of being bigots, while also
hurling the exact same accusation at those who don't adequately "inter-

pret" verses in the Quran that endorse in plain language the beheading of disbelievers or beating of wives. In a 2014 tweet, Reza Aslan gave Harris some unsolicited advice: "If you're constantly having to explain away horrid things you've written, don't write them in [the first] place."[14] Note that this is from a man who has partly made a career out of constantly explaining to people why violent passages in Scripture don't really mean what they say.

The cognitive dissonance of many of today's moderate Muslims, however, has an upside. The fact that half of them don't think the Quran should be read literally indicates an indirect acknowledgment of the issue on their part: they wouldn't be pushing for nonliteral readings if they didn't think reading the Quran *as it's actually written* was problematic. They know it is. This is only one step away from direct acknowledgment of the issue, which naturally leads to letting go of the notion of scriptural inerrancy—a necessary prerequisite for any kind of reform.

The concept of "reformation" is a tricky one, not least because the term is so loaded. There was the Protestant Reformation, which might have been a necessary precursor to the Enlightenment, but didn't happen without years of violence, immense bloodshed, and virulent anti-Semitism. And then, there is what some Muslims consider to be an Islamic reformation orchestrated by Muhammad ibn Abd Al-Wahhab, an eighteenth-century Sunni preacher who brought to Arabia the doctrine of Salafism, or a return to the original, pure Islam practiced by Muhammad and the first three generations of Muslims. To be clear, this wasn't really a "reformation" at all, but the opposite—an outright rejection of the innovations and reforms to the faith by Muslims through the centuries, including entire sects like Shiaism.

A common counterargument to calls for Islamic reformation involves invoking Martin Luther or Abd Al-Wahhab and saying, "See? That's why Islam shouldn't have a reformation." This, of course, is a juvenile attempt at shutting down the conversation by clinging to semantics. It should be obvious that no one today is advocating for a thirty-year war, the murder of millions, or the demonization of Jews for not converting. Reformation in the current context simply means an effort at modernizing Islam and finding ways to make it compatible with the twenty-first century.

As a rationalist, I would ideally want to see a truly enlightened world, liberated from religion and superstition entirely; this is where I diverge somewhat from my pro-reform friends and family, most of whom are believers. I am, however, pragmatic enough to know that changes of this magnitude happen in increments, and thankfully, our goals are aligned along the same spectrum. The dynamic is similar to how I approach devout Catholics who accept evolution. Although I am personally unable to see any way that religious faith can be compatible with evolution, or even science overall (see chapter 5), I do support religious authorities like Pope Francis accepting evolution as reality, creating the potential for millions of young children from Catholic families to be exposed and receptive to it. Sometimes, setting the stage for a conversation is just as important as, if not more than, the conversation itself. In this spirit, I see any potential path to enlightenment in the Muslim world comprising four incremental steps:

1. Rejection of scriptural inerrancy
2. Reformation
3. Secularism
4. Enlightenment

Most of the world's non-Muslim countries are at Step 3: they are secular states where religion and state are separate. In contrast, few Muslim-majority countries have even gotten to Step 1. Can they?

Rejection of scriptural inerrancy entails looking at the Quran not as the word of God, but as the word of man, even if it's divinely inspired. It also means seeing Muhammad not as an infallible figure to be emulated for all time, but as a historical figure who can be seen critically in the context of his time, like Jefferson or Churchill—respected and revered widely for the good he did in the time he lived, while honestly acknowledging flaws in many of his views and actions that are not applicable in the modern world.

If you find this to be an incredulous proposal, you're not alone. In her book *Heretic: Why Islam Needs a Reformation Now,* Ayaan Hirsi Ali outlined five tenets of the faith that must be reformed, the first of which was exactly this: the rejection of "Muhammad's semi-divine and infallible status along with the literalist reading of the Qur'an, particularly those parts that were revealed in Medina."[15] This left many Muslim commentators shaking their heads. Reviewing the book for *Religion Dispatches,* Muslim columnist Haroon Moghul lamented, "Hirsi Ali must know that no Muslim would accept these conditions."[16]

Moghul isn't completely wrong, at least in the short term. Reading Hirsi Ali's book, or this one, isn't going to set believing Muslims running to reject what they have been taught is a fundamental tenet of their faith. As I mentioned earlier, large majorities of Jews and Christians also believed their holy books to be the perfect word of God for centuries, and might also have gasped like Moghul when someone suggested otherwise. But these things do change, and indeed have changed, gradually, over generations.

I have been asked countless times by my peers why I do what I do. "Who are you trying to convert? You're not going to change people's minds by attacking their beliefs." First of all, this isn't true, and almost anyone who does this kind of work will tell you that. But for now, let's set that aside and bring out another smoking analogy: *my goal isn't to get smokers to quit, but rather, to help prevent young people from picking up the habit in the first place.* I have actually had members of my extended family criticize my work and passionately debate me late into the night, only to wake up the next morning to an e-mail from their adolescent son, saying, "Uncle Ali, I agree with your ideas and so do my friends. Please keep doing what you do and don't tell my parents I sent you this." This has happened many times—and my fellow secularists from the Muslim world will tell you similar stories. Apart from family, I also hear every day from young people across the world who are part of Muslim families they simply can't speak to openly about this one topic. As the world becomes more interconnected, children from Muslim families around the globe are becoming increasingly exposed to a plethora of new ideas at the tap of their fingers that their parents never had access to growing up. And when you do impart your ideas, they really want you to make the case. They want reasons. They want to be convinced that they're being told the truth. Blind belief and dogma just don't have the sway they once did, and the archaic precepts of Abrahamic scriptures, even in their most liberal interpretation, simply aren't resonating in the Information Age like they did in generations past.[17] So, while Moghul may be correct in assuming that few adult Muslims today will be willing to give up the beliefs they have been indoctrinated with since childhood, I would wager that he might be surprised at how this plays out over the next generation or two, as it has happened before. And we're very close to it: calls to reject literalism typically precede calls to reject inerrancy, the natural next step, because both are essentially founded on the same insight: that these passages, read as they're actually written, are problematic.

With this, the path to reformation becomes much clearer. Rejecting precepts like infallibility is an indispensable prerequisite for any kind of meaningful progress to even begin. Without this, innovation—which lies at the heart of reform—becomes blasphemy. And innovation itself cannot happen without open exploration of ideas, dialogue, or challenging the status quo.

For the most part, it is the Muslims who live in secular societies that appear most open to modernization and reform. For example, Turkey, perhaps the most secular Muslim-majority country in the world, has held an annual gay pride parade in Istanbul, its largest city, for over a decade. In this country that lies at the crossroads between Europe and the Middle East, alcohol isn't taboo, nightlife is vibrant, and men and women intermingle as they do in any other European country. It's true that under the presidency of Tayyip Erdoğan, there has been justified concern about resurgent Islamization in Turkey; the last few years have seen attempts at restricting access to alcohol, and police attacked participants of the 2015 LGBT pride parade with pepper spray and water cannons because it took place during the holy month of Ramadan.[18] Despite these regressions, however, Turkey towers above its peers as a Muslim success story.

Muslims also display more moderation and openness as minorities in pluralistic, democratic societies. This is certainly true for Muslims in the United States and Canada, as I discussed in chapter 4. And it is also the case at a much larger scale in India, which hosts the second-largest

Muslim population in the world (third, by some accounts), albeit one that makes up less than 15 percent of its total population. It is notable that Indian Muslims, numbering over 170 million, are relatively moderate compared to their co-religionists in Muslim-majority countries. There are several factors that account for this, such as the oft-cited contrast between Sufi mystic influences on Muslims in India versus Sunni Arab influences in Pakistan; but the real reason is much more obvious. Indian Muslims are the product of, and participants in, a democratic, pluralistic society where they are less prone to intimidation by fundamentalists and more likely to challenge them. They also make up a large enough minority to play a significant role in India's political system. While not perfect by any means, it is this kind of secular, pluralistic society where religious moderation can thrive.

Islam today, however, needs more than just moderates. It needs reformers. It should come as no surprise that it is from within non-Muslim secular societies that we are hearing more and more reformist voices standing up to the dogmatism of fundamentalists and apologism of moderates alike. They include ex-radicals like Maajid Nawaz, who runs the Quilliam Foundation, an increasingly influential counterextremist U.K. think tank; Raheel Raza and former *Wall Street Journal* columnist Asra Nomani of the Muslim Reform Movement, pushing for "peace, human rights, and secular governance";[19] Raquel Saraswati, who was featured alongside Raheel Raza in the documentary *Honor Diaries*, highlighting violence against women in the Muslim world; Irshad Manji, the Canadian LGBT Muslim author of *The Trouble with Islam: A Muslim's Call for Reform in Her Faith*; and, more recently, the vocally secular new mayor of London, Sadiq Khan, the first mayor of a major Western capital to come from a Muslim background. All of them identify as believing Muslims, and some have openly questioned the inerrancy and supremacy of the Quran. All have generated great controversy around their ideas, yet are steadily gaining popularity among a younger generation of Muslims looking for more options and role models than what they see on TV and in their local mosque. All are galvanizing a younger generation of Muslims seeking a group identity that reflects the modern values and ideals of their lives in the twenty-first century.

What is a "moderate Muslim"? This is also a broad, loaded term. Strictly, religious moderates believe or practice their religion selectively or with less intensity than fundamentalists. In practice, moderates are the vast majority of Muslims around the world, excluding Islamists (who want to impose Islam on society) or jihadists (who are willing to use violence to achieve this). Moderates may be liberal or progressive, but most, especially in Muslim-majority countries, tend to be socially conservative. While many may not support the political tactics of Islamists, they might still see eye-to-eye with them on a range of issues, such as the status of women in society or capital punishment for apostates.[20] And a majority of moderate Muslims—including liberal and progressive Muslims in the United States, as we saw earlier—believe in the inerrancy of scripture and the infallibility of Muhammad.

Reformers, on the other hand, differ in that they acknowledge the problematic aspects of Islamic scripture, and desire either to reinterpret it in a way that is commensurate with modernity and secularism, or to find an altogether different element within Islam or the Muslim world to help unify Muslims and drive them forward toward progress.

Perhaps the earliest and most well known faction of reformist Muslims is the Mutazilites, who came to prominence in eighth-century Iraq. The group found its origin amid a successorship dispute following the death of Uthman, the third caliph of Sunni Islam. Like the earlier dispute after Muhammad's death, this one was also over Ali, Muhammad's cousin and son-in-law. Some wanted Ali to become the fourth caliph (which he ultimately did), and others didn't. The Mutazilites maintained a neutral position, consequently earning the label *mu'tazila*, which means "those who withdraw."

Mutazilites are thought to be the earliest of the relatively few Muslim groups who rejected the idea that the Quran is God's word. For them, this assessment wasn't based on the content of the Quran—that was irrelevant. Rather, they thought it to be a logical extension of their foundational principle of *tawhid*, or unification, which establishes the absolute oneness of an eternal and therefore *uncreated* God. The conventional wisdom at the time was this: If God is uncreated and eternal, God's word is uncreated and eternal. And if the Quran is God's word, the Quran would have to be uncreated and eternal as well. The Mutazilites disputed this. They didn't believe that the revelations of the Quran had always existed.

In his book *Heaven on Earth: A Journey Through Shari'a Law from the Deserts of Ancient Arabia to the Streets of the Modern Muslim World*, Sadakat Kadri explains why. While traditionalists of the time believed the Quran had eternally existed, Mutazalites claimed this was impossible, because logically, God had to have preceded his own speech. This dispute might sound like a strange thing to fuss over now, but it had profound implications at the time. If God really had created the Quran, as the Mutazalites said, he must have created it at (and for) a certain time and place, and its message was therefore susceptible to change. This, writes Kadri, was "a conclusion that alarmed conservatives and excited reformists as much in the ninth century as it does in the twenty-first."[21]

While still rooted in Islam, Mutazilites favored using reason, logic, and rationality over scriptural ordinance (especially when the two were in conflict), and also consulted thought systems outside of Islam, like Greek philosophy, to formulate their worldview. Although they gradually faded from prominence around the tenth century, the Mutazilites significantly influenced some sects in Islam, notably the Shias.

Today, there are a handful of Islamic sects that can be considered reformist. Unfortunately for the rest of us, their beliefs and practices are so removed from mainstream Sunni Islam that they often find themselves having to choose between persecution and secrecy. Here, I will take the opportunity to discuss two of them.

Ahmadi Muslims, who are adherents of the *Ahmadiyya* movement, are one such group. Ahmadis have roots in the Indian subcontinent and have essentially made religious moderation the cornerstone of their faith—a characterization they may dispute, insisting there is no such thing as "moderate," because Islam itself is moderate. Agree with that or not, many welcome their approach, considering some of the alternatives we see today.

The Ahmadiyya movement was founded in the nineteenth century by Mirza Ghulam Ahmad, believed by his followers to be a divinely appointed messiah sent down to bring *tajdid*, which means renewal or reform, to Islam. Ahmad established this by claiming to be the *Mahdi*—the prophesized messiah in Islam—but with the spirit of Jesus. In the Ahmadiyya faith, Jesus is believed to have survived his crucifixion and lived on until he died an old man, making his resurrection more of a metaphorical phenomenon, in the form of Ahmad, than a physical one. Ahmad retained the belief that the Quran was perfect and inerrant, but used a very broad, liberal approach to interpret it to be consistent with his vision for Islamic revival: the reframing of jihad as a personal struggle for betterment rather than holy war; rejection of violence and bloodshed; and promotion of Islam as a religion of peace, allowing violence only as a last resort in response to extreme persecution.

Today, Ahmadi Muslims are among the most persecuted religious communities in the world. This is primarily because of Ahmad's claim of being a messiah and prophet who regularly received revelations directly from God. He did not claim to preach a separate religion, but rather a revival of what he believed to be Islam the way it was originally meant to be. He still maintained that the Quran was God's final revelation and did not consider his status to be independent of Muhammad's prophethood—but he did claim to be a prophet nonetheless. To many mainstream Muslims, this is a particularly egregious form of blasphemy that they consider to be deserving of death. They consider Ahmadis to be a heretical group that should not be called Muslims. In Pakistan, where every citizen's religion is displayed on his or her national identity card or passport, application forms for both require all Muslim applicants to sign a statement saying, "I consider Mirza Ghulam Ahmad an impostor prophet. And also consider his followers, whether belonging to the Lahori or Qadiani group [subdivisions within the Ahmadiyya movement], to be non-Muslims."[22]

Interestingly, Mirza Ghulam Ahmad once made the same kind of statement about those who didn't accept *his* divine status. In the book *Tadhkirah*, a collection of Ahmad's dreams and revelations, he is quoted as saying, "God has revealed to me that every single person who has heard my claim, and has not accepted me, that person is not a Muslim, and is subject to prosecution in front of God."[23]

To learn more about this quote, which labels anyone who rejects

Ahmad's claim to prophethood as a non-Muslim, I reached out to attorney and columnist Qasim Rashid, a strong advocate for the American Ahmadiyya community and author of a moving book, *The Wrong Kind of Muslim*, which chronicles the persecution that Ahmadi Muslims face around the world. I started by asking him whether Ahmadi Muslims believe this revelation to be correct. The conversation that followed reiterated for me how incompatible meaningful reform is with concepts like inerrancy and infallibility.

"Yes," replied Rashid. "Ahmadi Muslims believe Hazrat Ahmad that God conveyed that revelation to him." (*Hazrat* is an honorific title.) He said that Ahmad was not responsible for that quote, because he was merely channeling God's word. "It is God who makes that revelation, so whatever it says, it is God saying it," he told me. "Indeed, it would be strange if God did *not* say such a thing about His chosen prophet. Ahmadi Muslims aren't saying this, Ahmad himself isn't saying this, but instead it is God saying it. Therefore, whatever the content, it cannot be assigned as the opinion of Ahmad as he never said it of his opinion or his will . . . It was a revelation from God, and Ahmad conveyed it as that revelation from God."[24]

As the reader will appreciate, Rashid made his argument in clear, definitive words. And while it may have seemed perfectly cogent to a committed believer, it sounded very convoluted to me. Many months after this conversation, Rashid and I discussed the same topic again. This time, he told me to stop citing the quote—he was now convinced that it had been fabricated. "Mirza Ghulam Ahmad categorically rejects it as fraudulent . . . Mirza Ghulam Ahmad never said it," he wrote. "The error is in our part in not providing the full story in one place in *Tadhkirah*, thus leading to your confusion. Apologies for that and the newer translations of *Tadhkirah* explain this clerical lapse and has [sic] rectified it."

Indeed, the latest English translation of *Tadhkirah* no longer has the quote.[25] However, the Urdu version—available on the official website of the American Ahmadiyya community as of this writing—still has it. Remember, this is the same quote about which Rashid had reassuringly told me a few months earlier that it would be "strange if God did *not* say such a thing about His chosen prophet."

Whether the quote is really fabricated or just being quietly erased from the books because it harms the current Ahmadiyya narrative is not of much interest to me. Here's what is: as I've alluded to a few times already, this is the consequence of believing in scriptural inerrancy and the argument from authority: you consider the source of the information, determine that the information must be error-free because the source is error-free, and then defend it by any means necessary. And if it turns out the source was wrongly identified, your argument completely changes into its antithesis. It's not about the merit of the idea, but the authority of the one who articulates it.

To an atheist, this back-and-forth between mainstream Muslims and Ahmadi Muslims would never be an issue if its consequences weren't so deadly. In effect, it is similar to two groups fighting about whether the green or the blue unicorn is the right one. To me, it's clear that the amount of actual evidence supporting Muhammad's claim to prophethood is exactly the same as that supporting Ahmad's: none whatsoever. Yet the violence continues, with the Ahmadis disproportionately at the receiving end of it, for two reasons. First, they are a minority, and minorities generally don't fare well in Muslim-majority countries, especially those considered heretical. Second, they have successfully used the kind of argumentation displayed above to make the case that Islam and the Quran reject jihad and violence—no easy feat—and are therefore less prone to fighting. As a community, few minority sects are more laudable: Ahmadi Muslims speak of and practice an Islam that is peaceful, tolerant, and pro-secular. Whether they'll be able to find more compelling theological grounds to make their case remains to be seen.

The Nizari Ismailis, in contrast, are possibly the most interesting example of what Islam could look like if modernized. As I mentioned in chapter 5, their spiritual leader, Prince Karim Aga Khan, is a Swiss-born British national who lives in Paris, France. He is believed to be a documented descendant of the Prophet Muhammad, and is considered infallible by millions of Ismaili Shia Muslims scattered across South and Central Asia, Africa, Europe, and North America. He is pro-secular, pro-West, and socially liberal. His stepmother was actress Rita Hayworth, and his eldest son, Rahim, is married to American supermodel Kendra

Spears. He became the forty-ninth Imam of the Nizari Ismailis as a junior at Harvard, after the death of his grandfather.

The Ismailis are an offshoot of Shiaism. Mainstream Shias are sometimes called "Twelvers" (*Ithnasheri* in Arabic) because of their belief in twelve Imams, patrilineally descended from Ali ibn Abi Talib and Muhammad's daughter, Fatima. For them, the lineage stops at the twelfth Imam, Mahdi, who is believed to have gone into hiding until a time close to the Day of Judgment, when he is due to return and bring widespread justice to humanity. I was raised in a Twelver Shia family.

The Ismailis, however, split from the Twelvers long ago in a dispute—yet again—over successorship. Jafar As-Sadiq, considered the sixth Imam by the Twelvers, and the fifth by Nizari Ismailis,[26] had two sons, Ismail and Musa Kazim. Twelvers went with Musa Kazim as their seventh Imam, and the Ismailis went with his elder brother, Ismail, as their sixth. For this reason, Ismailis are sometimes called "Sixers."

Both Ithnasheri and Ismaili Shias believe that all of their Imams, as descendants of Muhammad and members of the Ahl Al-Bayt ("people of the house"; see chapter 2), are divinely appointed and infallible, infused with the spirit of Allah himself. For the Ithnasheris, who haven't had an Imam since their last one went into hiding in the ninth century, there is still heavy reliance on Quranic scripture and the millennium-old documented guidance of their twelve Imams.

This is not the case for Nizari Ismailis. They have a living Imam—right here on Earth, with the same infallible stature as Ali ibn Abi Talib—who is a Parisian multimillionaire Harvard graduate with British citizenship, avidly enjoys thoroughbred horse racing, is a generous philanthropist, and whose son, the possible future Imam-in-waiting for twelve million Ismaili Muslims, is married to an American supermodel.

How does it work when you have a living, breathing, and divine representative of God on Earth? Do you consult a 1300-year-old holy book when you can go right to the source? To be sure, no Nizari Ismaili will tell you that the Quran is not revered in his or her faith; they will insist that there is no contradiction between the teachings of the Aga Khan and the holy text. However, to the objective observer, it's inevitable in this situation that the Quran becomes a secondary source, a historical reference book at most. Indeed, the Aga Khan's modern, progressive views and rulings have resulted in the Nizari Ismaili community becoming arguably the most well-integrated, secular, apolitical, nonviolent, and generally pro-West Muslim community in the world.

It's no wonder that we don't hear much about Nizari Ismailis in our mainstream discourse, and they like it that way. They are discouraged from speaking about their faith, or proselytizing, for reasons of security—they don't want to end up like Ahmadis and other minorities who are mercilessly persecuted in countries like Pakistan and Saudi Arabia for bringing innovations and reform to what the mainstream largely considers an immutable faith.

As some readers might have picked up, all of this can also easily backfire. I am repeatedly specifying that these are "Nizari" Ismailis, because the split after Jafar As-Sadiq's death wasn't the only one. Later splits resulted in another group of Ismailis, the *Mustaali* Ismailis, the largest group of which is the Dawoodi Bohras. The Bohras are worlds apart from Nizari Ismailis in their religious conservatism. As an article of faith, the men keep beards, the women wear burka-like dresses, and female genital mutilation is widely practiced. This contrast between Nizari and Mustaali Ismailis (particularly the Bohras) demonstrates that when reform is contingent upon one individual with godlike authority, things can really go either way. To have any kind of meaningful reform give way to enduring secular values will require much more than that, and this won't come without its obstacles.

Historically, the Muslim world has had a difficult relationship with secularism. And for a host of reasons, encouraging Western-style secularism in Muslim-majority countries comes with a great set of challenges.

For millions of Muslims, secularism doesn't necessarily connote the kind of individual freedom and liberty that it does in the West. Many associate secularism with negative, even humiliating aspects of their past. Set aside the centuries of Western imperialism and colonialism that chewed away at their indigenous identities; even when it has come from within, secularism has too often impinged on the individual rights of Muslim people rather than bolstering them. Mustafa Kemal Atatürk's enforced secularization of Turkey, for example, effectively killed off any remnants of the Ottoman Empire, the last great Islamic caliphate. He dismantled the Sharia, replacing it with an antitheocratic legal system. He banned the wearing of veils and turbans. He strictly regulated what could be preached in mosques and other religious institutions. He introduced a Turkish version of the *adhaan*, the Muslim call to prayer. He even did away with the Arabic script that had been used to write the Turkish language for over a thousand years, replacing it with the Latin alphabet. Though a hero to many, others saw him as an enemy of Islam for his enforced reforms.

Then there are the secular dictatorships that millions of Muslims have lived under for decades. For many of them, secularism isn't associated as much with liberal democracy as it is with dictators keeping religion down and at a distance, believing that a religious uprising would be an existential threat to them. Leaders like Gaddafi, Saddam Hussein, Bashar al-Assad, and Hosni Mubarak have all played this game: you could grow your beard and praise Allah—that helped them—but if that beard got a little too long and your voice a little too loud, they'd whisk you away in the middle of the night. In these scenarios, religious uprisings have sometimes come in the form of democratic *resistance* to secular dictatorial rule, whether it's the Iranian Revolution of 1979, the election of Mohammad Morsi and the Muslim Brotherhood to power after the fall of Mubarak in Egypt, or the resistance to Assad in Syria today. The Iranian Revolution that made Iran the theocracy it is today was a response to the U.S.-backed dictatorial rule of the Shah, who was never forgiven by Iranians for working with the CIA and the British to overthrow their democratically elected prime minister, Mohammad Mosaddegh, in 1953. This was a catastrophic event that has repercussions to this day. Iranians and other Muslims often see this coup as proof that for all of its rhetoric about freedom and democracy, the United States isn't really any different behind the scenes from the dictators it has installed and supported for its own interests in Muslim-majority countries. Even today, when you express skepticism about any of a number of outlandish anti-American conspiracy theories pervasive in the Muslim world, there will always be someone that says, "Did you forget Mosaddegh?"

This is a problem. *Secularism*, *liberalism*, and *democracy* are loaded words for many in these societies. Far from guaranteeing their religious freedom, secularism is often perceived—wrongly—as an attack on it. How to get over that hump? Is there an in-between area where elements of nominal religiosity can be incorporated into a functionally secular system that these countries can call their own? Or must it necessarily exist as the hard separation of religion and state that it is in the West?

What will it take for Muslim-majority societies to warm up to secularism? Will they eventually learn to tolerate the taboos of apostasy and blasphemy? What has changed since the days of the Salman Rushdie affair? What factors have been responsible for this change? How can we engage in critical dialogue if we're unable to create an environment for the dialogue to happen in the first place? Can mainstream Muslims—like mainstream Jews and Christians—form a community based on shared experience instead of shared ideology?

This isn't about what *kind* of conversation needs to take place within Muslim communities. It's about *facilitating an environment* where these conversations can happen in the first place.

Secularism is the only system that allows such an environment to flourish. Secularism is not antireligion; it is simply the separation of religion from the affairs of the state. It allows both freedom of and freedom from religion. It not only allows citizens to practice their religion freely, but also protects the freedom of others to challenge it. Secularism isn't the opposite of theocracy, but rather the middle road between theocracy and antireligious discrimination. While theocracy favors the power of one religion over all others, secularism allows a plurality of religious belief and practice, where people of all faiths and no faith can coexist and engage in dialogue without fear of censorship or retribution.

NINE

Letting Go (Part II): The Silver Lining

A few years ago, I got a message from an old friend I'd known from Riyadh. Her father had recently died, as had mine years ago. She wrote, "He's dead and in the ground. I take great comfort in thinking that he's in a good place. Do we just become fertilizer, end of story? I am not questioning your beliefs and the why or where of it. I'm just asking what you think is the next step. If you think it's fertilizer, please lie to make it more interesting."

For all the talk of rationality, intellectual honesty, and objectivity we engage in as atheists, this is one of the most uncomfortable questions we have to wrestle with. What can we offer as a substitute for the emotional comfort religion offers believers in facing their own death, or that of their loved ones? What should we say to our believing family and friends when they are acutely grieving these losses? How do we address our irrational human needs using rational means?

Reading my friend's note, I was reminded of the 2009 Ricky Gervais comedy *The Invention of Lying*. The movie is about a world where no one has the ability to lie, until one day when Gervais's character, Mark, suddenly develops it. He is at his mother's bedside as she is dying. "I'm so scared," she tells him, through tears. "This is it, Mark. A few more hours like this, and then an eternity of nothingness."

And this is when he tells the very first lie ever told by anyone in that fictional parallel universe.

"Mum . . . you're wrong about what happens after you die," he says. He tells her she will go to a wonderful place, be reunited with everyone she loves who died before her, and be young again. She begins to smile. He continues. There will be no pain, he says, and there will be only love and happiness, for all eternity.

How does one substitute for that?

My friend's note jolted me. Not because I didn't have a response. I did. I just wasn't sure how to articulate it in a way that was both honest and emotionally supportive, her loss being so recent. It also forced me to revisit the death of my own father, with whom I had a very close relationship.

Processing a horrific experience like the loss of a loved one using rationality and logic does help during those times when you're trying to make sense of things, but not as much when you're feeling helpless and emotionally vulnerable. And everyone who has been through it knows that we experience both. Most people can understand how believing in a personal god can help here.

But what do believers do with this god? Do they rage at him for taking their parent, spouse, or child away from them, often cruelly? Or do they surrender to their helplessness, thanking him for putting their loved ones "in a better place" and begging him to reunite them one day?

I wrote back to her the same day, but revisited what I wrote many times in the next few months, adding to it. Here is what I would write to her today.

Hi, Amber.

Thank you for your message. I am so sorry for your loss.

My father died over a decade ago, and the question you asked ran through my mind then as well. After struggling for a while with trying to make sense of it all, I eventually decided to approach it by separating my thoughts into two categories: what I know, and what I don't know.

I know that we're alive through our offspring. You are physically an embodiment of your father's biological and genetic essence. This includes everything from how you look to many of the behavioral and personality traits you have. In other words—and this is not an exaggeration—your father is literally alive through you, as mine is through me. For me, knowing that is incredibly powerful and comforting.

I know that we continue to exist through the Earth. This is my attempt at being euphemistic about your fertilizer theory. As part of this huge reservoir of terrestrial carbon, we die and become part of the Earth, which gives rise to new life, as it once gave rise to us. That is also very powerful to me, in a more collective, worldly sense.

I also know that I've only been conscious for some forty years out of the 13.8 billion years that the universe has been in existence. Everything from plankton, to dinosaurs, to the formation of the U.N., to the moon landing happened before I was even remotely self-aware. I don't miss those things, nor do I recall that huge chunk of time as horrible or upsetting. I simply can't recall it at all—because I didn't exist.

Not knowing anything else, I work on the assumption that after death, we simply go back into the prebirth phase. I don't feel like that would bother me any more than it did during those first 13.8 billion years. This is actually a really comforting, peaceful idea when you give it some thought. Especially because it makes me value this little sliver of time I have of a few decades as a conscious, living being a lot more than if I thought it was just transit time to someplace else. It also helps me not take my life, or the lives of others, for granted.

There are other things I know, but I don't know what they mean.

I know that according to the law of conservation of energy, energy can neither be created nor destroyed, but can be changed from one form to another, or be transferred from one object to another. I know that the subatomic particles that constitute you, me, and all of the matter we see around us can exist outside of the realm of time, travel through extra dimensions, and even temporarily violate conservation of energy by literally popping in and out of existence. I know there is a possibility that we're part of a multiverse and may exist in several universes simultaneously. I know that even nothing is still something.

All of those things are true. But I don't want to make any inferences from them à la Deepak Chopra, because I am not completely sure what they mean. I'm cautious about making connections between these ideas and the experience of human existence, or the process of human death. I am not a physicist, and I am skeptical of those who do make these connections as if they were facts. But this is still more compelling and awe-inspiring to me than the notion of angels, or rivers of wine, or the pearly gates, or eternal torment in hellfire. There is so much we don't know, and that should be humbling.

Here, read this passage from Aaron Freeman about why you'd want a physicist to speak at your funeral:

> You want a physicist to speak at your funeral. You want the physicist to talk to your grieving family about the conservation of energy, so they will understand that your energy has not died. You want the physicist to remind your sobbing mother about the first law of thermodynamics; that no energy gets created in the universe, and none is destroyed. You want your mother to know that all your energy, every vibration, every Btu of heat, every wave of every particle that was her beloved child remains with her in this world. You want the physicist to tell your weeping father that amid energies of the cosmos, you gave as good as you got.
>
> And at one point you'd hope that the physicist would step down from the pulpit and walk to your broken-hearted spouse there in the pew and tell him that all the photons that ever bounced off your face, all the particles whose paths were interrupted by your smile, by the touch of your hair, hundreds of trillions of particles, have raced off like children, their ways forever

changed by you. And as your widow rocks in the arms of a loving family, may the physicist let her know that all the photons that bounced from you were gathered in the particle detectors that are her eyes, that those photons created within her constellations of electromagnetically charged neurons whose energy will go on forever.

And the physicist will remind the congregation of how much of all our energy is given off as heat. There may be a few fanning themselves with their programs as he says it. And he will tell them that the warmth that flowed through you in life is still here, still part of all that we are, even as we who mourn continue the heat of our own lives.

And you'll want the physicist to explain to those who loved you that they need not have faith; indeed, they should not have faith. Let them know that they can measure, that scientists have measured precisely the conservation of energy and found it accurate, verifiable and consistent across space and time. You can hope your family will examine the evidence and satisfy themselves that the science is sound and that they'll be comforted to know your energy's still around. According to the law of the conservation of energy, not a bit of you is gone; you're just less orderly. Amen.[1]

I don't take this to mean more than it does. But again, it reminds us of the mystery and wonder of the universe we're in, and how lucky we are to have this short life, this tiny opportunity, to learn as much as we can about it.

It's often said that religion was created by humans as a means to cope with their own mortality—a powerful defense mechanism that arose from an irresolvable conflict almost unique to humans: having the same instinct of self-preservation that insects have when they run for their lives sensing they are about to be stomped upon, yet simultaneously harboring a central nervous system advanced enough to comprehend the reality that we will all die one day. This is not an

easy conundrum to grapple with, and I can understand why
the faithful exist, even if I don't understand the faith. But I
made the personal choice to ask real questions instead of taking comfort in false answers.

You asked me what I think is the next step.

Well, no one has reported back from the other side, none
of us who are alive have been to the other side, and we don't
have any factual evidence supporting a life (as we know it) after
we die. To me, believing what I want to be true can be very
comforting—but that doesn't make it true. And I find more
comfort in what I know to be true. For the things I don't
know, I prefer saying just that—*I don't know*—instead of entertaining supernatural guesses or made-up answers from
a time when humans didn't know anything about the carbon cycle that keeps life moving, or the structure of the
DNA molecules that your father passed on to you, his living, breathing daughter.

You said that if I didn't have the answers, I should "lie to
make it more interesting." But I have always found things
most interesting when I didn't have to lie. That is why I am
an atheist.

Admitting ignorance is humbling. It reminds us that as
fleeting inhabitants of this vast universe, we are part of something much bigger. It forms a foundation for the curiosity
that defines us as human beings, that drives us to contem-
plate our existence, educate ourselves, and to grow and evolve
as individuals and as a species.

To lose that is a much worse death than physical death.

I wish you the strength and resolve to cope with your loss.
Mourn his death, but also celebrate the life that he helped
give you. That's what he would have wanted.

In solidarity,
Ali

Along with the physical and emotional costs of giving up religion that
we explored in chapter 3—becoming estranged from one's family, ostra-
cized from the community, and even being persecuted by the state—
Muslims who leave their religion often have to rethink a range of big

questions. These questions have easy answers when we believe. But once we're on our own, we have to ask them all over again; and the answers aren't as easy. We have to become comfortable with not knowing everything. We have to learn to value truth over comfort—and comfort is what religion is so good at giving us, at least temporarily, until we can learn to derive comfort from the truth. The way we deal with the difficult human challenges of morality and grief has to be rethought, and can be really trying, but—as difficult as it is to imagine for believers—is ultimately much more fulfilling and satisfying than the superficial comfort that age-old supernatural beliefs can ever provide.

I was about twelve when I met my first real-life atheist. He was the new kid in school and sat next to me in class, so we quickly became friends. His family had moved to Riyadh from Sweden for his father's work. One day, as we were learning about the different religions of the world in class, I asked him what religion he was.

"I don't know," he said.

"You don't know?" I asked. "How could you not know what religion you are?"

"I don't think I have a religion."

"What about your parents? What do they believe?"

"I don't know. We've never talked about it."

"Are you guys Christian?"

He laughed. "Oh, no, definitely not."

"Do your mom and dad believe in God?"

"I don't think so."

"What about you? Do you believe in God?"

"No. No God, no religion."

I remember being shocked. Not just because he didn't know what religion he was, or if he even had a religion, but because he was responding like he'd never even *thought* about it. I could tell that no one had ever asked him these questions before. It was as if they were irrelevant.

If we'd been a little older, I might have asked him where he thought we all came from, or whether he'd ever wondered who created the universe. But at that point, there was one thing I was more curious about than anything else.

"So does that mean you can do anything?" I asked.

"What do you mean?"

"Like, steal, kill people, bad stuff like that?"

"No."

"Why? You don't believe in God."

I remember him being confused by my line of questioning. And I was just as confused that he didn't understand what I was getting at.

"Well, we don't do bad things because it's illegal. And you shouldn't do bad things."

"What do your parents tell you so you wouldn't do bad things?" I asked.

"They say, 'How would you like it if someone did it to you?'"

I thought about our conversation a lot, for many years afterward. I started noticing my own actions very consciously, as if I'd stepped out of my body and was watching myself. Years later, in Pakistan, my friends and I were walking back from a pizza place after having dinner. We'd all eaten way too much, and had the leftovers packed to take home. On the way, we came across a homeless beggar sitting at the side of the street. He was gaunt and haggard, barely able to speak. Without thinking twice, we all gave our leftovers to him. It wasn't a difficult decision—it was almost automatic.

I would later wonder why I had done this. No one had really told us to behave this way in this particular situation. The man was grateful, which made us feel nice, but that isn't why we gave him our food. And we certainly didn't do it thinking it would get us any reward from God, or that we'd get punished in the afterlife if we didn't do it. It was the furthest thing from our minds. Yet we did it, because *we know what it would feel like if we were in that man's position*. We knew what it felt like to be hungry, and could imagine how horrible he must have felt to be in the shape he was in. We did it because we could *empathize* with him.

I grew up thinking religion is the reason we are morally good. Without religion, without a god watching over us, what incentive would we have to be good people? But even the most devoutly religious people, I learned, ultimately did good things because they felt empathy for their fellow human beings and other living creatures—not to gain favor with

God. And in fact, recalling the second part of Hitchens's challenge (see chapter 6), it almost seemed like it was the other way around: when people traded in their firsthand conscience for a secondhand set of dos and don'ts from an ancient book—when they thought in terms of what's pious and sinful instead of what's right and wrong—it was a *corruption* of their morality, not a manifestation of it. Just as religion can lead its devotees to suspend reason for faith, it can also lead them to suspend morality for piety. Indeed, a growing body of evidence today suggests that morality might be innate in humans, and unrelated to religion.[2] And the Golden Rule—do unto others as you would have them do unto you— predates almost all of today's religions.

Questions of mortality, morality, and spirituality often loom heavy on the minds of those who leave their faith. These aren't easy questions, and we know too much about the world and the universe today to assume they have easy answers. They don't. But life isn't about answers. The most valuable insight I've gained from simply being alive is that the quest to know more never ends. For every answer you arrive at, a multitude of new questions arise. And so you move on, you move forward. This is how you grow, it's how you evolve.

What is the meaning of life? Well, it's a uniquely human thing to want to find meaning in things on that grand a scale. Evolutionarily, our advanced nervous systems have given us the gift of long-term memory, unparalleled by almost any other species.[3] This enhances our self-awareness, and affords us the capability to set long-term goals—which naturally nudges us to search for purpose and meaning. In essence, the meaning of life is whatever we want it to be. We decide what we want our lives to mean, and we create that purpose. For me, that purpose is to know as much as I can about the world and the universe during the short time that I'm here. More than anything, I'm driven by my instinct to explore and my quest for knowledge.

I once read an interview with the late, great, heavy metal singer Ronnie James Dio that stayed with me. He was asked about how he approaches his life. They say there's a pot of gold at the end of every rainbow, he said.

And we're all walking on that rainbow to get to that pot of gold. To be sure, we're never going to reach it. But look at what we're doing—*we're walking on the rainbow*. What could be more amazing than that?

Today, we know, thanks to science, that every rainbow is a circle. It never ends. And that's okay with me. I don't want it to.

Acknowledgments

When you've grown up in societies in which free thought is a risk and free speech a crime, you learn never to take these freedoms for granted. And parents in these societies who want to instill these values in their children have a harder job than most. I am grateful first and foremost to my mother, who taught me how to think, question, and imagine; my late father, who always taught me to see the other side; and my sister and brothers, for teaching me that love transcends all disagreements, however stark.

I want to thank my teachers at the American International School in Riyadh for imparting to me—to borrow from Mark Twain—not only schooling, but an education. I especially want to acknowledge Mr. Puffer, who taught me the importance of thoroughly understanding the rules before breaking them. I'm also greatly indebted to my cousin, Kamran Bhai, for introducing me to Bertrand Russell at a young age, and demonstrating by example that the only kind of diversity that really matters is the diversity of ideas.

I am grateful to Ibrahim Abdallah, Faisal Saeed Al-Mutar, Saraswati Apsara, Jerry Coyne, Anwar Khokhar, Soraya Mehdi, Eiynah Nicemangos, Caleb Powell, Simi Rahman, Faisal Rajan, Hussain Rizvi, and

Michael Spitz for their extremely useful notes and feedback on the proposal and/or manuscript. I'm also thankful to Kashif Ali, Raif Badawi, Wissam Charafeddine, Melissa Chen, Richard Dawkins, Marc Genesee, Kyle Grounds, Stephanie Renée Guttormson, Ensaf Haidar, Sam Harris, Seemi Jamil, Aly Lakhani, Armin Navabi Maajid Nawaz, Asra Nomani, Joe Rogan, Dave Rubin, and Kunwar Khuldune Shahid for their invaluable support and inspiration. To the folks at *Huffington Post*—thank you for giving my thoughts an outlet. To the Center for Inquiry, Richard Dawkins Foundation for Reason and Science, Movements.org, Quilliam Foundation, Council of Ex-Muslims of Britain, and Muslimish—thank you for your unparalleled work helping to give dissidents and reformers of the Muslim world a voice and platform. To the countless liberals and freethinkers who have corresponded with me over the years from Saudi Arabia, Pakistan, Egypt, Malaysia, Iran, Bangladesh, and more—this book is for you. To those who have been imprisoned, flogged, persecuted, and killed for speaking your mind—this book is for you. You are heroes.

I am deeply grateful to my agent, Don Fehr, for his help, support, and encouragement at every stage in this project's development. And without the dedicated guidance and enthusiasm of my editor, Karen Wolny, this book wouldn't be in the form it is today. Thanks also to Alan Bradshaw, Bill Warhop, Laura Apperson, and the rest of the St. Martin's team for helping bring this book to life.

My greatest debt of gratitude in both work and life remains to my wife and partner-in-crime, Alishba. Her indispensable insights and contributions helped make this book so much more than it would otherwise be. I am enormously fortunate to have her patience, love, and support.

Notes

Chapter One

1. Charles M. Sennott, "Saudi Schools Fuel Anti-US Anger," *Boston Globe*, March 4, 2002, http://www.boston.com/news/packages/underattack/news/driving_a_wedge/part2.shtml.

2. Nina Shea, "This is a Saudi textbook. (After the intolerance was removed.)," *Washington Post*, May 21, 2006, http://www.washingtonpost.com/wp-dyn/content/article/2006/05/19/AR2006051901769_2.html; Center for Religious Freedom of Freedom House with the Institute for Gulf Affairs, *Excerpts from Saudi Ministry of Education Textbooks for Islamic Studies: Arabic with English Translation* (Washington, DC: Freedom House, 2005–6).

3. The crew and callers, radio talk show interview by Howard Stern, *Howard Stern Show*, September 11, 2001, https://youtu.be/kfguSwWeXOw at 17:20 (accessed March 10, 2016). The full *Howard Stern Show* broadcast on September 11, 2001, which I listened to live as the events unfolded, is now classic radio widely available online.

Chapter Two

1. John Adams, Thomas Jefferson, "From the Commissioners to John Jay," March 28, 1786, Grosvenor Square, in *The Diplomatic Correspondence of the United States of America*, vol. 1, *1783–89*, ed. U.S. Secretary of State, Blair & Rives, 1837, 605.

2. Robert Davis, "British Slaves on the Barbary Coast," *BBC History*, February 17, 2011, http://www.bbc.co.uk/history/british/empire_seapower/white_slaves_01.shtml

3. U.S. Department of State Office of the Historian, "Barbary Wars, 1801–1805 and 1815–1816," https://history.state.gov/milestones/1801–1829/barbary-wars (accessed March 10, 2016).

4. John Adams, Thomas Jefferson, "From the Commissioners to John Jay."

5. Thomas Jefferson Encyclopedia, "Jefferson's Religious Beliefs," https://www.monticello.org/site/research-and-collections/jeffersons-religious-beliefs (accessed March 10, 2016).

6. Thomas Jefferson, *Notes on the State of Virginia* (First published in Paris, 1785) (New York: Penguin Books, 1999), 165.

7. John Ferling, *Adams vs. Jefferson: The Tumultuous Election of 1800* (New York: Oxford University Press, 2005), 154.

8.   Kendra Marr, "Newt Talks Faith at Texas Church," *Politico*, March 28, 2011, http://www
     .politico.com/story/2011/03/newt-talks-faith-at-texas-church-052023.
9.   Denise A. Spellberg, *Thomas Jefferson's Qur'an: Islam and the Founders* (New York: Vintage,
     2014), 271.
10. Ibid.
11. Kevin J. Hayes, "How Thomas Jefferson Read the Quran," *Early American Literature* 39, no. 2
     (2004): 247–61.
12. Christopher Hitchens, "Jefferson's Quran," *Slate*, January 9, 2007, http://www.slate.com
     /articles/news_and_politics/fighting_words/2007/01/jeffersons_quran.html.
13. Thomas Jefferson, *Autobiography of Thomas Jefferson 1743–1789*, ed. Paul Leicester Ford and
     George Haven Putnam (New York and London: G. P. Putnam Sons and the Knickerbocker
     Press), 71.
14. Frank Lambert, *The Barbary Wars: American Independence in the Atlantic World* (New York:
     Hill and Wang, 2005), 8.
15. "Treaty of Peace and Friendship between the United States of America and the Bey and Sub-
     jects of Tripoli of Barbary," November 4, 1796, Tripoli, in *Treaties and Other International Acts
     of the United States of America*, vol. 2, *1776–1818*, ed. Hunter Miller, United States Government
     Printing Office, 1931, 365.
16. "Pasha" was an honorary title for high-ranking officials of the Ottoman Empire.
17. Frank Lambert, *The Barbary Wars: American Independence in the Atlantic World* (New York:
     Hill and Wang, 2005), 8.
18. "Last words of a terrorist," *The Guardian*, September 30, 2001, http://www.theguardian.com
     /world/2001/sep/30/terrorism.september113.
19. "CNN Presents: Soldiers of God," CNN, September 29, 2001, http://www.cnn.com
     /TRANSCRIPTS/0109/29/cp.00.html.
20. Fareed Zakaria, "The Politics of Rage: Why Do They Hate Us?," *Newsweek*, October 14, 2001,
     http://www.newsweek.com/politics-rage-why-do-they-hate-us-154345.
21. Middle East, "Saudi Man Executed for 'Witchcraft and Sorcery,'" *BBC News*, June 19, 2012,
     http://www.bbc.com/news/world-middle-east-18503550; Agence France-Presse, "Raif Badawi
     Tells of Flogging Ordeal in Letter from Saudi Prison," *The Guardian*, March 27, 2015, http://
     www.theguardian.com/world/2015/mar/27/raif-badawi-tells-of-flogging-ordeal-in-letter
     -from-saudi-prison; Schams Elwazer and Bryony Jones, "Saudi Protester Ali Al-Nimr's Cruci-
     fixion Could Happen 'At Any Moment,'" CNN, October 21, 2015, http://www.cnn.com/2015
     /10/21/middleeast/ali-al-nimr-crucifixion-beheading-father-plea/.
22. Martha Kirk, *Green Sands: My Five Years in the Saudi Desert* (Lubbock: Texas Tech University
     Press, 1994), 78.
23. Natasha Culzac, "Saudi Arabia Executes 19 in One Half of August in 'Disturbing Surge of
     Beheadings,'" *The Independent*, August 22, 2014, http://www.independent.co.uk/news/world
     /middle-east/saudi-arabia-executes-19-during-half-of-august-in-disturbing-surge-of
     -beheadings-9686063.html.
24. Anthony Bond, "Video: Gruesome Footage Showed a Blood-Stained Michael Adebolajo Shortly
     after Butchering Lee Rigby," *Mirror*, December 19, 2013, http://www.mirror.co.uk/news/uk
     -news/lee-rigby-murder-trial-gruesome-2943281.
25. Polling and Analysis, "Mapping the Global Muslim Population," Pew Research Center, Octo-
     ber 7, 2009, http://www.pewforum.org/2009/10/07/mapping-the-global-muslim-population/.
26. Reza Aslan, interview by Jon Stewart, "Exclusive: Reza Aslan Extended Interview," *The Daily
     Show with Jon Stewart*, May 13, 2015, http://www.cc.com/shows/the-daily-show-with-jon-stewart
     /interviews/8dwtnx/exclusive-reza-aslan-extended-interview.
27. E. van Donzel, B. Lewis, and C. Pellat, eds., *Brill Encyclopaedia of Islam*, vol. 4, *1954–2005*
     (Leiden: Brill Academic Pub, 1997), 171.
28. Erasmus, "A Liberal Muslim and a Non-believer in Search of Common Ground," *The Econo-
     mist*, October 3, 2015, http://www.economist.com/blogs/erasmus/2015/10/muslim-atheist
     -debate.

29. Kunwar Khuldune Shahid, "Liberal Takfiris," *Friday Times*, March 7, 2014, http://www
.thefridaytimes.com/tft/liberal-takfiris/.

30. Christopher Hitchens and Andrew Sullivan, interview by Tim Russert, *CNBC's Tim Russert*,
September 5, 2004, https://youtu.be/esRy1gnbVoE.

31. "The Book Pertaining to the Turmoil and Portents of the Last Hour (Kitab Al-Fitan wa Ashrat
As-Sa'ah)," *Translation of Sahih Muslim* Book 41 (University of Southern California: Center
for Jewish-Muslim Engagement), Number 6985, http://www.usc.edu/org/cmje/religious-texts
/hadith/muslim/041-smt.php#041.6985 (accessed March 10, 2016).

32. Barack Obama Administration, George W. Bush Administration, Bill Clinton Administration,
George H. W. Bush Administration, Ronald Reagan Administration, Jimmy Carter Administration, Gerald Ford Administration, Richard Nixon Administration, Lyndon Johnson
Administration, "Statements from U.S. Government Officials Concerning Israeli Settlements," in *Peace Library*, ed. Churches for Middle East Peace http://www.cmep.org/content/us
-statements-israeli-settlements_short (accessed March 10, 2016).

33. Michael Lipka, "More White Evangelicals Than American Jews Say God Gave Israel to the Jewish People," Pew Research Center, October 3, 2013, http://www.pewresearch.org/fact-tank
/2013/10/03/more-white-evangelicals-than-american-jews-say-god-gave-israel-to-the-jewish
-people/.

34. Jodi T. Allen and Alec Tyson, "The U.S. Public's Pro-Israel History: In Mid-East Conflicts,
Americans Consistently Side with Israel," Pew Research Center, July 19, 2006, http://www
.pewresearch.org/2006/07/19/the-us-publics-proisrael-history/.

35. Michael Lipka, "More White Evangelicals Than American Jews Say God Gave Israel to the Jewish People."

36. Ian Black, "Saudi Girl, Eight, Married Off to 58-Year-Old Is Denied Divorce," *The Guardian*,
December 23, 2008, http://www.theguardian.com/world/2008/dec/23/saudi-arabia-human
-rights.

37. Ayatollah Sayyid Ruhollah Musavi Khomeini, "Fi Ba'ad Adab wa Ahkaam," *Tahrir Al Wasileh*,
Kitabun-Nikah (Iran: Official website of the Supreme Leader), Maslaa 12, http://www.leader.ir
/tree/index.php?catid=13 (accessed March 10, 2016).

38. UNICEF, "When and how is FGM/C performed?" *Female Genital Mutilation/Cutting: A Sta-
tistical Overview and Exploration of the Dynamics of Change*, New York, UNICEF Statistics and
Monitoring Section, http://www.unicef.org/media/files/FGCM_Brochure_Lo_res.pdf (accessed March 10, 2016).

39. Reza Aslan, interview by Don Lemon, "Reza Aslan: Maher's Facile Generalizations of
Islam the Definition of Bigotry," September 30, 2014, http://www.realclearpolitics.com/video
/2014/09/30/reza_aslan_mahers_facile_generalizations_of_islam_the_definition_of
_bigotry.html.

40. Meiwita Budiharsana, Lila Amaliah, Budi Utomo, Erwinia, "Prevalence of Female Circumci-
sion," *Research Report: Female Circumcision in Indonesia—Extent, Implications and Possible
Interventions to Uphold Women's Health Rights* (Jakarta: Population Council, United States
Agency for International Development, September 2003), 24, http://pdf.usaid.gov/pdf_docs
/Pnacu138.pdf (accessed March 10, 2016); Abigail Haworth, "The day I Saw 248 Girls Suffering
Genital Mutilation," *The Guardian*, November 18, 2012, http://www.theguardian.com/society
/2012/nov/18/female-genital-mutilation-circumcision-indonesia.

41. A. Bouhdiba, "The Different Aspects of Islamic Culture," *The Individual and Society in Islam*
(Paris: UNESCO, 1998), 436.

42. "*Hadith*" may refer to a single account of Muhammad's words or actions, or the entire body of
accounts as a whole. "*Ahadith*" refers to multiple accounts.

43. University of North Carolina, "Islamic Jurisprudence & Law," *Islamic Discourses on Veiling*,
http://veil.unc.edu/religions/islam/law/ (accessed March 10, 2016); Reetika Subramanian,
"Bohra Women Go Online to Fight Circumcision Trauma," *Hindustan Times*, December 9,
2011, https://en.wikipedia.org/wiki/Dawoodi_Bohra#cite_note-bohrawomen-21; Farhanaz
Zahidi, "Female Genital Mutilation: Many Pakistani Women's Painful Secret," *Express Tribune*,

February 6, 2013, http://blogs.tribune.com.pk/story/15979/female-genital-mutilation-many
-pakistani-womens-painful-secret/.

44. Anonymous, "Saying 'It's the Culture, Not the Religion' Is Fairly Meaningless," *reddit exmuslim*, July 22, 2014, https://www.reddit.com/r/exmuslim/related/2bfue8/saying_its_the_culture
_not_the_religion_is_fairly/.

45. John Leland and Elizabeth Bumiller, "Islamic Scholars Split Over Sea Burial for Bin Laden,"
New York Times, May 2, 2011, http://www.nytimes.com/2011/05/03/world/asia/03burial.html.

46. Antony Flew, *Thinking About Thinking: Or, Do I Sincerely Want to be Right?* (London: Fontana/
Collins, 1975), 47.

47. Polling and Analysis, "Religious Commitment," *The World's Muslims: Unity and Diversity*, Pew
Research Center, August 9, 2012, http://www.pewforum.org/2012/08/09/the-worlds-muslims
-unity-and-diversity-2-religious-commitment/.

48. "N.C. Suspect Had 13 Guns, Ammo Stash. He's Charged with Murder of Three Muslim Students," *The Columbian*, February 14, 2015, http://www.columbian.com/news/2015/feb/13/nc
-suspect-had-13-guns-ammo-stash/.

49. Daniel Burke, "CNN Newsroom," CNN, February 12, 2015, http://edition.cnn.com
/TRANSCRIPTS/1502/12/cnr.07.html.

50. Elizabeth Bruenig, "The Chapel Hill Murders Should Be a Wake-Up Call for Atheists," *New
Republic*, February 11, 2015, http://www.newrepublic.com/article/121036/chapel-hill-muslim
-murders-show-atheism-has-violent-extremists-too.

51. Reza Aslan, Twitter, February 11, 2015, https://twitter.com/rezaaslan/status/565670891397591041.

52. Glenn Greenwald, Twitter, February 11, 2015, https://twitter.com/ggreenwald/status/565511
572374949889.

53. Adrian Blomfield, "Osama Bin Laden Enters Global Warming Debate," *The Telegraph*, January 29, 2010, http://www.telegraph.co.uk/news/earth/environment/climatechange/7104143
/Osama-bin-Laden-enters-global-warming-debate.html; Theresa Cook, "New OBL Tape: Iraq,
Democratic Control," *ABC News*, September 9, 2007, http://blogs.abcnews.com/politicalradar
/2007/09/new-obl-tape-ir.html; "Publicly Available U.S. Government Documents," *Bin Laden's
Bookshelf*, Office of the Director of National Intelligence, http://www.dni.gov/index.php
/resources/bin-laden-bookshelf?start=3 (accessed March 10, 2016).

54. Barack Obama, "Transcript: President Obama's Remarks on the Execution of Journalist James
Foley by Islamic State," *Washington Post*, August 20, 2014, https://www.washingtonpost.com
/politics/transcript-president-obamas-remarks-on-the-execution-of-journalist-james-foley
-by-islamic-state/2014/08/20/f5a63802-2884-11e4-8593-da634b334390_story.html.

55. Swati Sharma, "Islamic State Claims Responsibility for Paris Attacks," *Washington Post*,
November 14, 2015, https://www.washingtonpost.com/news/worldviews/wp/2015/11/14
/islamic-state-claims-responsibility-for-paris-attacks/.

56. Ruma Paul, "Publisher of Slain Blogger Hacked to Death in Bangladesh," Reuters,
October 31, 2015, http://www.reuters.com/article/2015/10/31/us-bangladesh-writers-idUSKCN
0SP0M520151031.

Chapter Three

1. *Ar-Rahmaan* and *Ar-Raheem* are two of the ninety-nine names given to Allah according to
Islamic tradition, meaning "compassionate" and "merciful" respectively.

2. Jessica Ravitz, "This Oklahoma Atheist Isn't Thanking the Lord," *The CNN Belief Blog*,
May 22, 2013, http://religion.blogs.cnn.com/2013/05/22/this-oklahoma-atheist-isnt-thanking
-the-lord/.

3. Stacy Simon, "Childhood Leukemia Survival Rates Improve Significantly," *American Cancer
Society*, March 27, 2012, http://www.cancer.org/cancer/news/childhood-leukemia-survival
-rates-improve-significantly.

4. Gillian Mohney, "Cancer-Stricken Infant Who Was Kissed by Pope Is Responding to Treatment, Parents Say," *ABC News*, November 24, 2015, http://abcnews.go.com/Health/cancer
-stricken-infant-kissed-pope-responding-treatment-parents/story?id=35394172.

5. Bertrand Russell, *Why I Am Not A Christian*, March 6, 1927, London, England, viewed online at Carnegie Mellon University, https://goo.gl/POKcof (accessed March 10, 2016).

6. Robert Evans, "Atheists Face Death in 13 Countries, Global Discrimination: Study," Reuters, December 9, 2013, http://www.reuters.com/article/2013/12/10/us-religion-atheists-idUSBRE9B 900G20131210#WTcyWposMdKyEGHP.97; these countries are Afghanistan, Iran, Malaysia, Maldives, Mauritania, Nigeria, Pakistan, Qatar, Saudi Arabia, Somalia, Sudan, United Arab Emirates, and Yemen.

7. Adam Withnall, "Saudi Arabia Declares All Atheists Are Terrorists in New Law to Crack Down on Political Dissidents," *The Independent*, April 1, 2014, http://www.independent.co.uk/news /world/middle-east/saudi-arabia-declares-all-atheists-are-terrorists-in-new-law-to-crack -down-on-political-dissidents-9228389.html.

8. Max Fisher, "Majorities of Muslims in Egypt and Pakistan Support the Death Penalty for Leaving Islam," *Washington Post*, May 1, 2013, https://www.washingtonpost.com/news/worldviews /wp/2013/05/01/64-percent-of-muslims-in-egypt-and-pakistan-support-the-death-penalty -for-leaving-islam/.

9. The Editorial Board, "Bangladesh's Descent into Lawlessness," *New York Times*, May 8, 2016, http://www.nytimes.com/2016/05/09/opinion/bangladeshs-descent-into-lawlessness.html

10. Daniel C. Dennett, *Breaking the Spell: Religion as a Natural Phenomenon* (New York: Penguin Books, 2006), 14–15.

11. Simon Cottee, *The Apostates: When Muslims Leave Islam* (London: Hurst, 2014), xii–xiii.

12. *Encyclopaedia Britannica Online*, s.v. "Anomie, Sociology," http://www.britannica.com/topic /anomie (accessed March 10, 2016).

13. Council of Ex-Muslims of Britain, official website, http://ex-muslim.org.uk/ (accessed March 10, 2016).

14. Muslimish, official website, http://www.muslimish.com/ (accessed March 10, 2016).

15. Ex-Muslims of North America, official website, http://www.exmna.org/ (accessed March 10, 2016).

16. Ali A. Rizvi, "#ExMuslimBecause: Thousands of Former Muslims Are Speaking Out After Paris—and It's Amazing," *Huffington Post Politics* (blog), November 23, 2015, http://www .huffingtonpost.com/ali-a-rizvi/post_10571_b_8615610.html.

17. Richard Dawkins, Twitter, November 21, 2015, https://twitter.com/RichardDawkins/status /667988900087005184.

18. Sarah Ager, Twitter, November 19, 2015, https://twitter.com/SaritaAgerman/status/66757 2379334402048; https://twitter.com/SaritaAgerman/status/667572926208675840; and May 17, 2015; https://twitter.com/SaritaAgerman/status/599906320775585792.

19. Jeff Goodell, "The Steve Jobs Nobody Knew," *Rolling Stone*, October 27, 2011, http://www .rollingstone.com/culture/news/the-steve-jobs-nobody-knew-20111027.

20. Catherine Smith, "Egypt's Facebook Revolution: Wael Ghonim Thanks the Social Network," *Huffington Post*, November 2, 2011, http://www.huffingtonpost.com/2011/02/11/egypt-facebook -revolution-wael-ghonim_n_822078.html.

21. Sami Ben Hassine, "Tunisia's Youth Finally Has Revolution on Its Mind," *The Guardian*, January 13, 2011, http://www.theguardian.com/commentisfree/2011/jan/13/tunisia-youth -revolution; Elizabeth Dickinson, "The First WikiLeaks Revolution?," *Foreign Policy*, January 13, 2011, http://foreignpolicy.com/2011/01/13/the-first-wikileaks-revolution/.

22. Robert Mackey, "Qaddafi Sees WikiLeaks Plot in Tunisia," *The Lede* (blog), *New York Times*, January 17, 2011, http://thelede.blogs.nytimes.com/2011/01/17/qaddafi-sees-wikileaks-plot-in -tunisia/.

23. Jim Sciutto, Evan Perez, Kevin Liptak, and Z. Byron Wolf, "Why Did Obama Declare ISIS 'Contained' the Day Before Paris Attack?" *CNN Politics*, November 16, 2015, http://www.cnn .com/2015/11/14/politics/paris-terror-attacks-obama-isis-contained/.

24. Thomas L. Friedman, "How ISIS Drives Muslims From Islam," *New York Times*, December 6, 2014, http://www.nytimes.com/2014/12/07/opinion/sunday/thomas-l-friedman-how-isis -drives-muslims-from-islam.html.

Chapter Four

1. Mark Tran and Matthew Weaver, "ISIS Announces Islamic Caliphate in Area Straddling Iraq and Syria," *The Guardian*, June 30, 2014, http://www.theguardian.com/world/2014/jun/30/isis-announces-islamic-caliphate-iraq-syria.

2. Olivia Ward, "Yazidi Girls Kidnapped by Islamic State Return Traumatized," *The Star*, April 9, 2015, http://www.thestar.com/news/world/2015/04/09/yazidi-girls-kidnapped-by-islamic-state-return-traumatized.html.

3. Christopher Hitchens, *God Is Not Great* (New York: Twelve, 2007), 129.

4. Fareed Zakaria, "I am a Muslim. But Trump's views appall me because I am an American," *Washington Post*, December 10, 2015, https://www.washingtonpost.com/opinions/i-am-a-muslim-but-trumps-views-appall-me-because-i-am-an-american/2015/12/10/fcba9ea6-9f6d-11e5-8728-1af6af208198_story.html.

5. Cally O'Brien, "Eriksonian Identity Theory in Counterterrorism," *Journal of Strategic Security* 3, no.3 (2010): 27–38.

6. Robert Siegel, "Sayyid Qutb's America," National Public Radio, May 6, 2003, http://www.npr.org/templates/story/story.php?storyId=1253796.

7. O'Brien, "Eriksonian Identity Theory in Counterterrorism," 30–31.

8. George Carlin, excerpt from "It's Bad for Ya," HBO, March 2008, https://youtu.be/iOmQP9guIl0 (accessed March 10, 2016).

9. Toni Johnson, "Muslims in the United States," Council on Foreign Relations, September 19, 2011, http://www.cfr.org/united-states/muslims-united-states/p25927.

10. Azmat Khan, "America and Muslims: By the Numbers," Public Broadcasting Service, September 26, 2011, http://www.pbs.org/wgbh/frontline/article/america-and-muslims-by-the-numbers.

11. Sam Hodges, "Gallup: Muslim Americans the Most Diverse U.S. Religious Group," *Dallas Morning News*, March 2, 2009, http://religionblog.dallasnews.com/2009/03/gallup-muslim-americans-the-mo.html/.

12. Martin Chulov, " 'The Best Employee We Ever Had': Mohammed Emwazi's Former Boss in Kuwait," *The Guardian*, March 2, 2015, http://www.theguardian.com/world/2015/mar/01/mohammed-emwazi-best-employee-we-ever-had-former-boss-kuwaiti-it-firm.

13. Cally O'Brien, "Eriksonian Identity Theory in Counterterrorism," *Journal of Strategic Security* 3, no.3 (2010): 29.

14. Seth J. Schwartz, Curtis S. Dunkel, and S. Waterman, "Terrorism: An Identity Theory Perspective," *Studies in Conflict and Terrorism* 32, no. 6 (2009): 537–59.

15. Erik H. Erikson, "Foundations in Observation," in *Identity: Youth and Crisis* (New York and London: W. W. Norton & Company, 1968), 89.

16. Alishba Zarmeen, Twitter, August 4, 2013, https:/twitter.com/SecularlyYours/status/364196032210411520.

17. Re-Enlightenment (pseudonym), "Did You Hear the One About the Alcoholic, Atheist Muslim?" *The Blog of the Re-Enlightenment*, August 7, 2012, https://enlightenmentlover.wordpress.com/2012/08/07/did-you-hear-the-one-about-the-alcoholic-atheist-muslim/.

18. Phil Zuckerman, interview by Sam Harris, "The Frontiers of Secularism," *Sam Harris: The Blog*, December 3, 2014, http://www.samharris.org/blog/item/the-frontiers-of-secularism.

Chapter Five

1. *Oxford Dictionaries*, "Definition of *atheism* in English," http://www.oxforddictionaries.com/definition/english/atheism (accessed March 10, 2016).

2. Don Hirschberg, "Calling Atheism a Religion . . ." Metro State Atheists, October 24, 2008, https://metrostateatheists.wordpress.com/tag/don-hirschberg/.

3. *Real Time with Bill Maher*, "New Rules," Episode 236, February 3, 2012, http://www.hbo.com/real-time-with-bill-maher/episodes/0/236-episode/article/new-rules.html.

4. *Oxford Dictionaries*, "Definition of *theism* in English," http://www.oxforddictionaries.com/us/definition/american_english/theism (accessed March 10, 2016).

5. *Oxford Dictionaries*, "Definition of *deism* in English," http://www.oxforddictionaries.com/us/definition/american_english/deism (accessed March 10, 2016).

6. Associated Press, "Letters from Einstein About God (and Toys) Sell for $420,625," *NBC News*, June 11, 2015, http://www.nbcnews.com/science/science-news/letters-einstein-about-god-toys-sell-420-625-n373991.

7. Albert Einstein, "The Word God Is the Product of Human Weakness," in *Letters of Note*, ed. Shaun Usher, http://www.lettersofnote.com/2009/10/word-god-is-product-of-human-weakness.html (accessed March 10, 2016).

8. Albert Einstein, excerpts from *Ideas and Opinions* (New York: Crown Publishers, 1954), in *Einstein: Science and Religion*, ed. Arnold V. Lesikar, http://einsteinandreligion.com/scienceandreligion.html (accessed March 10, 2016) and http://einsteinandreligion.com/scienceandreligion2.html (accessed March 10, 2016).

9. Richard Dawkins, "First Chapter: The God Delusion," *New York Times*, October 22, 2006, http://www.nytimes.com/2006/10/22/books/chapters/1022-1st-dawk.html?pagewanted=all.

10. Albert Einstein, *Albert Einstein, the Human Side*, ed. Helen Dukas and Banesh Hoffman (Princeton: Princeton University Press, 1981), 39.

11. Albert Einstein, *The World as I See It* (New York: Citadel, 2001), 7.

12. Time Staff, "Ayaan Hirsi Ali: They Simply Wanted Me to be Silenced," *Time*, April 9, 2014, http://time.com/56111/ayaan-hirsi-ali-they-simply-wanted-me-to-be-silenced/

13. Carl Sagan, *Pale Blue Dot: A Vision of the Human Future in Space* (New York: Random House, 1994).

14. Francis Collins, " 'God Is Not Threatened by Our Scientific Adventures,' " *Beliefnet*, August 22, 2006, http://www.beliefnet.com/News/Science-Religion/2006/08/God-Is-Not-Threatened-By-Our-Scientific-Adventures.aspx.

15. Contrary to popular perception, the widely referenced number of "seventy-two" virgins in Paradise is not mentioned in the Quran. It is derived from a variety of *ahadith*, the authenticity of which is a matter of continuous debate among different scholars.

16. Richard Dawkins and Mehdi Hasan, debate, "Is Religion Good or Evil?" *Al Jazeera*, July 20, 2013, http://www.aljazeera.com/programmes/general/2012/12/2012121791038231381.html at 14:30.

17. Ibn Warraq, "Virgins? What Virgins?," *The Guardian*, January 12, 2002, http://www.theguardian.com/books/2002/jan/12/books.guardianreview5.

18. Staff writers, "Scientist Richard Dawkins Slaps Down Science Cynic," news.com.au, April 3, 2013, http://www.news.com.au/technology/science/dawkins-bitchslaps-anti-science-cynic/story-fn5fsgyc-1226611489475.

19. This quote is thought to be misattributed to George Carlin. There is no record of it in his writings or performances. The real source of the quote is unknown.

20. Bertrand Russell, "Is There a God?" (commissioned, but never published, by *Illustrated* magazine in 1952). In this article, Russell created an analogy to demonstrate that the one who makes unfalsifiable claims carries the burden of proof, not others. He wrote, "If I were to suggest that between the Earth and Mars there is a china teapot revolving about the sun in an elliptical orbit, nobody would be able to disprove my assertion provided I were careful to add that the teapot is too small to be revealed even by our most powerful telescopes. But if I were to go on to say that, since my assertion cannot be disproved, it is intolerable presumption on the part of human reason to doubt it, I should rightly be thought to be talking nonsense. If, however, the existence of such a teapot were affirmed in ancient books, taught as the sacred truth every Sunday, and instilled into the minds of children at school, hesitation to believe in its existence would become a mark of eccentricity and entitle the doubter to the attentions of the psychiatrist in an enlightened age or of the Inquisitor in an earlier time." The full paper can be accessed here: http://russell.mcmaster.ca/cpbr11p69.pdf (accessed March 14, 2016).

21. "Neil deGrasse Tyson—A Conversation about Communicating Science," The Science Network, January 20, 2011, https://youtu.be/1ulkX-DA9BM.

22. Pervez Hoodbhoy, *Islam and Science: Religious Orthodoxy and the Battle for Rationality* (London: Zed Books, 1991), xiv.

23. "Richard Dawkins—Why There Was No 'First' Human," Ideas at the House, October 24, 2013, https://youtu.be/u7O7EfQpJcc.

24. Lawrence M. Krauss, "Ben Carson's Scientific Ignorance," *New Yorker*, September 28, 2015, http://www.newyorker.com/news/news-desk/ben-carsons-scientific-ignorance.

25. "Celebration of Creation | Ben Carson, MD," https://youtu.be/Z6ChFtIDUbg at 43:30.

26. Keith L. Moore, Shaykh Abdul-Majeed A. Azzindani, "Foreword, Acknowledgement," *The Developing Human: Clinically Oriented Embryology with Islamic Additions* (Saudi Arabia: Abul Qasim Publishing House, 1983).

27. Daniel Golden, "Western Scholars Play Key Role in Touting 'Science' of the Quran," *Wall Street Journal*, January 23, 2002, http://www.wsj.com/articles/SB1011738146332966760.

28. Joseph Needham, revised with the assistance of Arthur Hughes, *A History of Embryology* (Cambridge: The University Press, 1959), 82.

29. Heinrich von Staden, "The Discovery of the Body: Human Dissection and Its Cultural Context in Ancient Greece," *Yale Journal of Biology and Medicine* 65, no. 3 (1992): 223–41, http://www.ncbi.nlm.nih.gov/pmc/articles/PMC2589595/pdf/yjbm00051-0069.pdf.

30. David Williams, "Jihadis Paraded Severed Heads of Their Victims through Our Village: Yazidi Mother Gives Harrowing Account of Islamic State's Bloody Tirade Across Iraqi Mountains," *Mail Online*, August 13, 2014, http://www.dailymail.co.uk/news/article-2724414/Jihadis-paraded-severed-heads-victims-village-Yazidi-mother-gives-harrowing-account-Islamic-State-s-bloody-tirade-Iraqi-mountains.html.

31. Aristotle, *Generation of Animals*, English trans. A. L. Peck (Cambridge: Heinemann/Harvard University Press, 1953), 197 (740a).

32. "Aristotle's Biological Practice," in *Aristotle's Biology* (Stanford: Stanford Encyclopedia of Philosophy, 2011), http://plato.stanford.edu/entries/aristotle-biology/#AriBioPra (accessed March 14, 2016).

33. *The O'Reilly Factor*, Fox News, January 4, 2011, http://www.foxnews.com/transcript/2011/01/04/o039reilly-debates-atheist-group-president-over-religions-are-039scams039-billboard/.

34. Haroon Moghul, "Dear Trolls," Facebook, December 21, 2005, https://www.facebook.com/hsmoghul/posts/1684330225115703

35. J. B. S. Haldane, *Possible Worlds* (New Brunswick: Transaction Publishers, 2002), 286.

36. "Curiosity: Did God Create the Universe?" Season 1, Episode 1, *Discovery Channel*, August 7, 2011, http://store.discovery.com/curiosity-with-stephen-hawking-dvd/detail.php?p=366989.

37. Barb Mattson, "100 Years of General Relativity," *Blueshift*, National Aeronautics and Space Administration, November, 25, 2015, http://asd.gsfc.nasa.gov/blueshift/index.php/2015/11/25/100-years-of-general-relativity/.

Chapter Six

1. *Snyder v. Phelps*, Supreme Court of the United States, October Term, 2010, http://www.supremecourt.gov/opinions/10pdf/09-751.pdf (accessed March 14, 2016).

2. The reason this can be seen as a somewhat flawed argument is that anti-Semitism targets a group of people simply on the basis of their identification as Jews, while the cartoons target Islam (an idea/ideology), and Muhammad (a long-dead public figure). A more appropriate comparison would be satirical speech against the *religion* of Judaism, or cartoons of Moses. However, this is also a legitimate argument because there is good reason to believe that saying something like, "Judaism is a cult of death," would be seen as much more hostile than, "Islam is a cult of death." In France, these distinctions are dangerously blurry.

3. Ali A. Rizvi, "A Conversation Between Two Atheists from Muslim Backgrounds (Part 1)," *Huffpost Politics* (blog), Huffington Post, March 26, 2014, http://www.huffingtonpost.com/ali-a-rizvi/a-conversation-between-two-atheists_b_4623831.html.

4. Dr. Ijaz Shafi Gilani, Ms. Rushna Shahid, and Irene Zuettel, "Global Index of Religiosity and Atheism," Gallup International, 2012, http://www.wingia.com/web/files/news/14/file/14.pdf (accessed March 14, 2016).

5. Charles Haviland, "Bangladesh Blogger Niloy Neel Hacked to Death in Dhaka," *BBC News*, August 7, 2015, http://www.bbc.com/news/world-asia-33819032.

6. Evelyn Beatrice Hall, *The Friends of Voltaire* (London: Smith, Elder, & Co., 1906), 199.
7. Peter W. Galbraith, *The End of Iraq: How American Incompetence Created a War Without End* (New York: Simon and Schuster, 2006), 83.
8. Kacem El Ghazzali, "Reading 'The God Delusion' In The Arab World," *The Huffington Post*, May 9, 2016, http://www.huffingtonpost.ca/kacem-el-ghazzali/the-god-delusion_b_9867606.html.
9. Richard Dawkins, "Militant Atheism," TED Talk Official Conference, February 2002, https://www.ted.com/talks/richard_dawkins_on_militant_atheism?language=en.
10. Richard Dawkins, *The God Delusion* (New York: Houghton Mifflin Harcourt, 2008), 51.
11. Hitchens v Hitchens Debate, *Hauenstein Center*, April 3, 2008, https://youtu.be/ngjQs_QjSwc.
12. Jimmy Carter, "Rushdie's Book Is an Insult," *New York Times*, March 5, 1989, http://www.nytimes.com/1989/03/05/opinion/rushdie-s-book-is-an-insult.html.
13. Nicholas Birch, "Dawkins' Publisher Faces Jail over 'Atheist Manifesto,'" *The Independent*, November 29, 2007, http://www.independent.co.uk/news/world/europe/dawkins-publisher-faces-jail-over-atheist-manifesto-761063.html; Riazat Butt, "Turkish Court Bans Richard Dawkins Website," *The Guardian*, September 18, 2008, http://www.theguardian.com/world/2008/sep/18/turkey.
14. Al-Fayhaa TV, "Iraqi Researcher Defies Scientific Axioms: The Earth Is Flat and Much Larger Than the Sun (Which Is Also Flat)," *MEMRI TV*, October 31, 2007, http://www.memritv.org/clip/en/1684.htm.
15. Jeremy Koselak, "The Exaltation of a Reasonable Deity: Thomas Jefferson's Critique of Christianity," *Lost in Thought: Undergraduate Research Journal* 2 (1999): 59.
16. Will M. Gervais, Azim F. Shariff, and Ara Norenzayan, "Do You Believe in Atheists? Distrust Is Central to Anti-Atheist Prejudice," *Journal of Personality and Social Psychology* 1, no. 6 (2011): 1189–1206.
17. John Allen Paulos, "Who's Counting: Distrusting Atheists," *ABC News*, April 2, 2006, http://abcnews.go.com/Technology/story?id=1786422; Jeffery M. Jones, "Some Americans Reluctant to Vote for Mormon, 72-Year-Old Presidential Candidates." Gallup, February 20, 2007, http://www.gallup.com/poll/26611/some-americans-reluctant-vote-mormon-72yearold-presidential-candidates.aspx; Lydia Saad, "Support for Nontraditional Candidates Varies by Religion" Gallup, June 24, 2015, http://www.gallup.com/poll/183791/support-nontraditional-candidates-varies-religion.aspx?utm_source=Politics&utm_medium=newsfeed&utm_campaign=tiles.
18. Kelly Murray, "He Studies Where Morals Come From," CNN, May 16, 2013, http://www.cnn.com/2013/05/07/health/lifes-work-de-waal/.
19. Bill Maher, *Real Time with Bill Maher*, HBO, October 3, 2014, Episode 331.
20. Web Desk, "Muslim Schoolgirl in New York Called 'ISIS,' Put into Headlock and Punched," *Express Tribune*, December 8, 2015, http://tribune.com.pk/story/1006029/muslim-schoolgirl-in-new-york-called-isis-put-into-headlock-and-punched/.
21. Reza Aslan, interview by Jesse Singal, "Reza Aslan on What New Atheists Get Wrong About Islam," *New York Magazine: Science of Us*, October 14, 2014, http://nymag.com/scienceofus/2014/10/reza-aslan-on-what-the-new-atheists-get-wrong.html.
22. Max Fisher, "Majorities of Muslims in Egypt and Pakistan Support the Death Penalty for Leaving Islam," *Washington Post*, May 1, 2013, https://www.washingtonpost.com/news/worldviews/wp/2013/05/01/64-percent-of-muslims-in-egypt-and-pakistan-support-the-death-penalty-for-leaving-islam/.
23. Global Attitudes and Trends, "Muslim Publics Divided on Hamas and Hezbollah: Views of Hezbollah," Pew Research Center, December 2, 2010, http://www.pewglobal.org/2010/12/02/muslims-around-the-world-divided-on-hamas-and-hezbollah/#prc-jump.
24. Reza Aslan, "Bill Maher Isn't the Only One Who Misunderstands Religion," *New York Times*, October 8, 2014, http://www.nytimes.com/2014/10/09/opinion/bill-maher-isnt-the-only-one-who-misunderstands-religion.html (accessed March 14, 2016).
25. Christopher Massie, e-mail, October 9, 2014.
26. Ayaan Hirsi Ali, interview by Sam Harris, "Lifting the Veil of 'Islamophobia,'" *Sam Harris: The Blog*, May 8, 2014, http://www.samharris.org/blog/item/lifting-the-veil-of-islamophobia.

27. John Plunkett, "BBC Revises Muhammad Ban As BBC1 Bulletin Features Charlie Hebdo Cover," *The Guardian*, January 9, 2015, http://www.theguardian.com/media/2015/jan/09/bbc-revises-muhammad-ban-bbc1-news-bulletin-features-charlie-hebdo-cover.

28. Maajid Nawaz, "ISIS Is Just One of a Full-Blown Global Jihadist Insurgency," *Daily Beast*, November 19, 2015, http://www.thedailybeast.com/articles/2015/11/19/isis-is-just-one-of-a-full-blown-global-jihadist-insurgency.html.

29. Kevin Johnson, "Justice Dept. reverses course on redacting transcript of Orlando gunman," *USA Today*, June 20, 2016, http://www.usatoday.com/story/news/nation/2016/06/20/fbi-release-orlando-911-transcripts/86130520.

30. Karla Adam, "Obama ridiculed for saying conflicts in the Middle East 'date back millennia,'" *Washington Post*, January 13, 2016, https://www.washingtonpost.com/news/worldviews/wp/2016/01/13/obama-ridiculed-for-saying-conflicts-in-the-middle-east-date-back-millennia-some-dont-date-back-a-decade.

31. Jeffrey Goldberg, "The Obama Doctrine," *The Atlantic*, April 2016, http://www.theatlantic.com/magazine/archive/2016/04/the-obama-doctrine/471525.

32. Jeryl Bier, "Kerry: We Must 'Put Real Islam Out There,'" *Weekly Standard*, September 16, 2014, http://www.weeklystandard.com/kerry-we-must-put-real-islam-out-there/article/805207.

33. Eliza Collins, "Kerry Sees 'Rationale' in Charlie Hebdo Murders, Unlike Friday's Attacks in Paris," *Politico*, November 17, 2015, http://www.politico.com/story/2015/11/john-kerry-paris-attacks-charlie-hebdo-215992#ixzz3rmmpySzj.

34. Adam Taylor, "John Kerry Keeps Calling the Islamic State 'Apostates.' Maybe He Should Stop," *Washington Post*, February 3, 2016, https://www.washingtonpost.com/news/worldviews/wp/2016/02/03/john-kerry-keeps-calling-the-islamic-state-apostates-maybe-he-should-stop/.

35. Maajid Nawaz, "Don't call me 'Porch Monkey,'" *Daily Beast*, September 21, 2015, http://www.thedailybeast.com/articles/2015/09/21/don-t-call-me-porch-monkey.html.

36. Biography, "Nathan Lean," Berkley Center for Religion, Peace & World Affairs, http://berkleycenter.georgetown.edu/people/nathan-lean (accessed March 14, 2016); "About" section, Prince Alwaleed bin Talal Center for Muslim-Christian Understanding, Georgetown University School of Foreign Service, https://acmcu.georgetown.edu/about.

37. Nawaz, "Don't call me 'Porch Monkey.'"

38. Jamie Smith, "The Rise of the Regressives," *Futile Democracy*, December 31, 2015, https://futiledemocracy.wordpress.com/2015/12/31/the-rise-of-the-regressives/.

39. Kaveh Mousavi, "The Unbearable Toxicity of 'Native Informant,'" Patheos: On the Margin of Error, January 1, 2016, http://www.patheos.com/blogs/marginoferr/2016/01/01/the-unbearable-toxicity-of-native-informant/.

40. Deepa Kumar, quoted in John Sargeant, "McCarthyism, Muslims, and Ex Muslims," *Homo Economicus' Weblog*, June 11, 2015, https://homoeconomicusnet.wordpress.com/2015/06/11/mccarthyism-muslims-and-ex-muslims/.

41. Max Fisher, "Majorities of Muslims in Egypt and Pakistan Support the Death Penalty for Leaving Islam," *Washington Post*, May 1, 2013, https://www.washingtonpost.com/news/worldviews/wp/2013/05/01/64-percent-of-muslims-in-egypt-and-pakistan-support-the-death-penalty-for-leaving-islam/; Pew Research Center's Forum on Religion & Public Life, "The World's Muslims: Religion, Politics and Society," Pew Research Center, April 30, 2013, http://www.pewforum.org/files/2013/04/worlds-muslims-religion-politics-society-full-report.pdf.

42. Muhammad Syed, Facebook, February 16, 2016.

43. Christopher Hitchens, Dinesh D'Souza, introduced by Marvin Olasky, "Is Christianity the Problem?," Debate at King's College, C-Span, October 22, 2007, at 21:15, http://www.c-span.org/video/?201727-1/christianity-problem&start=1295.

Chapter Seven

1. Entertainment Desk, "Richard Dawkins Mansplains Feminism to Muslim Women, Bhutto Hits Back," *Dawn*, July 24, 2015, http://www.dawn.com/news/1196079.

2. Paula Stockley, "The Baculum," *Current Biology* 22, no. 24 (December 18, 2012): R1032.

3. Richard Dawkins, *The Selfish Gene. 30th Anniversary Edition* (London: Oxford University Press, 2006), Endnotes to Chapter 9, 307.

4. Scott F. Gilbert and Ziony Zevit, "Congenital Human Baculum Deficiency: The Generative Bone of Genesis 2:21–23,"*American Journal of Medical Genetics* 101, no. 3 (2001): 284–85.

5. Ziony Zevit, "Was Eve Made from Adam's Rib—or His Baculum?" *Biblical Archaeology Review* 41, no. 5 (2015), September/October.

6. Christopher Hitchens, *God Is Not Great* (New York: Twelve, 2007), 22–23.

7. Reza Aslan, "How to Read the Quran," *Slate*, November 20, 2008, http://www.slate.com /articles/arts/books/2008/11/how_to_read_the_quran.single.html.

8. A group of anonymous ex-Muslim and non-Muslim Arabs have done exhaustive research on every single use of the word *daraba* and its derivatives in the Quran, and demonstrated how the meaning of the word—to hit, strike, or smite—stays the same in each case. Their article is hosted on Wikislam, a controversial website that I am citing here only because it uses the Quran and *hadith* alone as sources. The article on verse 4:34 can be accessed here: https:// wikiislam.net/wiki/Beat_your_Wives_or_Separate_from_Them_-_Quran_4-34.

9. There are three main *ahadith* regarding the verse 4:24.

    1. Abu Dawud 11:2150:
    Abu Said al-Khudri said: "The apostle of Allah sent a military expedition to Awtas on the occasion of the battle of Hunain. They met their enemy and fought with them. They defeated them and took them captives. Some of the Companions of the apostle of Allah were reluctant to have intercourse with the female captives in the presence of their husbands who were unbelievers. So Allah, the Exalted, sent down the Quranic verse, 'And all married women (are forbidden) unto you save those (captives) whom your right hands possess. That is to say, they are lawful for them when they complete their waiting period.' "

    2. Sahih Bukhari 5:59:459:
    Narrated by Ibn Muhairiz: I entered the Mosque and saw Abu Said Al-Khudri and sat beside him and asked him about Al-Azl [i.e. coitus interruptus]. Abu Said said, "We went out with Allah's Apostle for the Ghazwa of Banu Al-Mustaliq and we received captives from among the Arab captives and we desired women and celibacy became hard on us and we loved to do coitus interruptus. So when we intended to do coitus interruptus, we said, "How can we do coitus interruptus before asking Allah's Apostle who is present among us?" We asked (him) about it and he said, 'It is better for you not to do so, for if any soul (till the Day of Resurrection) is predestined to exist, it will exist."

    3. Sahih Muslim 8:3432:
    Abu Sa'id al-Khudri (Allah be pleased with him) reported that at the Battle of Hunain Allah's Messenger (may peace be upon him) sent an army to Autas and encountered the enemy and fought with them. Having overcome them and taken them captives, the Companions of Allah's Messenger (may peace be upon him) seemed to refrain from having intercourse with captive women because of their husbands being polytheists. Then Allah, Most High, sent down regarding that: "And women already married, except those whom your right hands possess."

10. Stoning to death as a punishment is never mentioned in the Quran, but appears in the *hadith*. According to several *ahadith*, notably in *Ibn Majah*, 3:9:1943, Muhammad's youngest wife, Aisha, claims that the verses commanding stoning to death were revealed, but the paper they were written on was eaten by a sheep shortly after Muhammad died. The *hadith* reads as follows: "It was narrated that Aisha said, 'The verse of stoning and of breastfeeding an adult ten times was revealed, and the paper was with me under my pillow. When the Messenger of Allah died, we were preoccupied with his death, and a tame sheep came in and ate it.' "

11. Vicky Baker, "Rape Victim Sentenced to 200 Lashes and Six Months in Jail," *The Guardian*, November 17, 2007, http://www.theguardian.com/world/2007/nov/17/saudiarabia.international;

"Saudi Woman to Get 200 Lashes after Being Raped," *Middle East Monitor*, March 6, 2015, https://www.middleeastmonitor.com/news/middle-east/17365-saudi-woman-to-get-200-lashes-after-being-raped.

12. Although the Quran restricts Muslim men to four wives at a time, Muhammad, as the prophet of God, was an exception to this; he is believed by most Muslims to have had eleven wives.

13. Between 2006 and 2016, U.S. bombs had fallen at some point in seven Muslim-majority countries: Iraq, Afghanistan, Pakistan, Libya, Somalia, Yemen, and Syria.

14. *Ibn Majah*, 3:9:1943.

15. Donald J. Trump, Twitter, February 28, 2016, https://twitter.com/realdonaldtrump/status/703900742961270784.

16. Chuck Todd, *Meet the Press*, NBC, February 28, 2016 http://www.nbcnews.com/meet-the-press/meet-press-february-28-2016-n527506.

17. Kevin Alfred Strom, *All America Must Know the Terror That Is Upon Us* (Sarver: America First Publishers, 1993), http://www.amfirstbooks.com/IntroPages/ToolBarTopics/Articles/Featured_Authors/strom,_kevin/kevin_strom_works/Kevin_Strom_1991–1994/Kevin_A._Strom_19930814-ADV_All_America_Must_Know_the_Terror_That_Is_Upon_Us.html.

18. Adolf Hitler, *Mein Kampf*, transl. James Vincent Murphy (London: Hurst and Blackett, 1981). An online version of the section of the book with these quotes is available here: http://www.hitler.org/writings/Mein_Kampf/mkv1ch03.html (accessed March 14, 2016).

Chapter Eight

1. E. A. Foster et al., "Jefferson Fathered Slave's Last Child," *Nature* 396, no. 6706 (1998): 27–28.

2. The *ahadith* supporting Aisha's prepubertal age at marriage and/or consummation include: *Sahih Bukhari* 5:58:236; *Sahih Bukhari* 7:62:64; *Sahih Bukhari* 7:62:65; *Sahih Bukhari* 7:62:88; *Sahih Bukhari* 7:62:163; *Sahih Bukhari* 8:73:151; *Sahih Bukhari* 5:58:234; *Sahih Muslim* 8:3309; *Sahih Muslim* 8:3310; and *Sahih Muslim* 8:3311. These are only the *ahadith* from *Sahih Bukhari* and *Sahih Muslim*; there are several more in other *hadith* collections.

3. Maryam Usman, "Bill Aiming to Ban Child Marriages Shot Down," *Express Tribune*, January 15, 2016, http://tribune.com.pk/story/1027742/settled-matter-bill-aiming-to-ban-child-marriages-shot-down/; Ishaan Tharoor, "Bill Banning Child Marriage Fails in Pakistan after It's Deemed 'Un-Islamic,'" *Washington Post*, January 15, 2016, https://www.washingtonpost.com/news/worldviews/wp/2016/01/15/bill-banning-child-marriage-fails-in-pakistan-after-its-deemed-un-islamic/.

4. "CNN/YouTube Republican Presidential Debate," CNN, November 28, 2007, http://www.cnn.com/2007/POLITICS/11/28/debate.transcript/index.html and http://www.cnn.com/2007/POLITICS/11/28/debate.transcript.part2/index.html?iref=nextin.

5. Jeffrey M. Jones, "In U.S., 3 in 10 Say They Take the Bible Literally," Gallup, July 8, 2011, http://www.gallup.com/poll/148427/say-bible-literally.aspx.

6. Abigail Pobregin, Gary Ginsberg, and Michael Lynton, "America's Top 50 Rabbis for 2012," *Daily Beast*, April 2, 2012, http://www.thedailybeast.com/galleries/2012/04/02/america-s-top-50-rabbis-for-2012.html.

7. Rabbi David Wolpe, "Did God Write the Bible?" *My Jewish Learning*, April 2, 2012, http://www.myjewishlearning.com/article/did-god-write-the-bible/

8. "U.S. Public Becoming Less Religious," Pew Research Center, November 3, 2015, 58–59. An online PDF version of the survey is available here: http://www.pewforum.org/files/2015/11/201.11.03_RLS_II_full_report.pdf.

9. "The World's Muslims: Unity and Diversity," Pew Research Center, August 9, 2012, http://www.pewforum.org/2012/08/09/the-worlds-muslims-unity-and-diversity-executive-summary/.

10. Pew Research, "U.S. Public Becoming Less Religious," 58.

11. Sam Hodges, "Gallup: Muslim Americans the Most Diverse U.S. Religious Group," *Dallas Morning News*, March 2, 2009, http://religionblog.dallasnews.com/2009/03/gallup-muslim-americans-the-mo.html/.

12. Hijab may be implied in verses like 24:31, which tells women to "wrap [a portion of] their head-covers over their chests," but circumcision isn't even hinted at in the Quran.

13. Anonymous, online communication, December 17, 2014. (Translated from Urdu by myself and Alishba Zarmeen.)

14. Reza Aslan, Twitter, October 12, 2014, https://twitter.com/rezaaslan/status/521425356306538496.

15. Ayaan Hirsi Ali, *Heretic: Why Islam Needs a Reformation Now* (New York: HarperCollins, 2015), 74.

16. Haroon Moghul, "Ayaan Hirsi Ali's *Heretic*: With Friends Like These, Who Needs Jihadis?," *Religion Dispatches*, April 1, 2015, http://religiondispatches.org/ayaan-hirsi-alis-heretic-with-friends-like-these-who-needs-jihadis/.

17. Among the young people I have corresponded with, I've noticed a hunger for authenticity, which they either find among the fundamentalists who back up their actions with scriptural passages they can cite on demand, or those who have rejected the faith and can provide solid arguments against it. To young people who can see the words of the Quran in multiple languages with a quick search and a few clicks, the decontextualized interpretations of scripture by "moderates" are increasingly unconvincing from what I've seen. As one young reader told me, "When ISIS does terrible things, it actually looks like what the words say."

18. Ashley Fantz, Gul Tuysuz, and Arwa Damon, "Turkish Police Fire Pepper Spray at Gay Pride Parade," CNN, June 29, 2015, http://www.cnn.com/2015/06/28/world/turkey-pride-parade-lgbt-violence/.

19. Muslim Reform Movement, official website, http://muslimreformmovement.org/ (accessed March 14, 2016).

20. Some moderates are ideologically allied not just with the goals of Islamists, but with jihadists as well, even if not condoning violence firsthand. And jihadists come in several varieties: globally oriented jihadists who want to establish a caliphate (like the Islamic State); anti-West jihadists who want to fight and ultimately destroy the United States (like Al Qaeda); regional, geographically focused, nationalism-driven jihadists like Hamas and Hezbollah in Palestine and the Taliban in Afghanistan; and others. Each outfit might have a sizeable number of moderate Muslims supporting it. To be sure, some of these are legitimate grievances, and when state governments fail to deal with them satisfactorily, militant groups fill the vacuum.

21. Sadakat Kadri, *Heaven on Earth: A Journey Through Shari'a Law from the Deserts of Ancient Arabia to the Streets of the Modern Muslim World* (New York: Macmillan, 2012), 77.

22. Mohammed Hanif, "Why Pakistan's Ahmadi Community Is Officially Detested," *BBC News*, June 16, 2010, http://news.bbc.co.uk/2/hi/8744092.stm.

23. *Tadhkirah*, 4th ed. [Urdu] (Rabwah, Pakistan: Zia-ul Islam Press, 2004), 519. Available online at http://www.alislam.org/library/books/tadhkirah/?page=519 (accessed March 14, 2016).

24. Qasim Rashid, online communication, June 11–13, 2014; May 29, 2015.

25. *Tadhkirah, English rendering of the divine revelations, dreams and visions vouchsafed to Hadrat Mirza Ghulam Ahmad of Qadian, The Promised Messiah and Mahdi, on whom be peace* [English] (Tilford, Surrey: Islam International Publications, 2009), 797–908. Available online: https://www.alislam.org/library/books/Tadhkirah.pdf (accessed March 14, 2016).

26. The Twelver Shias consider the first three Imams to be Ali, his older son Hassan, and his younger son, Husayn, respectively. Therefore, Husayn's great-grandson, Jafar As-Sadiq, is the sixth Imam for Twelvers. The Nizari Ismailis, on the other hand, don't consider Hassan to be an Imam, and take Husayn to be the second Imam. Another major Ismaili sect, the Mustaali Ismailis, don't consider Ali to be the first Imam, but do take both Hassan and Husayn as the first two Imams, respectively. For both Nizari and Mustaali Ismailis, therefore, Husayn is the second Imam, and Jafar As-Sadiq the fifth.

Chapter Nine

1. Aaron Freeman, "Planning Ahead Can Make a Difference in the End," NPR, June 1, 2005, http://www.npr.org/templates/story/story.php?storyId=4675953. Reproduced by permission of Aaron Freeman.

2. Wilhelm Hofmann, Daniel C. Wisneski, Mark J. Brandt, and Linda J. Skitka, "Morality in Everyday Life," *Science* 345, no. 6202 (September 12, 2014): 1340–43. Ingrid Storm, "Morality in Context: A Multilevel Analysis of the Relationship between Religion and Values in Europe," *Politics and Religion* 9, no. 1 (March 2016): 111–38.
3. Johan Lind, Magnus Enquist, and Stefano Ghirlanda, "Animal Memory: A Review of Delayed Matching-to-Sample Data," *Behavioural Processes* 117 (2015): 52–58.

Index